MAKING
WAVES

MAKING WAVES

THE *RAG RADIO* INTERVIEWS

THORNE DREYER

BRISCOE CENTER
FOR AMERICAN HISTORY
THE UNIVERSITY OF TEXAS AT AUSTIN

DISTRIBUTED BY TOWER BOOKS, AN IMPRINT
OF THE UNIVERSITY OF TEXAS PRESS

Copyright © 2022 by Thorne Dreyer
Preface © Briscoe Center for American History
All rights reserved
Printed in the United States of America
First edition, 2022

Requests for permission to reproduce material from this work should be sent to:
    Office of the Director
    Dolph Briscoe Center for American History
    University of Texas at Austin
    2300 Red River Stop D1100
    Austin, TX 78712-1426

∞ The paper used in this book meets the minimum requirements of ANSI/NISO z39.48-1992 (r1997) (Permanence of Paper).

Library of Congress Control Number: 2021944128

ISBN 978-1-953480-09-5 (hardcover)
ISBN 978-1-953480-11-8 (ebook)

DEDICATED TO THE MEMORIES OF:

Tom Hayden
Paul Krassner
Margaret Moser
Al Reinert
Bob "Daddy-O" Wade

CONTENTS

PREFACE by Don Carleton · ix

INTRODUCTION · 1

STORYTELLERS
    Dan Rather and Robin Rather · 19
    Bill Minutaglio and Kaye Northcott on Molly Ivins · 41
    Ronnie Dugger · 59
    Paul Krassner · 79
    Al Reinert · 101
    Harry Hurt III · 115

VISUAL ARTISTS
    Pete Gershon · 133
    Margo Sawyer · 157
    Bob "Daddy-O" Wade and Jason Mellard · 175

IMPRESARIOS
    Eddie Wilson · 193
    Margaret Moser · 209

MUSIC MAKERS
    Bill Kirchen · 231
    David Amram · 243
    Ed Sanders · 261

POLITICIANS
    Bernie Sanders   281
    Jim Hightower   295

NEW LEFTIES
    Tom Hayden   315
    Bernardine Dohrn and Bill Ayers   333

RIGHTS FIGHTERS
    Leon McNealy   353
    Frances "Poppy" Northcutt   371
    Roxanne Dunbar-Ortiz   387

PREFACE

In April 2018 I received an email from political activist, progressive journalist, underground newspaper pioneer, and alternative-views radio personality Thorne Dreyer. "I was having a late breakfast with Bill Minutaglio at Cisco's yesterday," Dreyer wrote, "and he encouraged me to contact you. I have a uniquely valuable oral archive collection that I've put together over the nine years I've been doing *Rag Radio*. Maybe a visit? I'm at your service."

Thorne's breakfast mate, Bill Minutaglio, is a journalist and bestselling author whose in-depth research materials for *First Son*, his book about George W. Bush, are housed in the archives of the Dolph Briscoe Center for American History. Cisco's restaurant, an iconic East Austin breakfast hangout founded in 1948, has long been favored by journalists, politicians, community leaders, and University of Texas staff and faculty. An uncountable number of deals, alliances, proposals, and ideas have been hatched at Cisco's, which made it a fitting place for Thorne to get the idea to contact me. *Rag Radio* is Thorne's weekly interview program broadcast over KOOP-FM, a community radio station in Austin.

I quickly responded to Thorne's email. I had often tuned in to his program, on which Thorne interviewed a wide range of political activists, writers, community organizers, and individuals who had played influential roles in the so-called counterculture of the late '60s and early '70s. The Briscoe Center is busy documenting the history of the activists associated with that era, as well as the life and work of prominent participants in the liberation, social justice, and antiwar movements that followed the heyday of the counterculture and that continue to the current day. There was no doubt in my mind that Thorne possessed material that should be preserved for historical research and teaching. I was keen to talk to him, but I was also eager to finally meet him in person.

By the time I received Thorne Dreyer's email, I had been closely following his career in Houston and Austin for nearly fifty years. We had often worked, played, and lived in places quite near each other, and we had mutual acquaintances.

While I was in graduate school in Houston at the beginning of the 1970s, I was an avid reader of *Space City!*, an underground newspaper that Thorne played a major role in founding as well as editing. During those same years I listened to a program Thorne hosted on Houston's Pacifica radio station, KPFT. I lived in Houston's Montrose neighborhood, which was just a few blocks from the KPFT studio. A few of my graduate student colleagues and I frequented a bar in Montrose called Prufrock's Tavern, which was one of Thorne's hangouts and the subject of a profile he wrote for *Texas Monthly*. We were both deeply involved in Houston in Senator George McGovern's quixotic presidential campaign. When I wrote my doctoral dissertation on McCarthyism in Houston, I wrote about Thorne's father, Martin Dreyer, a reporter for the *Houston Chronicle* who was a fierce critic of the Red Scare. After I became director of the Houston Metropolitan Research Center in the late 1970s, I had the center's oral historian interview Thorne's father. Our parallel lives continued after we both moved to Austin, but due to the vagaries of life, we wouldn't actually meet, at least as far as we are aware, until after Thorne sent me that email.

Thorne and I finally met in the Briscoe Center's facility on the campus of the University of Texas at Austin, and the deal was made. Thorne generously agreed to place in the center's archive the recordings of about four hundred hour-long interviews he has conducted on his *Rag Radio* program since 2009. His interviewees include Paul Krassner, John Sinclair, Ed Sanders, Paul Buhle, Tom Hayden, Todd Gitlin, Judy Gumbo Albert, Bernardine Dohrn, Bill Ayers, and dozens of other important players in American progressive movements.

The *Rag Radio* archive is a valuable addition to the center's growing body of material related to the history of social justice, antiwar, civil liberties, and other progressive movements in American history. The center's holdings include one of the largest collections of the archives of photojournalists and documentary photographers—including Flip Schulke, Charles Moore, R. C. Hickman, Spider Martin, and Stephen Shames—who visually documented the civil rights and Black power movements. The center also has the papers of John Henry Faulk, James Farmer, Ramsey Clark, Frances Tarlton "Sissy" Farenthold, Alice Embree, and Abbie Hoffman, among many other figures and organizations closely identified with progressive causes. Thorne has or had important connections to many of these figures, including the late Abbie Hoffman, with whom he worked in New York City for an underground newspaper syndicate, and Alice Embree, his close friend and collaborator who was his colleague at *The Rag*, the pioneering underground newspaper in Austin during the late 1960s. The Briscoe Center has also published Embree's insightful memoir, *Voice Lessons*.

A few months after the center acquired the *Rag Radio* archive, I accepted Thorne's proposal that the Briscoe Center publish his favorite interviews from the collection in an anthology, which would include his overall introduction as well as short introductions to place each interview in context. That work has now been completed. I am pleased to present for your enjoyment and edification the Briscoe Center's publication of Thorne Dreyer's *Making Waves*.

I want to thank Thorne Dreyer for choosing the center as the permanent home for his archive. I am grateful, as always, to Holly Taylor, the Briscoe Center's head of publications, for her skilled work on *Making Waves*. The Briscoe Center's audio recordings archivist, Justin Kovar, was responsible for integrating the interviews into our sound archives. Echo Uribe, the Briscoe Center's director for administration, oversaw the project to transcribe Thorne's interviews.

Finally, please accept my invitation to visit the Briscoe Center's main facility on the campus of the University of Texas at Austin, adjacent to the Lyndon B. Johnson Library and Museum, or online at briscoecenter.org.

Don Carleton
Executive Director and J. R. Parten Chair in the Archives of American History

MAKING
WAVES

INTRODUCTION

For a few years in the 1970s I worked at KPFT-FM, the listener-supported Pacifica radio station in Houston. I hosted a show called *The Briarpatch* and even put in a stint as general manager of the station. There are five independently operated Pacifica stations around the country, and they're a unique and eccentric bunch. The nonprofit Pacifica Foundation was founded in 1946 by pacifists E. John Lewis and Lewis Hill, and the stations are known for their progressive politics (and their frequent money struggles). *Democracy Now!*—with Amy Goodman—is considered Pacifica's flagship operation.

In 1970, KPFT was the target of a suddenly revitalized Knights of the Ku Klux Klan. KPFT went on the air on March 1, 1970, playing a recording of the Beatles' "Here Comes the Sun," and the Klan, wasting no time, blew up the station's transmitter on May 12. Thankfully, the transmitter was located in Stafford, Texas, and KPFT's downtown studios weren't damaged and no one was hurt. The Klan blew the station off the air a second time, on October 6, 1970. A recording of Arlo Guthrie's "Alice's Restaurant" was playing when the blast occurred, and when the station came back three months later, Guthrie was in the studio, playing the song live. KPFT is the only radio station in the country to have been blown off the air—even once.

My next radio gig came some four decades later in Austin, as host and producer of the weekly *Rag Radio* program. *Rag Radio*, which features hour-long in-depth interviews, airs on Austin's KOOP-FM, another unique community station, and is syndicated on several other outlets. Founded in 2009, *Rag Radio* has broadcast more than five hundred original shows; on September 27, 2019, we celebrated our tenth anniversary. We post all of our shows as podcasts at the Internet Archive.

KOOP (pronounced "co-op," not "coop") wasn't exactly blown off the air like KPFT, but the station survived three debilitating fires; two, which were accidental, occurred in 2006, and the second knocked KOOP off the air for fourteen days. After that, the station moved to its current location at 3823 Airport Boulevard, where in 2008, a third fire resulted in $300,000 in damage. This fire, no accident, was started by a disgruntled volunteer who was upset with changes in the musical programming. He served a short prison sentence, and the station was off the air for a few weeks.

Being knocked off the air multiple times is not the only thing that KOOP and KPFT have in common. They are both known for their progressive politics and wide range of community programming. KOOP's mission is "to engage, connect, and enrich the whole community, including the underserved, through creating diverse, quality, educational music and news programming." KOOP is a nonprofit, noncommercial, solar-powered radio station that is cooperatively run by its volunteers and staff. To my knowledge, it is the only such cooperatively run radio station in the United States.

Rag Radio comes from a long and storied tradition. *The Rag*, an underground newspaper published in Austin from 1966 to 1977, was one of the first and longest-running underground papers of the '60s and '70s. And among the most influential. It was the sixth underground paper, and there would ultimately be as many as one thousand of these upstart little tabloids, made possible by the advent of the offset press (which made things a whole lot cheaper). The papers filled a major gap in US journalism, reporting on civil rights, the Vietnam War, and the '60s counterculture, and later became a strong voice for women, gay people, antiwar GIs, high school activists, and community organizers. I was a founding editor of *The Rag* in 1966 (and later of *Space City!* in Houston, a second-generation underground paper).

Carol Neiman (*left*) and Thorne Dreyer (*right*), founding editors of Austin's pioneering underground newspaper *The Rag*, attend the national congress of the United States Student Press Association in Minneapolis in 1967. © Peter Simon.

In his book *The Paper Revolutionaries*, Laurence Leamer called *The Rag* "one of the few legendary undergrounds." The paper helped pull together Austin's antiwar and student power movements and its large countercultural community and merge them into a political force. Though it was far from slick, the paper was generally quite literate with political analysis and cultural coverage. And it was always full of its own brand of great Texas humor. Gilbert Shelton's *Fabulous Furry Freak Brothers* comic strip—arguably the most cherished of the era's underground "comix"—debuted in *The Rag* in 1968. As of 2019, according to *Forbes*, "Freak Brothers comics have been translated into 14 languages with more than 40 million copies sold." Jim Franklin's legendary surrealistic armadillos graced many of *The Rag*'s covers, and noted underground artists such as Micael Priest, Kerry Awn, and Jack Jackson (Jaxon) were frequent contributors.

Historian John Moretta believes that *The Rag* played a major role in the evolution of Austin into what it is today—that it helped start the whole process of making Austin "weird." Or what Kinky Friedman

Staff photo originally published as a wraparound cover in the Houston underground newspaper *Space City!*, April 8, 1971. Thorne Dreyer is seated, second from right. Photo by Jerry Sebesta / *Space City!* Thorne Dreyer Collection, Houston Metropolitan Research Center (HMRC).

refers to as the "long-haired, hippie, pot-smoking, hell-raising Gomorrah of the Western world."

The Rag, in fact, became a community in its own right, and much of that community is still active today. Two *Rag* reunions, the first on Labor Day weekend in 2005 and the second in October 2016, brought together dozens of former *Rag* staffers and fellow travelers from parts wide and far. The reunions—which included a series of social gatherings, panel discussions, concerts, and art exhibits—reignited a dormant energy that brought that community back together. This led to a plethora of new projects and political activity. *The Rag Blog*, a progressive internet news magazine that was founded in 2005, gained a national following; a three-part film about the paper's history was produced by People's History in Texas; and, with Alice Embree and Richard Croxdale, I coedited a three-hundred-page book, *Celebrating 'The Rag': Austin's Historic Underground Newspaper*, which *Kirkus Reviews* called "a raucous, absorbing excursion back to the 1960s and '70s." We also

INTRODUCTION / 5

produced *Rag Blog* benefit concerts and other community events. The nonprofit New Journalism Project was formed to coordinate these projects and to serve as a publishing house for our books.

Rag Radio went on the air on September 29, 2009, with a show about the original *Rag* and the underground press, and it is still going strong. During the pandemic, all KOOP radio shows have been produced via Zoom from our home studios, but we haven't missed a beat. In his 2020 book *All-American Rebels*, historian Robert Cottrell wrote that *Rag Radio*, "a weekly syndicated radio program based out of Austin, Texas, maintained the Movement spirit associated with the legendary underground newspaper" that inspired it. He wrote that "host and *Rag* founder Thorne Dreyer [has] deftly interviewed hundreds of guests," including a number of historical figures. In his history of modern Austin, *Austin to ATX*, Joe Nick Patoski wrote, "Thorne Dreyer reimagined *The Rag*, the underground newspaper he founded and edited in the late sixties and early seventies, into a multiplatform information delivery system that included an online blog, a weekly radio program that aired on KOOP community radio, a book, and a three-part documentary film."

The *Rag Radio* group at our tenth-anniversary show in Austin, September 27, 2019. *Front row, left to right:* Tracey Schulz, Allen Campbell, Roger Baker. *Back row, left to right:* Roy Casagranda, Beverly Baker Moore, Thorne Dreyer, Alice Embree, Suzy Shelor. Photo by Charlie Martin.

I must add that I am given way too much personal credit for these efforts: others have played significant if not equal roles. Alice Embree helped found the original *Rag* and has been indispensable in leading its digital-age rebirth. People's History in Texas produced the *Rag* movie, and I could never have done *Rag Radio* without the able assistance of engineer and associate producer Tracey Schulz.

* * * * *

In 1940, Martin Dreyer arrived in Houston from Chicago, rented a room in drama teacher Nydia Dallas's basement studio complex in the Beaconsfield Apartments on Main Street, and started teaching creative writing. In a 1979 story titled "The Way We Were," written for the *Houston Review*, he reported that his small room "featured a cot and battered Underwood typewriter." "I was in business," he said. It was in this rather bohemian setting that he met—and soon married—artist Margaret Lee Webb, who, in his words, was "tall, dark-haired, amiable, a version of Garbo who didn't 'vant to be alone.'"

Dreyer was already a critically acclaimed short story writer who had been cited as *Esquire*'s "Discovery of the Month"; published in the era's prestigious "Little Magazines," like the *Prairie Schooner*; and "starred" in collections of the best short stories of the year. By the time I was born, in 1945, my father had begun a three-decade stint at the *Houston Chronicle* as a reporter, feature writer, and editor. He would be considered by many, including his fellow reporters, to be the best creative writer working in Houston journalism.

Margaret Webb Dreyer, a painter and muralist who also taught art in private classes and for the City of Houston, was to become one of the city's most celebrated and, in art historian Pete Gershon's words, "most beloved" artists. Mimi Crossley, art writer for the *Houston Post*, remembered that "Maggie's absolute freedom, her hospitality, big floppy hats and committed heart put the art scene in Houston on the side of human rights and general soul. To a large extent, she made it an art-for-artist's scene, and set the stage for those of us who walk on it now."

In 1976, after she died from cancer way too early, more than two hundred of my mother's closest friends gathered at the Rothko Chapel to tell "Maggie stories." In a eulogy, Houston's progressive young mayor

Fred Hofheinz said of my mother, "There are some people who by only living their lives enrich the lives of everyone around them."

Speaking at that gathering, the late Houston artist Bob Riegel told how Maggie Dreyer "completely changed my life one afternoon." My father wrote about it later: "As a youth living in our neighborhood, [Riegel] was shooting mockingbirds with his new slingshot. Suddenly he felt a disapproving presence hovering over him. It was my bird-loving wife who, said Bob, 'took me in right then and gave me my first art lesson.'" "I guess she thought this was a real case of misdirected energy," Riegel told the Rothko gathering. "Before I knew it, I was wielding a paintbrush instead of a slingshot."

That year, Houston's Contemporary Arts Museum staged a posthumous exhibition of Margaret Webb Dreyer's final paintings, and in 1979, the University of St. Thomas followed with a lovely retrospective of her life's work.

In 2001, Martin Dreyer died at the age of ninety-two. He was still getting up every morning and putting in an hour or two on his latest manuscript. Thankfully, he had upgraded from that "battered Underwood" typewriter on which he had taught creative writing in the 1940s.

When I was a youngster, we lived in the Montrose area (which was already becoming the Greenwich Village of Houston) before we moved southwest to follow the schools. In 1959, my elderly grandmother, Eula Richey Webb, moved in with us and, in turn, her former two-story house on San Jacinto became Dreyer Galleries. My mother added on a long gallery room with an outside deck above it. Later, after I had flown the proverbial nest, my parents would move into the upstairs of the gallery. Dreyer Galleries, which was run by both of my parents with an occasional assist from young Thorne and others, was one of the first galleries in boomtown Houston to focus on local, Texas, and Latin American painters and to show the work of young Black and women artists (the most prominent galleries in town at that time were satellites of the New York art scene).

When famed Houston artist and art teacher Arthur Turner retired from the Museum of Fine Arts' Glassell School of Art in 2011, he remembered that when he was nineteen and attending North Texas State University, he made a cold call at Dreyer Galleries and met my mother. According to a feature story in the *Houston Chronicle*, he was clutching his portfolio under his arm, and she greeted him, "Darlin', come in, would you like a drink?" "Three hours later, I had a show," he said—his first of many to come.

A Uruguayan painter named Rodriguez Candhales came to Dreyer Galleries for a one-man show and decided to remain in Houston for a while. My mother invited him to stay at the gallery and to help out in his spare time. He ended up living for several months in a converted kitchen and sleeping on a plywood board over a bathtub. He painted a portrait of me that I still have. Two of my mother's gallery attendants (whom she also helped nurture) included Kerry Awn, who would become a noted cartoonist and poster artist, comic, and musician on the Texas underground scene, and screen actor Sonny Carl Davis, whose film work has included roles in *Bernie*, *The Whole Shootin' Match*, and *Melvin and Howard*.

Some folks bought art, of course, but the gallery openings were best known as gathering spots for the artists themselves and the local bohemian community, and for literary types, academics, local politicians, and political activists. In an article titled "The Most Influential Houstonians of All Time," *Houstonia* magazine wrote, "People loved Margaret Webb Dreyer's Saturday night salons . . . where today's celebrated art scene may well have been born." Guests, they reported, included Jane Fonda and "renegade filmmaker" Robert Altman. Other regular visitors were politicians like Mayor Hofheinz and US Representative Mickey Leland. Jane Fonda once spoke to a group of peace activists spread out on the gallery floor; she stood on a chair amid what my father referred to as "obstacles d'art," which included large African and pre-Columbian artifacts.

My family's public opposition to the war in Vietnam and support for human rights angered local right-wingers, and night riders shot bullets through the front door of Dreyer Galleries, a bullet lodging in a mosaic wall. They left behind a calling card that said, "The Knights of the Ku Klux Klan is watching you." Around the same time, the Klan also threw a concussion grenade into the offices of *Space City!*, another underground newspaper I helped publish—because we had invited yippie Abbie Hoffman to town to speak at several events, including a rally at Hermann Park. My colleague Sherwood Bishop was living in the office and was an eyewitness to this and other Klan attacks, including an arrow shot from a crossbow into the front door of *Space City!*'s Wichita Street digs. We gave the arrow to Abbie Hoffman as a going-away present. The *Space City!* office was located about three blocks from Dreyer Galleries. The Klan distributed its own "underground" newspaper—giving new meaning to the concept of a "throwaway"—called the *Rat Sheet*. A special edition featured the "Infamous Dreyer Rats"—Martin, Margaret, and yours truly.

When I was a child, my mother would take me to see my father at the *Chronicle* city room, where we were greeted by city editor Zarko Franks and a cast of characters, some of whom looked like they'd just stepped out of the movie *Front Page*. The police reporter brought out photos of murder victims for me to see, and I would get a guided tour of the printing presses. I would go to the Press Club with my mother, where we sat at the bar and I drank ginger ales while my father beat the reporters and other media types at pocket billiards. He was Press Club champ and even had a plaque that said so.

My father had some innate talent at art, and my mother gave him a few lessons and critiqued his paintings. His work was modernist with a surrealistic bent. One year, in 1947, my dad decided to submit one of his oil paintings to the Texas General Exhibition, open to artists all over the state. He made the show—which traveled to museums in Houston, Dallas, and San Antonio—and received an "honorable mention" for his painting. My mother, who often won purchase prizes at these shows, was, as they say, "booted out." He bragged about it for years.

One of my father's gigs at the *Houston Chronicle* was travel editor, which meant I got included in the occasional "junket." When I was fifteen or sixteen, the three of us went to the grand opening of a fancy resort on the bay of Puerto Marqués, just south of Acapulco. We made friends with a woman who, despite having only one arm, drove race cars in France. She had a lovely daughter about my age. One day I accompanied the two of them—in an open-sided jeep—on a trip into town. The mother drove at least ninety on this narrow mountain road with hairpin curves. If you dared to look through your white knuckles, you saw straight down to the ocean. When we got to town, the race car driver left her daughter and me at a small Mexican movie theater while she went shopping. The daughter took my hand and we headed for the balcony to unwind.

"The Infamous Dreyer Rats." *Clockwise from left:* Margaret Webb Dreyer, Thorne Dreyer, and Martin Dreyer (with dog), ca. 1970. This picture was taken before the three Dreyers went to Houston City Hall to complain to—and be ignored by— city council about the violent activities of the local Ku Klux Klan. The Klan put out a mimeographed paper called the *Rat Sheet* and dedicated one issue to the "Infamous Dreyer Rats" and the family's progressive political activities. Photo by Victoria Smith. Thorne Dreyer personal collection.

Margaret Webb Dreyer at Thorne's thirtieth birthday party on August 1, 1975, at Chaucer's, the artists' bar at the Plaza Hotel in Houston. Photo by Janice Rubin.

My family took a vacation every summer, usually driving to Mexico, where we went to out-of-the-way places. In Ajijic, an art colony near Guadalajara, we visited a gallery that showed actual *paintings* by two of my heroes, *Mad* magazine cartoonists Don Martin and Frank Kelly Freas. Another summer my mother took me with her to San Miguel de Allende, where we rented a small cottage for a few months. She took art classes at the renowned Instituto Allende, sometimes letting me tag along. Once I attended a glassblowing class, where I got sick because I sucked in instead of blowing out.

My mother did her best to bring out my artistic potential. She would sit me down and teach me how to "break up space" by scribbling wildly all over the page and then looking for monsters and filling them in with vivid colors using crayons or tempera paint. This was a method she used in some of her own work, though she had mostly graduated from monsters. I got pretty good at it and entered one of my pieces—a finger painting—in the Scholastic Art Show. It was accepted, won a gold key, and was chosen for a national touring group. A few years later, I did an acrylic portrait of my girlfriend Carol in a red-and-white striped shirt against a blue background, but all I actually painted was the shirt as if she were in it. No head, no arms. Carol pretended to love it and my mother hung it in the gallery.

That was my art career.

I wrote some poetry and occasional prose and was an editor of the high school yearbook. My father would critique my work. In one piece I referred to young children as "kids." "No," my father said. "Kids are *goats!*" He of course thought I was the next Hemingway.

So, as an only child parented by a newspaperman and an abstract expressionist, I naturally decided I wanted to be an *actor*. At Bellaire High School, I studied theater with the legendary Cecil Pickett, who later taught at the University of Houston. He was a national treasure. His theater at Bellaire was often referred to as "Little Broadway," and show people from all over the city attended our plays. The talent he developed at Bellaire and UH included his daughter, Cindy Pickett, perhaps best known as Matthew Broderick's mom in *Ferris Bueller's Day Off*; brothers Randy and Dennis Quaid; Brent Spiner (Data on *Star Trek*); and Trey Wilson (*Raising Arizona* and *Bull Durham*). His student Thomas Schlamme produced *The West Wing* with Aaron Sorkin.

I starred in several shows at Bellaire, including the musical *Daddy Long Legs*. I was cast in the part Fred Astaire played in the movie, but it soon became clear that I couldn't sing a lick or dance without falling on my face, so other actors were recruited to sing and dance my part. I traveled to numerous speech tournaments sponsored by the University Interscholastic League and won prizes in acting and poetry-reading categories.

I was in a play at the revered Alley Theater in 1963, back when it was located in a converted fan factory on Berry Street, then studied acting in New York with William Hickey at HB Studios and in Austin at the University of Texas. By the 1960s, Austin was already known as "Nirvana in the Hills" and I was smitten. It was the place to be and the time to be there. Soon I dropped out (down?) into the underground; I joined the Students for a Democratic Society (SDS), directed some street theater and worked with Gary Chason's Curtain Club, and became heavily involved in civil rights and the movement to end the war in Vietnam. When I helped create and edit *The Rag*, that upstart little underground tabloid seduced me into a new career.

After a few months as an editor at Liberation News Service in New York, which supplied editorial content to alternative media around the country, I moved back to Houston in the summer of 1969, helped to steer the underground paper *Space City!*, and worked in progressive political campaigns and as a public-information officer for the City of Houston. I was on the Texas staff of antiwar presidential candidate George McGovern, and my business partner Teague Cavness and I managed Kathy Whitmire's campaign for city controller. Kathy was the first woman elected to citywide office in Houston and later served five terms as the city's mayor. I wrote for *Texas Monthly* magazine and

Left to right: Thorne Dreyer, Kinky Friedman, Houston First Lady Mac Hofheinz, and Mayor Fred Hofheinz at Liberty Hall, Houston, mid-1970s. Photographer unknown, copy in Thorne Dreyer personal collection.

other publications, owned and operated a public relations business, managed a downtown jazz club called Mums and a jazz singer named Cy Brinson, and then worked with two bookstores and ran an online bookselling business.

But the *Rag* reunion in 2005 romanced me back to Nirvana, and I've been in Austin ever since, editing *The Rag Blog*, hosting and producing *Rag Radio*, and engaging in the random adventure.

* * * * *

The interviews in *Making Waves* shine a light on my personal history and interests. The passions of those I've interviewed, and in some cases their lives, are intertwined with mine. In this book, I've divided my guests into somewhat arbitrary and overlapping categories: storytellers, visual artists, impresarios, music makers, politicians, New Lefties, and rights fighters.

Gathering at Thorne Dreyer and Kathy Gresham Dreyer's Montrose home in Houston in the mid-1970s. *Left to right:* Harry Hurt III, Thorne Dreyer, Dustin Dreyer (*on Thorne's shoulders*), Mitch Green, Laura Viada, Jeff Nightbyrd, and Al Reinert. Hurt (*far left*) and Reinert (*far right*) were each guests on *Rag Radio* some forty years later, and their interviews appear in this book. Photo by Kathy Gresham Dreyer.

It's clear that my father the journalist and my mother the artist—and all the people I met around them and at their gatherings—played a major role in the trajectory of my life and, ultimately, in the makeup of this book. The turn toward political and social activism and the influence of the visionaries I worked with in SDS and the underground press—and my later work in progressive politics—gave me an abiding sense of purpose. And lots of contacts! And the stage acting reinforced the ham in me. Put it all in a blender and *Rag Radio* was bound to whip up.

I like to know and interview people doing significant work in this world. I like to visit with interesting folks, and I never discourage laughter. I always tell my guests to relax, that I want the discussion to be informal. "We're going to record some important history here," I say, "but we also want to have fun."

* * * * *

In addition to Alice Embree and Tracey Schulz, I'd like to thank Jeff Shero Nightbyrd, who thought we should start an underground paper in the first place, and Carol Nieman, who joined me as coeditor of the original *Rag*. Much of the decision-making at the paper was done collectively, but others (among many!) who were instrumental players include Judy Fitzgerald, Dennis Fitzgerald, Gary Thiher, David Mahler, Judy Smith, Trudy Minkoff, Alan Pogue, and Glenn Scott. Richard Jehn was the original editor of *The Rag Blog* in 2005, before I took over the next year. Carlos Lowry, and before him James Retherford, designed the *Rag Blog* site and masthead. Sherwood Bishop, who had been a member of the *Space City!* editorial collective in 1969 and the early '70s, is president of the New Journalism Project Board of Directors. Allan Campbell helped mentor me at KOOP, and Suzy Shelor has been a *Rag Radio* mainstay, as have Roger Baker, Glenn Smith, Roy Casagranda, and many more. Larry Yurdin and Danny Samuels were driving forces at KPFT in Houston and provided inspiration. And both Kimberly McCarson, who was general manager at KOOP when we started *Rag Radio*, and Federico Pacheco, who holds that position as I write, have been very supportive of our efforts.

Much gratitude to Thomas Zigal—his help and encouragement have been indispensable—and to Holly Taylor, my editor; Abby Webber, my copy editor; and Derek George, the book's designer; and to Don Carleton, executive director of the Briscoe Center for American History at the University of Texas, for nurturing this project.

Thorne Webb Dreyer
Austin, Texas

STORYTELLERS

Legendary newsman Dan Rather (*left*) was our *Rag Radio* guest September 27, 2013. He was joined by his environmentalist daughter Robin (*right*) in their first father-daughter interview. Photo by Roger Baker.

DAN RATHER AND ROBIN RATHER

Hearts can inspire other hearts with their fire.

In their first ever father-daughter interview, Dan Rather and Robin Rather talk about baseball, idealism, the environment, and the concentration of media ownership.

Dan Rather was anchor and managing editor of the CBS Evening News for twenty-four years. Born in Wharton, Texas, Dan started his journalistic career in Houston with the Houston Chronicle, KTRH Radio, and KHOU-TV. He has received virtually every honor in broadcast journalism, including numerous Emmy and Peabody Awards. On October 13, 2013, three weeks after this broadcast, Rather joined a very exclusive group, including Edward R. Murrow and Walter Cronkite, as a recipient of the prestigious Trustees Award of the National Academy of Television Arts and Sciences. He lives in New York but also has a home in Austin.

Robin Rather, the daughter of Dan Rather and Jean Goebel, is an Austin-based environmental activist and sustainability consultant. Robin was chair of the board of the Save Our Springs (SOS) Alliance, which has played a major role in the preservation of the Edwards Aquifer and Austin's Barton Springs. She has also been a consultant on a volunteer basis for community radio station KOOP-FM, where this show was originally broadcast.

Dan Rather and my father, Martin Dreyer, were friends and colleagues. I first met Dan in person when I was about ten years old and he was working at the Chronicle, *and I have followed and admired him on radio and television ever since. This was the first time I had the pleasure of meeting Robin, though I was already an admirer of her work. Five decades separated my first meeting with Dan Rather and the first time I met his daughter.*

Rag Radio *engineer Tracey Schulz joins us on this show.*

SEPTEMBER 27, 2013

THORNE DREYER: It's really great to have the two of you here, in your first ever father-daughter interview.

ROBIN RATHER: I love this radio station.

DREYER: And this radio station loves you.

There's so much to talk about. For one thing, I want to discuss the old days in Houston, where I grew up. You were my idea of a newsman, Dan; I followed you on radio and TV in Houston.

You also did some sports broadcasting. I listened to your play-by-play of the Houston Buffs on the radio—when you did that year of broadcasting the games in 1959. I want to ask you something: Did you go on the road with the team?

DAN RATHER: No, we did re-creation.

DREYER: Re-creation?

D. RATHER: It's great to be with you this afternoon. And I have such memories of radio in Houston before I got into television. Doing play-by-play sports for the University of Houston, Southwest Conference in football, and the Buff baseball.

But to answer your question. The Buffs had moved into Triple-A.

DREYER: Right.

D. RATHER: This was the year before Houston got its major league franchise.

DREYER: They had always been in the Double-A Texas League.

D. RATHER: That's right. But we did not travel with the team. We didn't have the money, and I'm not sure the team particularly wanted us to travel with them. It was not a good team, if you recall. Marty Marion, the great St. Louis Cardinals shortstop, had bought the team.

But at any rate, we did re-creation, which I know is hard for people to imagine. Ronald Reagan, of all people, did the same thing back in the 1930s. When the team went, for example, to Minneapolis or Saint Paul or Omaha—they were all Triple-A teams—a Western Union man would be at the game.

R. RATHER: This is even more low-tech than I could have possibly imagined.

D. RATHER: This was the ultimate low-tech. He would put it on ticker tape, which would then show up in our Houston studio. I'd be standing in front of a microphone, very much as you're standing in front of one today. The sound engineer would be in a glass-enclosed booth off to the side, and he would have a record of crowd noise. So, if it were a single, the telegraph would say, "Fridley"—Jim Fridley was the cleanup hitter—"Fridley, ground ball, shortstop, BH, base hit." That's what you'd have on the tape.

"Fridley with a sharp ground ball, deep shortstop, throw to first, not in time, base hit." And the sound engineer would play a crowd record commensurate with a single at the ballpark. Now, if it were a home run or a very close play at the plate, give him the fist and the crowd noise would build as you say, "He rounds third, he's going to try for home. Delsin in center is with the ball, here's the throw, Reeder to the plate, not in time." Great roar of the crowd.

DREYER: Did anybody ever make a mistake and do the wrong sound effects?

D. RATHER: Oh, lots of times. And I made a lot of mistakes. Sometimes the Western Union man would be drinking an adult beverage as he was sending this game from Omaha or Minneapolis, and he would get confused. For example, he would say, "Delsin walks," so I would say, "Ball four and Jim Delsin takes first base."

A few minutes later when the next hitter was up, the telegraph operator would say, "By the way, Delsin *didn't* walk. The umpire called him out on strikes." Well, thank you very much. I've got Delsin on first base.

So, naturally I had the pitcher make a pickoff play, and he was picked off first.

DREYER: When I was a kid, I listened to every game. And when the Buffs were at bat, I'd be up there with my bat every pitch, and when we were in the field, I would be throwing the ball.

D. RATHER: You know, Robin became a very good softball player; she was an excellent athlete when she grew up. When I had the Buffs play-by-play, Robin was one year old.

R. RATHER: I don't remember any of this.

D. RATHER: No, you don't remember, but I always thought you were a good athlete and good softball player partly because your mother would turn up the radio. She would monitor my play-by-play of the Houston Buffs while nursing Robin or taking care of Robin as an infant, and the radio would be so loud that occasionally the neighbors would call over and say, "Jean, I know you want to hear Dan do the game, but could you turn it down just a tad."

DREYER: And you probably don't remember, Robin, when the tree fell into the house, when Hurricane Carla hit [in 1961].

R. RATHER: No, actually, I don't remember it except very vaguely. Both my mother and I have been really afraid of big rainstorms ever since then. It was just a tough night in our whole neighborhood. And one of the things I was going to say that's strange about having a journalist father—there are lots of great things, but one of the strange things is when really bad things happen, they're not there.

So you learn really early to be extremely independent. And I do want to give a shout-out to Mom. We always say she's the best of the Rathers, and she has an almost unbelievable amount of common sense—because my father was out doing things like standing in the hurricane, you know, so he could feel how much rain there was and then report on that.

DREYER: But he did not tie himself to the tree. And we're thankful for that.

I want to talk about Hurricane Carla, not only because it was a significant news event, and one that affected all of our lives, but I also think it tells a lot about you, Dan, as a newsman, and your approach—and certainly the whole thing about the radar and the way that got developed. And, of course, it was when CBS discovered you.

D. RATHER: True.

DREYER: Okay. Your grandmother told you that a hurricane would get you very close to God, I think—something to that effect.

D. RATHER: My Grandmother Page, who was my maternal grandmother down in Bloomington, Texas, taught me, "First of all, Danny, you should fear only God and hurricanes."

DREYER: God and hurricanes, all right.

D. RATHER: And then she said it would be very difficult, if not impossible, to get closer to God than you are when you are in the middle of a hurricane.

DREYER: I remember Carla very well. It was a heavy-duty hurricane that hit just south of Galveston.

D. RATHER: That's right, the year was 1961, September 1961. It was at the time—and I think still is, in terms of geographical size—the largest hurricane on record in the Gulf of Mexico, and at one time it had winds gusting two hundred miles an hour and above.

DREYER: I think the story of how you covered Carla, how it came about, how you sold your news director on doing it—you sold him on getting there early because you knew that the island was going to be closed off and other reporters wouldn't be able to get there—and what happened with your innovation with radar, is all very telling.

Galveston was where the Weather Bureau was, and my father, who was a newsman, moonlighted as a weatherman. I mean, they didn't really have weathermen. My father would—after he got off work at the *Chronicle*, he and his photographer, because my father didn't drive, would get in the car and go to Galveston, check in at the Weather Bureau, call back in to KTRH news, and give a weather report.

But everything was new. It was a time of incredible innovation.

D. RATHER: Well, that's the point. Speaking of technology overcoming and helping us time after time. The radar was developed during World War II. It was not being used for weather forecasting; no radio or television station in the nation had radar.

The Weather Service, sort of belatedly, started using radar, experimenting with it to predict weather patterns—and particularly they put it in Galveston because it's an island and faces the Gulf of Mexico—saying to themselves, "Maybe it can be useful, particularly with hurricanes." So, when Hurricane Carla came—this huge hurricane, the largest geographical size on record, a particularly fierce hurricane—naturally I said this could be a real story.

DREYER: You actually plotted the course.

D. RATHER: Well, I had done that as kind of a hobby since I was a child.

I had just come into television and convinced the people who owned the station—they were from Boston and Pittsburgh and didn't know anything about hurricanes. And I said, "This could be an historic hurricane and we should go to Galveston because Galveston has this new radar." I explained to them that the radar had the potential to spot the hurricane.

And so we went to Galveston knowing that as the hurricane got closer, the island would be cut off. The island *was* cut off. I made arrangements with the Weather Bureau to just give me a look at the radar, and it really knocked my eyes back because you could see this monster hurricane, for the first time, see an image. Before that, people had to make do with their imaginations.

So, the idea came up to give people an idea of its size and strength: Let's put a scale map of Texas, superimpose that on transparent plastic over the radar, and it will show you how huge and dangerous this is. Once I saw it, I said, "Boy, that would be something for the audience to see." The Weather Bureau was reluctant because they feared it might panic people. Eventually they became convinced it would be a public service because it might convince people that, yes, you need to get out of low lands.

And so we put it on the air. It made such an impact that other television stations in the state—nobody else could get on the island to do this kind of work—picked up our coverage, and the national news began to pick up the coverage. And as a result—I'm not saying it was only because of what we did with showing the picture of the hurricane on the radar on the television screen—but at the time it effected the largest peacetime evacuation in the history of the country.

DREYER: So, those are some interesting decisions you made. The other good decision you made was not to follow up on the idea of tying yourself to a tree.

D. RATHER: Well, it did enter my mind and we did try it.

DREYER: You actually did try it?

D. RATHER: Before the hurricane, the winds were up, the waves were up, before it came in. The idea was to stand outside and be outside in the hurricane. But, we asked, "How are you going to stand up in it?" So we said, "Well, look, maybe we can tie ourselves around a tree, maybe I can chain myself around a tree." I know it sounds crazy; it is crazy.

R. RATHER: It is crazy.

D. RATHER: But we dismissed it very quickly as an impractical idea. For one thing—and it had not occurred to me—but snakes, like people, go for the high ground in hurricanes. Galveston has a slight ridge at the top, and snakes were becoming increasingly apparent on the outside. And so, this idea of chaining oneself or tying oneself to a tree was dismissed pretty quickly.

DREYER: And we're thankful about that. But after the Carla story, you were actually hired, and you went to CBS News.

Okay, Robin and I have something in common, although the actual experience is very different in that we were both what they used to call "journalism brats." My father was a newspaperman, worked for the *Houston Chronicle*, was a reporter and editor. He also worked with you, Dan, for the year that you worked at the *Chronicle*.

D. RATHER: That's true. He was a star at the *Houston Chronicle*; he was a big byline regular with the newspaper. I was trying to catch on, and partly because I was, and remain, a terrible speller, I didn't make my tryout at the *Chronicle*. They took one look at my atrocious spelling and said, "You might have a future in radio." And because the newspaper owned a radio station, they sent me over to the radio station, and that's how I came to work at KTRH.

The *Chronicle* was not only a very influential newspaper in Houston, but it was an influential newspaper in the state. It was owned by the Jesse Jones interests: Jesse H. Jones, who was part of the Roosevelt cabinet for a while, one of the saviors of the country.

DREYER: Part of the "good old boy" network that ran Houston, too.

D. RATHER: Absolutely. And a good old boy network indeed ran it. Some argue how *good* the good old boys were—but one thing, they all had tons of money.

DREYER: Yes.

D. RATHER: None more than the Jones interests. And the Jones family, which has since become one of the more philanthropic families in Texas—and that's saying a lot—but they owned the *Chronicle*, and the *Chronicle* was a very influential newspaper on a state basis. It was a very stable place to work. It's hard for many people in newspapers today.

DREYER: Another person, by the way, who worked for a short period of time at the *Chronicle* was Molly Ivins, and I remember my father talking about this kind of free spirit who was working as an intern. And he said, "She goes around barefoot in the city room." He thought that was very cool.

D. RATHER: He thought that was very cool, but let me tell you, the *Chronicle* was not very kind to free spirits, your father excluded. But the superstructure of the newspaper was very conservative, and going without a tie, never mind going without your shoes, was frowned upon.

DREYER: I want to talk about what it means to be a newsman now, as opposed to the old days, when in Houston we had three newspapers— the *Houston Chronicle*, the *Houston Post*, and the *Houston Press*. [The *Press* was the first to go, closing shop in 1964, and the *Chronicle* bought out the *Post* in 1995.] It wasn't exactly like *Front Page* . . .

D. RATHER: . . . But it was close.

DREYER: The *Press* being a Scripps-Howard newspaper, the other two being Houston owned. The Hobby family owned the *Post*—the Hobbys being another good old boy family—and Hobby, Bill Hobby, was lieutenant governor of Texas.

It's a whole different era, you know. You had your three network television stations. Things certainly have changed.

D. RATHER: The biggest thing was that there were three separate newspapers. They were independent newspapers. There was real competition in the papers. And while both the *Post* and the *Chronicle* had their sacred cows, which is to say big people in the community about whom no bad things would be written, the *Post* sort of kept the balance.

And you also had the locally owned radio stations. I think at this time—we're talking the period of the late 1950s into the early 1960s—there were no fewer than half a dozen, and I'd want to say nine or ten, locally owned radio stations. Now, compare that with today.

DREYER: Most of them are owned by Clear Channel.

R. RATHER: I thought they all were.

D. RATHER: Exactly. And then you've had one merger after another, one purchaser getting ever bigger in both radio, television, and for that matter, with newspapers. And so we've reached the point where something more than 80 percent of the true national distribution of news is owned by no more than six conglomerates—very large corporations. Light years of difference.

So, when people say, "Well, okay, that's the case, but what difference does it make?" Here's the difference that it makes: very big media is in bed with very big government, whether that government is run at any time in Washington by Democrats or Republicans, and this does

---

> "... very big media is in bed with very big government, whether that government is run at any time in Washington by Democrats or Republicans, and this does not serve the public interest when it comes to news."

---

not serve the public interest when it comes to news. And that's the difference between today and the era we're talking about, the late '50s or early '60s.

DREYER: Okay, I want to talk about Austin and the environment and what's happening now with the incredible growth and how, as an environmentalist, Robin, how you see the possibilities of Austin actually surviving as something like Austin used to be.

But first, I want to address a topic that Robin suggested. Robin Rather has a sociology degree and did her honors thesis on utopian societies. And she told me that her father once called her the single most idealistic person that he had ever known. She said this was not necessarily a compliment!

To be a journalist and be a serious journalist you have to be practical and pragmatic, but you also have to be something of an idealist, I would think, in order to keep doing it, to keep butting your head against the wall. What's your feeling looking back now, both of you, on that question of idealism?

D. RATHER: Idealism in some ways, I think, has gone a little out of fashion lately because it's so easy to be cynical.

DREYER: As have utopian societies.

D. RATHER: That's true.

R. RATHER: "Snarky" is in.

D. RATHER: Journalists are trained to be skeptical but not cynical; there's a great difference between skepticism and cynicism. But today there's so much cynicism; cynicism has kind of run amok. I do agree with you that not everybody, but most people who get into journalism get into it from a certain amount of idealism.

Being idealistic, you want to belong. You want to be part of something bigger than yourself, you want to be part of something that matters, and you want to contribute. And that leads to an idealistic view of life, and I plead guilty to being an idealist. Robin has taught me a great deal about keeping idealism alive and how you can't let the flame go out.

And it is true that journalism is filled with idealistic people; there are those who don't like what journalists do sometimes—who think, well, they're *too* idealistic and that it leads to what these critics say is "bias." But there's no doubt that it is an important part of journalism.

But more importantly, I think idealism and being idealistic is central to being an American. That we were founded by forward-looking, optimistic, idealistic people. And it's very much in the American character to be idealistic. The whole idea of the frontier people who were constantly moving forward. Yes, there's great danger out there—who thinks you can civilize this western part of this continent? Well, we did. We are still frontier-minded people. Going into the cosmos—searching deep probes into our cosmos and beyond—is built on idealism.

Now, it is true that I said that of Robin, because I do believe she's the most idealistic person I've ever met. If Robin is walking along the street and someone puts a pistol in her ribs and says, "Give me your money," the first thing in Robin's mind is, "I wonder what caused this person to reach this point in their life, and what can I do to turn this person around?"

With a gun in your ribs, the answer is "not much." But Robin's a true believer, there must be something.

DREYER: Robin, you were involved in Save Our Springs [a nonprofit created to protect Austin's Barton Creek and the Edwards Aquifer ecosystem], which was certainly an idealistic kind of undertaking, but you were also involved in some very pragmatic decisions involving that. To be effective, maybe we have to temper our idealism with pragmatism.

"I think even living in an almost idyllic place like Austin—for me at least—even here I think it's hard to keep your idealism going. . ."

R. RATHER: A couple of things. First of all, I get up almost every day and, in my own fashion, pray that I don't become bitter, cynical, or exhausted. And a lot of days that's hard. I think even living in an almost idyllic place like Austin—for me at least—even here I think it's hard to keep your idealism going, and I think it's particularly hard right now.

Dad talked about idealism being part of the American DNA, if you will. I think this may be the hardest time it's ever been to be an idealistic American. And I say, and I'm going to say this regretfully, but I think in the Obama administration—because we all had so many hopes for him, or many of us did—that it's been very difficult to keep idealism about the country going when we've been in multiple wars, we've had some really tough constitutional rollbacks, we've had *Citizens United* [the landmark Supreme Court decision that allowed unlimited corporate spending on elections], and, you know, the role of money in every industry and every aspect of government.

I agree with Dad. I think idealism is very important. And it's one of the reasons I like having these kinds of conversations as a community. But it's also just very difficult to see the way forward. I think that the link between journalism and environmentalism is this: "Okay, things are tough, where do we go from here? Who's got a good plan? Who's got the vision? How do you start to visualize that?"

DREYER: I brought the newspaper with me today because there's a story about the City of Austin approving development on a family's ranchland. It says here the council voted six-to-one to give the family permission for somewhat more extensive development than would normally be allowed under the Save Our Springs environmental rules. And this is going to be, I think, a fairly major development.

R. RATHER: It's a total cave by the city council, and it's a rollback of the SOS ordinance that's been, you know, so hard fought for so long. We could talk the whole rest of the hour about my thoughts on how ridiculous that is.

DREYER: Tell us what SOS, Save Our Springs, is and why it was important.

R. RATHER: Most people think of it as not just the leading environmental advocacy group in this part of the country but one of the more popular and successful groups in the sense that—and I didn't live in Austin when the first round of SOS successes happened—but they used the citizens' petition as a way to force the council at that time to adopt stricter rules that would protect our freshwater sources.

And Austin is so blessed; one of the reasons that Austin is so magical to so many people is we have our own aquifer. Our people go swimming in Barton Springs, that's our iconic, soulful touch point as a community. And it has been since all the way back to the time of the Native Americans.

The SOS Ordinance, which went into effect by citizens' petition, was supposed to have been in effect for twenty years or more. At first it was just the state legislature that would bear down on Austin and prevent it from implementing its own ordinance. But, and what's outrageous to me, is that it's not the legislature doing it now, it's our own freely elected, mostly "green" city council that's doing it.

And you know, Dad said before that idealism is out of fashion. I'm concerned that in Austin real environmental protection, both of water and air, is going out of fashion, and we shouldn't let it.

DREYER: Austin has this image of being this very progressive city. And the city council as being this very progressive city council. And yet, Austin, last year, voted down an affordable-housing move—and is still a very segregated city.

R. RATHER: I think you can call Austin progressive only by Texas standards. I think if you look around the country, we're not even in the top fifty for what I consider super-progressive cities. Austin has so many strong points, so many great, talented, creative people. It always has. But most people I talk to feel like we're losing it. I know it's almost a cliché to say that. With every generation of new Austinites, everyone says, "Oh, it was better in the '60s." "Well, Austin in the '50s was better," and so forth.

But a lot of people feel that, around the time Formula 1 racing came to Austin [in 2012]—when that decision was made—that's when people were like, "Oh, we're totally losing it now." And it does seem to a lot of people that, as we've grown both in population and in our economic strength—which is phenomenal, and not something to take for granted—we're going to have to be even more vigilant about our clean air and clean water resources in the age of climate change than we've ever been before.

So, these kinds of rollbacks that you're talking about, it's extremely dangerous. And it's unfortunate, and I think our council should be ashamed of themselves. They're not holding the line as they should be.

DREYER: I grew up in Houston, but we regularly came to Austin, came back and forth to Austin—and Austin was "Nirvana in the Hills."

D. RATHER: Right.

DREYER: People came to Austin from wherever, and they just didn't leave. Especially in the early to mid-'60s, when I first moved here, it was just amazing. But Austin is now undergoing this incredible growth spurt. It's become a high-tech center, one of the fastest-growing tech centers in the country. And it's becoming unaffordable for the people who in some ways made it what it is, especially the musicians that it's famous for. Is it possible to retain at least something of a livable city with that kind of growth?

D. RATHER: Absolutely. I'm very optimistic about Austin. One reason is that Austin has so many people like Robin Rather: idealistic, courageous, not afraid to speak up.

And I sort of quarrel with the word "environmentalist." Robin and I have discussions all the time. What they're talking about is "conservation," *conserving* clean air, clean water, and ground [water]. And I think there's a consensus—whether people consider themselves progressives or liberals on the one hand, or conservatives or reactionaries on the other hand—there is common ground.

And I've seen Robin work. Like when she was helping to lead Save Our Springs. Robin is the kind of person, she walks into a room and says, "Look, folks. There are a hundred things on which we can't agree, but can we find one or two things—common ground—in which we can work?" Now, this spirit has carried Austin forward through its incredible growth, with still a reputation—I think a justified reputation—of being a green city. A progressive city in the sense that it's interested in conserving clean air, clean water—that's the spirit. That's the DNA of Austin. I think it's still here.

Now, it's easy at a time when the city council makes what Robin calls an outrageous vote, to say, "Well, it's all gone with the wind." I don't think so. I used to always refer to Robin as "Robin the Land-Hearted." As long as they have "land-hearted" people like Robin who are willing to speak up, who are willing to try to find common ground, then I remain optimistic about Austin's future.

R. RATHER: Well, I appreciate that, Dad.

There is an army of phenomenal expert environmentalists in this town, and I am just one of many. The thing is, though, you have to be vigilant. In Austin, I think our biggest problem is we think we're a lot greener than we are. And I think there's an aspect of resting on our laurels and taking it for granted by the elected officials who say, "Oh, yeah, yeah, we used to be a very environmental town, but now we're, you know, we're focused on other things."

And I think the affordability—I am so glad you raised that. To me they are linked: Austin's either going to be the kind of place, not that just musicians could live in, but that teachers and firemen and emerging journalists and lots of different kinds of people—or it's going to become sort of like Aspen, where it's really just a playground for the F-1 crowd.

And I know that seems far-fetched. But if you're really on the ground here, it doesn't feel even like it felt as recently as seven or ten years ago.

[*Break music plays.*]

DREYER: All right, Tracey Schulz, what was the music we were just listening to?

TRACEY SCHULZ: That was "What's the Frequency?" done by R.E.M.—a song that's been linked to our guest, Mr. Rather.

R. RATHER: Please don't look that up on YouTube. Dad with R.E.M. on Letterman—singing that song and actually dancing.

D. RATHER: R.E.M. recorded the song, and it had to do with an unfortunate incident that happened to me. [Rather was physically assaulted in 1968 on Park Avenue by a person with paranoid schizophrenia who shouted, "What's the frequency, Kenneth?"] And when they came to rehearse for a program in New York City, I came and sang along with them for about three or four bars until they realized I could not carry a tune in a bucket with a lid on it—and asked me to dance instead of sing.

DREYER: So, what we *don't* want to search is "Dan Rather on Letterman with R.E.M." Got it.

Okay. On another subject, Jeff Daniels recently won the Best Actor Emmy for playing Will McAvoy, the anchorman on *The Newsroom*. [The show created by Aaron Sorkin ran from 2012 to 2014. Daniels won the Primetime Emmy in 2013.] And I know, Dan, that you're a big fan of *The Newsroom* and you blog about it. I think you've blogged every episode.

D. RATHER: I do. It has brought to the screen—whether you're talking about big movie theater or television screen—the most authentic depiction of television news that's ever been in existence.

DREYER: Aaron Sorkin is a genius, too.

D. RATHER: He's masterful, as we learned with *A Few Good Men*, *The West Wing*, a long list of credits. This is the first time he's really faced a lot of criticism; he says so himself. Many people have been critical of *The Newsroom*, but I'm not among them because I'm intrigued. I do follow the story, I think it's a very strong story line, and it's so authentic that it intrigues me week to week. And I was so glad to see that Emmy come his way.

DREYER: I also follow it and also enjoy it a lot.

D. RATHER: Aaron Sorkin's idealistic—to use that word again—idealistic view of what news and newsrooms and news directors and an anchor *could* be is similar to *The West Wing*, which was his idealized version of what an ideal presidency would be and could be. And in that sense, I think it's inspiring.

DREYER: It's also a lot of fun to see Jane Fonda, as a friend says, "playing Ted Turner." Bit of irony there. But she's wonderful.

The story line of *Newsroom* has been very interesting, and I just wonder if anything there reminds you of your personal story—of the stuff that happened with you and CBS? [Rather was removed from the anchor desk and ultimately fired over a controversy stemming from his 2005 reporting about George W. Bush's service in the National Guard.]

D. RATHER: Well, of course, any number of things.

For those who don't know, very quickly, what it's about is this television news operation and this big-time cable news newsroom, and the whole news division has gotten in trouble because of a story it has run. It turns out their producer did some unethical things editing the videotape of an interview, and they had to retract it.

Aaron Sorkin and others have indicated this is based on a CNN case of some years ago in which CNN had to completely retract a story. Where the similarities are with my own case—with CBS News and the Bush military service—is that, in the case of this fiction, the corporate ownership of the news division stands by and stands up for its news division and its reporters, even though they had clearly made a mistake.

In our case we reported a truth. Let's don't go back over it, it takes too long. But it's interesting because in Sorkin's idealistic view, the ownership, the corporate ownership, said, "Okay, yes, our newsroom made a mistake, but you know what? We're going to stick up for them and stick by them." And they stuck up for their anchorman, as well.

R. RATHER: That would be similar, I guess—just to go back even further—to, during the Nixon administration, the whole, "Are you running for something?" Where the CBS management *did* back you up to the hilt. And so, it's not just idealistic; that has happened, and maybe those days aren't gone, but it certainly did happen and thankfully it did.

DREYER: That was at a press conference [in 1974] when Nixon asked you if you were running for something and you said, "Mr. President, are *you* running for something?"

D. RATHER: "No, sir, Mr. President. Are *you*?"

R. RATHER: It was in Houston, wasn't it?

D. RATHER: It was in Houston.

But Robin raises an interesting point—not to belabor this point—but in the 1970s, CBS News was owned and operated by CBS Inc., which was headed by William S. Paley, who *did* back his news division, *did* back his reporters.

R. RATHER: To the hilt.

D. RATHER: But what I like about *The Newsroom*, this HBO series, is that it reminds the public that it matters who owns these major news networks and what their attitude toward community service, public service is. Bill Paley, when he was alive and ran CBS News, he was interested in making money but he saw news as a public service and a public trust. And what Sorkin's outlining in *The Newsroom* is that it would be nice if things could go back to that. We all know they aren't going back to that, but boy, wouldn't it be nice?

DREYER: In *The Newsroom*, it was no given that they were going to support the news department. Because, with the character played by Jane Fonda—and her son, who was the hard character—they had been at odds with the news operation a lot, and so it wasn't just simple; it was complex.

D. RATHER: It was complex, which made the decision for the corporate side to stick by their news division maybe even more surprising to people who follow these things.

R. RATHER: We were talking in the car coming over here about the *Texas Tribune*, which is an online newsroom, if you want to call it that, and it's also a nonprofit. And I wonder, Dad, if you feel that the future of news is more in that direction? As a business model, does that provide greater reporter protection, greater freedom of expression, less corporate interference?

D. RATHER: Well, the short answer is "yes." And for transparency, let me say that I was among the founding people involved with the *Texas Tribune*. I wasn't able to contribute as much as I had hoped, but nonetheless people should know that.

But I think the answer is "yes," at least in the short term. What's necessary now for news—well, we're in this interregnum. The old order is dead and gone. The new order is not completely in place, which is why I used a term the Roman Catholic Church sometimes used. We're in an interregnum. A new business model needs to be found—a business model that can, on a continuing, sustained basis, support deep-digging investigative reporting, first-class international reporting, all of which requires a lot of money.

Nobody has come up with that, a business model that will do that. In the interim, nonprofits like the *Texas Tribune*, like, for that matter, KOOP radio, are filling a very important void for the public. I don't think it's the long-range solution, but in this interregnum period it's absolutely essential, especially for investigative reporting and first-class foreign news.

DREYER: Do you know Bob McChesney of Free Press?

D. RATHER: Yes.

DREYER: One of the things that he believes is that—and he's among others—in looking for that new model, it has to involve public support, public funding. Do you think that?

D. RATHER: I do. For example, we all treasure, or at least I treasure, and I think most people treasure National Public Radio. Why can't we have a companion National Public Television? It is true we have public television, but as you know, it's more balkanized. Why can't we have a National Public Television that's comparable with National Public Radio?

To answer your question, yes, I think public funding can provide a lot. But having spent all of my career in commercial radio and television, to sustain the kind of vigorous investigative reporting and first-class journalism, we need to find a way that it pays for itself.

DREYER: To monetize it.

D. RATHER: To monetize it to produce a profit.

DREYER: One thing that's true with the internet in so many different areas is that it's broken things down, it's compartmentalized things. And there are no new models that have come up. You know, in the old days it wasn't hard to get an audience. You had three television networks and everybody watched them.

D. RATHER: That's an important point. The fragmentation of the audience into smaller and smaller entities has made it all the more difficult to get some cooperative or some commercial operation that can command a large enough audience in the fierce competitive pit that is—what?—I think 850 television places on my tablet, something like that.

The fragmentation of the audience makes it ever increasingly more difficult to come up with a business model that will produce the kind of profits, spin off the kind of revenue that can finance sustained first-class reporting. But being the optimist that I am, we'll find that business model. I'm disappointed we haven't found it already.

R. RATHER: I just want to jump in and say, I think there are two other parts of the equation besides the business model. One of them is—and I want to get back to national leadership—I think we're really missing that person that has such a powerful vision. I think the biggest issue we have as a country, you know, crappy news—forgive my technical terminology—is one problem, but I think the much bigger problem is we don't have one or more national figures that can unify us around a central direction going forward.

A lot of people thought Obama would be that guy, but it turned out he wasn't. I think it's difficult for communications vehicles to unify up, if you don't have leaders that are unifying us up. And that's not to say we don't have mayors and elected officials here and there, but in general we just don't have that powerful voice that brings us together and automatically creates an audience that wants to hear something and discuss it honestly and not in a partisan way.

". . . we just don't have that powerful voice that brings us together and automatically creates an audience that wants to hear something and discuss it honestly and not in a partisan way."

DREYER: I don't want to be the pessimist, especially, you know, sitting opposite the optimist and the idealist. But we're also faced with gerrymandering and *Citizens United*, with the role of corporate money in politics, and with the rise of anti-intellectualism and anti-fact-ism and the incredible force of the right wing. Could one person make a difference at this point?

D. RATHER: I think one person can make a difference, and it occurred to me when Robin was talking. For example, in journalism, Ted Turner was a visionary.

DREYER: Yes.

D. RATHER: And what we are looking for in journalism now is another

Ted Turner or several Ted Turners, people who have a vision. Turner was laughed at when he had the idea of CNN, and in the very early years all kinds of people in network television predicted its rapid demise. Now, I'm not holding Ted Turner as the be-all and end-all, but let's face it, he was a visionary, effected a vision, and we could use a lot of that in journalism now for the nation as a whole.

We could spend the rest of the afternoon talking about it, but we do have to recognize that we're getting kind of bad about not wanting to face the facts. As of this moment, the very large corporations and their money—not exclusively, there's union money involved—very big money has virtually bought the government. And how we get it back from sheer money interests alone, I think, is the major challenge in our American time.

DREYER: And what is the path forward? Is part of it having some visionaries in leadership?

R. RATHER: I actually wanted to ask Dad about how, back in the day, activists like Martin Luther King were able to bring to bear some of what we're talking about. Are we past the point where activism, no matter who the leadership is, can effect change? Has money got such a solid grip that we can't get past it with straight-up activism, grassroots activism?

D. RATHER: We can get past it. And the short answer is "no," it's not a case of all is lost. Having covered Dr. Martin Luther King, Nelson Mandela, and others who had a dream, hearts can inspire other hearts with their fire.

Yes, it would be nice to have leaders such as some of the ones I've mentioned. But not all is lost, because "We the People"—put it all in caps, "WE THE PEOPLE"—still have, when we choose to use it, we have the winning hand.

Whether we can muster the will and whether we can put our own hearts on fire and thus inspire others, is the question of the day.

Author Bill Minutaglio (*right*), pictured here with Thorne Dreyer, joined former *Texas Observer* editor Kaye Northcott to discuss the late columnist and wit Molly Ivins, who was Kaye's coeditor at the *Observer*. The interview occurred December 8, 2009. Photo by Roger Baker.

BILL MINUTAGLIO AND KAYE NORTHCOTT ON MOLLY IVINS

"In the halls of justice, the real justice is in the halls."

Discussing the life, work, and wit of the late great Molly Ivins are Ivins's biographer Bill Minutaglio and her former Texas Observer *coeditor Kaye Northcott.*

Molly Ivins, one of the most influential American journalists of the twentieth century, was a widely syndicated columnist, satirist, and populist political commentator. Ivins was the subject of a 2009 biography, Molly Ivins: A Rebel Life, *written by Bill Minutaglio and W. Michael Smith; a 2010 stage play,* Red Hot Patriot: The Kick-Ass Wit of Molly Ivins, *starring Kathleen Turner; and a 2019 documentary film,* Raise Hell: The Life and Times of Molly Ivins. *Molly Ivins died of cancer on January 31, 2007, at the age of sixty-two.*

Bill Minutaglio is a former professor of journalism at the University of Texas at Austin. He's the author of several critically acclaimed books, including the first unauthorized biography of George W. Bush; the PEN Award–winning Dallas 1963, *cowritten with Steven L. Davis; and* The Most Dangerous Man in America: Timothy Leary, Richard Nixon and the Hunt for the Fugitive King of LSD, *a book he also discussed with us on* Rag Radio.

Kaye Northcott edited the Texas Observer *with Molly Ivins in the early*

'70s. Before that, Kaye was editor of the Daily Texan *at UT Austin, and she later worked as a freelance journalist and as a political writer and editor at the* Fort Worth Star-Telegram—*and also edited* Texas Co-Op Power, *with a circulation of 1.2 million.*

I first knew Kaye in the mid-'60s when she was at the Daily Texan, *and Molly when she edited the* Observer *with Kaye. Molly was a foot taller than Kaye, and they were even further apart in personal and reporting style, but they made a terrific team at the* Observer.

DECEMBER 8, 2009

THORNE DREYER: With me today to talk about the life and times of the great political writer Molly Ivins is Bill Minutaglio—author, with W. Michael Smith, of the terrific biography *Molly Ivins: A Rebel Life.* Also joining us is Kaye Northcott, who served with Ivins as coeditor of the *Texas Observer*.

Bill, you worked with Molly for a while, didn't you?

BILL MINUTAGLIO: I was at the *Dallas Morning News* while she was working—I wouldn't really say "for," but she was *with* the *Fort Worth Star-Telegram*. I think she really owned that place. She was down the hallway, and you knew when Molly was in the house because you could hear her, you could hear her laughing.

DREYER: And had it been radio, you would have been hearing the "bleeps" for whenever she . . .

MINUTAGLIO: That's true, too. The colorful language. You also knew when she was around because it was like the Vatican when the Vatican releases a puff of smoke to indicate a new Pope has been elected. There would be puffs of smoke coming out of the downtown office—where I think it was highly against the rules to smoke—but Molly was liberated to smoke in her office. Others were afraid; she was not.

So, you knew when she was around; she was just great fun to get to know. I had met her in the early to mid-1990s, kind of late to the Molly party, but I did get to know her a little bit, yeah.

DREYER: Kaye, you're—how tall are you?

KAYE NORTHCOTT: Five feet.

Kaye Northcott joined Bill Minutaglio for an interview about Molly Ivins. ©2007 Ave Bonar.

DREYER: And Molly was a foot taller. So Kaye and Molly were quite a pair and have been referred to as a Mutt and Jeff combination, but it was an interesting mix with very different styles, very different approaches.

Molly was hired by the *Texas Observer* after she had been working for the *Minneapolis Tribune*.

MINUTAGLIO: That's right.

DREYER: You all had a meeting at publisher Ronnie Dugger's house, I believe, and I guess that's where you first met her, Kaye?

NORTHCOTT: Yes.

DREYER: At first—because it developed, I think, into a wonderful friendship, working relationship—what was your first feeling about how the two of you would work together?

NORTHCOTT: Well, she was overwhelming. And, of course, we never felt very good standing next to each other. We would rather not even be in the same room if we could help it. Certainly, we didn't want our pictures taken together.

I thought she was pretty much an anecdote machine that day I met her, but her work was very good. I can still remember the stories she told us when we were interviewing her. I mean, that's what an impression she made.

DREYER: Molly came up out of Houston and out of a prep school background. Her father was a major player in the oil business, was one of the people who ran Tenneco, and she had this mix through her life—the influence of Texas and of an East Coast prep kind of mentality. So she had two things playing on her, which ended up working, I think, pretty well.

Bill, Molly started working at the *Houston Chronicle* as an intern originally, and I guess she did a couple of stints there.

MINUTAGLIO: The sense I got was that her folks were happy that she was going to take some summertime internships at the *Chronicle*. I think they thought it would be safe for her there and that she would maybe go to work in what was then, regrettably, called the women's pages. And she would be writing stories about high society, or whatever it was.

But Molly went there and kind of drank the Kool-Aid. She got a lot of ink in her veins very quickly and saw these real rascals and characters and people who were—I guess I would call them healthy skeptics about the way things worked in Houston. And it was a different world than the one that her father and mother had tried to ascribe for her, so she was exposed to a lot.

DREYER: Houston was kind of a wild place then, a boomtown, wildcatter center, very segregated city, but a very active city. A city with a lot of energy, and I guess the *Houston Chronicle* was an interesting place. And Kaye, you have some knowledge of that, too. You knew people who worked at the *Chronicle* during that period of time, and you came from Houston.

NORTHCOTT: Well, even when Molly and I came to the *Observer*, together—when we started editing it together in 1970—the *Chronicle* still wasn't paying attention to integration or poor people, or anything like that. It was very much an establishmentarian newspaper, and some parts of the city just weren't covered.

DREYER: Well, it was owned by the establishment.

NORTHCOTT: It was owned by the establishment, and one of the first things Molly did after she got to the *Observer* was write a piece about the *Chronicle*, which was—I think it was called "Forward to the Rear at the *Houston Chronicle*"—and it just was the current newspaper complaints about the *Chronicle*. And she had done the same when she left Minneapolis, about the newspaper she was on there.

But of course, this was funny—and devastating to some of the managers—and she provided their nicknames in the story. Like Everett Collier, who was managing editor, was called "Puddy Tat." And what happened is that we completely sold out of the *Observer* in Houston for that issue because Everett Collier got every one of them.

DREYER: He bought them all.

I grew up around the *Chronicle*, and the *Chronicle* had a lot of crusty characters. The *Chronicle* was kind of like an old-timey newspaper; it had a great big city room with all the desks, and you had some real characters working there. You almost had the guys with the fedoras with that tag on them that says "Press."

MINUTAGLIO: A lot of good Damon Runyon kind of characters.

DREYER: And guys who became fairly legendary: Billy Porterfield, Stan Redding, Zarko Franks. And my father, Martin Dreyer. And she immediately, I guess, gravitated to these—to the hard-drinking types—and she was hard-drinking and continually smoking, all of her life.

Which was, I guess, another difference between you and her, Kaye. Because you were a teetotaler.

NORTHCOTT: Oh, yeah. I'm just a little sissy. I have this tiny little body that doesn't take well to smoke or alcohol or staying up late, so Molly always called her smoking cessation efforts the "Northcott Memorial" efforts.

DREYER: I understand that whenever you had spent some time with her in a bar or somewhere, you had to go home and throw all your clothes in the washing machine.

You wrote, Bill, that it ended up being a really serendipitous relationship in terms of their two styles and how they were able to work together.

MINUTAGLIO: Absolutely. I'm going to say this right in front of Kaye, but I hope that someone writes a book about Kaye and her contributions—and yours, by the way, Thorne.

So, sure, when you meet Kaye and talk to her, there's a physical difference between her and Molly. But they were kindred souls and really being on the front lines and doing work that frankly nobody else was doing. And taking a look at that big state capitol of ours here in Austin in a way, and through a prism, that nobody else did—just tackling stuff and doing it.

In terms of writing about Molly and understanding her and even by extension Kaye, I began to realize you really have to view them through the prism of history and go back and try to put yourself in that time period and realize how difficult it was to do the work that they did.

DREYER: The book *Molly Ivins: A Rebel Life* is pretty remarkable in the way it deals with how history and these various elements shaped what Molly Ivins became. In high school, when she was young, she was always like a foot taller than any of the boys and felt very awkward and was not comfortable with her friends and with her schoolmates. She basically had a fantasy world and holed herself up and read lots of books.

And by the time that she was up at Smith College she had become this elegant, fashionable young lady.

MINUTAGLIO: She described herself growing up—she's written this—as a "Clydesdale among Thoroughbreds." She was kind of big and sturdy and, you know, big bones, and I think pushing six feet tall by the time she was eleven, twelve, thirteen years old. I think she felt a little awkward by most accounts.

I remember being at Kaye's house—she was generous enough to invite me over—and she had some photographs of Molly dressed *just so*, in this sort of '60s way. Pearls and so on and quite fashionable, and extremely elegant, if that's the standard of elegance. And some people describe her as looking like Jackie Onassis.

DREYER: By the time that you guys were working together, Kaye, you had a *Texas Observer* uniform that you had to sign for.

NORTHCOTT: Yes. It's sort of what you're wearing, which is a blue-jean shirt—we felt that that was appropriate for the legislature. I also carried Big Chief tablets.

DREYER: Molly Ivins had this incredible career at the *Observer*, working with politicians and becoming intimate with the movers and shakers. But some of the movers and shakers were a little bit crazy and a little bit wild.

And then she worked for the *New York Times* and as a freelancer and worked for the *Fort Worth Star-Telegram*, and then ultimately became one of America's most cherished columnists; she was, I think, syndicated in close to four hundred newspapers.

Well, Molly died in 2007 of cancer. And I guess she was fighting with it a number of years.

MINUTAGLIO: She was fighting it almost a decade, really.

DREYER: It was breast cancer, originally, and then it spread. And through that whole period of time she never stopped.

MINUTAGLIO: I think at one point it was just pretty safe to say that she was one of the most influential journalists in America. She had the three hundred—somewhere between three hundred and four hundred—newspapers, syndicated. Her books were perennially best sellers. She was on television, oft quoted, sought after, and she was so prolific. I just was humbled by that in learning about her. She seemingly could write so quickly and at such great length on anything that seemed to occur to her.

DREYER: When she started covering the legislature, she became friends with people like Ann and Dave Richards, before Ann Richards was governor. And [Lieutenant Governor] Bob Bullock, who was probably the most powerful politician in Texas and who later—I think much to Molly's dismay—threw in with George W. Bush.

Her way of dealing with covering politics had some of that gonzo journalism approach. She didn't make stuff up, but she presented what some critics might have called caricatures of Texans.

"One of the things I learned from Molly was to go ahead and be bold and say what I saw in people."

NORTHCOTT: But I think that she really did understand the people she wrote about. One of the things I learned from Molly was to go ahead and be bold and say what I saw in people. You've got a lot of impressions and go ahead and put them on paper. She could nail any character.

DREYER: There was a famous scene where she was in a bar with Bob Bullock, and she was trying to get out and he was blocking her—and she hip-checked him and knocked him onto the floor. And he said something like, "Son of a bitch, I love that Molly Ivins." Nobody else could get away with that, and there weren't any other women at this time doing that kind of thing—well, *that* kind of thing, certainly. That were playing the kind of role that she played. And I guess she was really a trailblazer. Both of you—you too, Kaye—were trailblazers for women.

NORTHCOTT: There were no other women. There had been a female bureau chief of the [Dallas] *Times Herald* at the capitol. But at the time we got there, there were no other women.

DREYER: And the *Texas Observer* at that time was, even though its circulation wasn't that large, was—and has continued to be—an influential force. It was read by everybody who was in power or who had any pretense towards power or wanted to understand the people in power. There were a lot of powerful people that you all were dealing with.

And Molly developed this persona. I guess she always had seen herself as becoming famous?

NORTHCOTT: Yes.

DREYER: A goal of hers or fantasy; a vision of hers from childhood.

MINUTAGLIO: Right. She had noted, at a young age, that she wanted to be famous later on. Just kind of thinking about her—and Kaye might disagree—but I felt that Molly wanted to be known for making a difference, as opposed to being a pop culture celebrity figure, that kind of famous. I think she wanted to go out there and do important work and wanted to be famous for that work.

NORTHCOTT: Yes. She was thinking in the context of being helpful and significant in journalism.

DREYER: According to Bill Minutaglio, "Northcott thought that Molly had the physical will to stay up late, smoke and drink—and to stare deeply into the eyes of people she considered existentially damaged, damaged salesmen of crooked dreams."

How did she look at the people that were running our state? Because she was attracted to it, she was pulled into that milieu.

"Molly wanted to be known for making a difference, as opposed to being a pop culture celebrity figure, . . ."

NORTHCOTT: Well, she looked at them eye to eye—or down—which I wish I could do. And she liked to get deep. She had so many different interests, and she could almost always find something to relate to a subject about. And you could just tell she was paying attention to you and wanted to know what you thought. And at the time you might not be thinking, "Oh, this is all going to come out in the newspaper tomorrow," because it seemed so intimate.

DREYER: Nothing was off the record with Molly Ivins, is that right?

MINUTAGLIO: I love the stories about Molly sneaking off to the restroom or just out in the hallway and filling up reporter's notebooks. All of her papers that she kept over the years are over at the University of Texas at the Briscoe Center for American History. And you can almost see her methodology there, where she would duck out from lunch—or maybe a cool beverage session with Bob Bullock or someone else—and I'll bet they were very, very surprised when they saw the story later on. You know, "Did I say that?" And Molly was writing it all down.

DREYER: There may have been things that she didn't report on because of those friendships—because maybe that helped her to learn more things that were more important.

MINUTAGLIO: Kaye could probably speak to this better than me, but I think Molly sought out people that could really help her understand or try to figure out the sort of inscrutable state government. And Ann Richards served a purpose in that way, and Bullock really did, because he was below deck looking at all the oily machinery and, you know, making it move. I think Molly figured out real quickly that that was a guy worth knowing.

There's an old Bob Dylan song, "In the halls of justice, the real justice is in the halls." The real way it works over there is that you have to go out in the hallways, sometimes to the wet bar in somebody's office at the state capitol or to a nightclub later, to really, as Kaye was saying, really kind of drill down and talk to some of these folks.

And Molly—with a great iron constitution that she inherited, maybe, or absorbed from a lot of those old newspaper cats—she stayed out later and drilled down deeper and was able to affix herself to personalities

"... she stayed out later and drilled down deeper and was able to affix herself to personalities who she knew really had quality information."

who she knew really had quality information. So she was a hellacious reporter in that regard.

DREYER: But wasn't there a rap on her sometimes that she—especially later, when she was a columnist—that she would depend, maybe too much, on just a string of anecdotes.

MINUTAGLIO: Some people would dismiss her that way, but probably illogically. The magic act that Molly had, I think, was, as she wrote frankly, or said in her very last column, that we should render the ridiculous—those who are in power who are ridiculous—write about them in a ridiculous way to paint the accurate portrait.

Kaye told me this when she met Molly: that Molly almost came fully formed as a voice, that she kind of hit the ground running when she came back down to Texas in 1970. That she had a way of having a little fun with Texas and injecting it in there. I maintain it was never mean-spirited, it was for a purpose and most of the time was, you know, pretty darned accurate.

And yeah, sure, maybe she was building a little mythology here and there, and Texas might have become kind of a cottage industry as a place to make fun of, but it was for a good end.

I think what you're getting at, Thorne, is that some people might read her work and say, "Well, gee, it's kind of funny, and there's a lot of cornpone in there." But just like Samuel Clemens or Will Rogers, just study it for a second and you'll see that she's delivering the medicine, making you eat your peas, but in a rather tasty way.

NORTHCOTT: Yeah, there will be nuggets, even in the funniest columns, that you can take home.

DREYER: Oh, I absolutely agree. I know that when she went to the *New York Times*, part of her appeal was that she talked about Texas and about Texans in a way that perhaps reinforced Eastern elitist images of Texas—some of which were certainly very accurate.

But did she, did she have problems with that at all, with the fact that maybe she played to those preconceptions?

MINUTAGLIO: I don't think so. I think she realized it was a utility and it was a way to get a point across. I've heard people say, "Oh, she objectified Texas to some degree that we all down here look like we ride around in the back of a truck filled with watermelons and are up to a lot of skullduggery." She really wasn't far from the truth on a lot of it. But yeah, she had fun. And I think it was always, again, with a wink and a nod and an affection for the state.

Lou Dubose, her colleague and coauthor on many great projects, said that Molly was trilingual: that she could speak real down-home Texan when she wanted to, she could speak fluent French—which she could because she had studied in France and was erudite and could read the great French philosophers in the original language—and then as well could speak this sort of New York, Upper East Coast, Smith College kind of language.

She was—I wouldn't say chameleonlike, but she was very adaptable, and that's why people liked her, I think. And she had friends across the board. She could go to a remote section of far West Texas or wherever and then, yeah, jet off to New York and mingle in those circles as well.

DREYER: Tell me about her relationship with John Henry Faulk. John Henry is another legendary character in Texas, who was a cultural folklorist and a civil libertarian and pretty much a radical—who became a radio personality and was gaining a very big following as kind of a Will Rogers-type storyteller. And then was brought down by Joe McCarthy-type red-baiting.

But he kind of took Molly under his wing and then later—when she came back and Faulk was on his deathbed—committed to him that she was going to take on his fight for civil liberties. And that relationship fed her a lot, didn't it?

NORTHCOTT: I think it did. I think it was one of the very most important relationships. She learned how to hone her anecdotes from him, she learned about the First Amendment, and inherited his deep purpose.

DREYER: Her lifestyle just always carried with her—and her drinking and her smoking—and I guess a lot of that caught up with her later in her life. She was one of these people who lived life so large that she didn't live it as long as we would have hoped. Because she was still in her prime.

Even in the days when she was suffering seriously from cancer and from the treatments for cancer, the chemotherapy and everything, she continued on. I saw her during that last period, at an ACLU benefit where she spoke. She was bald; she wouldn't wear a wig.

And she still had that—even though I guess it was affecting her brain because the cancer had moved into her brain at that time—she still had that courage. She refused to just stop and give up.

MINUTAGLIO: She really did enjoy life. I mean, that is unequivocal, and people said to me that it was like metal shavings to a magnet when Molly came into the room. Right through her later years, people just wanted to be around her. She filled up the room, really enjoyed life, squeezed every drop out of it. And laughed.

When we were trying to think of words that were redundant when we were working on her book, we noticed that laughter and laughing seemed to come up prevalently. It was just a constant theme in Molly's life. She wanted to have fun and render politics—which is so difficult—to render it funny. And almost reduce it, get it, knock it off its high horse, and say, "Some of this is actually funny."

DREYER: Speaking of the book, how did you put together her story? What did you do first, how did you approach it, how did you plan it out?

She saved everything, right, so you had lots of material.

MINUTAGLIO: That was the saving grace, in a way. Molly was a pack rat of extraordinary dimensions. She decided from the age of ten that she was going to keep everything—and she kept her report cards, you know, and unpaid parking tickets, all kinds of things in there. A hundred and fifty big banker's boxes, and they're all over at UT.

So, we began looking there and, frankly, just decided to do the only moderately logical thing, just approach her story chronologically. And then we had the great good fortune of talking to people like Kaye, who really had known Molly better than we ever could. We tried to talk to folks who were close to her and understood her evolution in history and in context.

And what it was like—this applies to Kaye, by the way—when Molly was the only woman in the room. She was often the only, literally, the only woman at the state capitol and in reporting circles and certain areas where you would try to gather news and be a good journalist—and it was extremely, you know, difficult. It was with the help of people like Kaye that we began to understand that.

NORTHCOTT: What are some of the most surprising things you found in Molly's archives?

MINUTAGLIO: This is acutely personal, I guess, but we didn't really understand that Molly had once been engaged to be married to a young man who politically and philosophically was just from another planet than the Molly that most people know and love as a great political commentator and journalist.

She was engaged to be married to a guy whose dad was a CIA operative; he was a high-ranking, very conservative member of the Eisenhower administration—a super-egotist kind of person. And it was so unlikely, it was so jarring, I'm still not sure it made any sense to me.

DREYER: Does it seem like an anomaly, or does it seem like part of a process?

MINUTAGLIO: Well, it seemed like the diminution of a process.

DREYER: He died tragically in a motorcycle accident.

MINUTAGLIO: Exactly, yeah.

DREYER: And that changed her life.

MINUTAGLIO: Molly was really being steered by her dad; folks in the family and friends used to call him General Jim. He was a pretty tough guy and had a lot of complex views about race, to put it mildly, in America. And Molly just grew up resisting everything he stood for. And one thing he stood for was her getting married at some point and having kids and probably settling into a life above the cloud line in Houston as a socialite.

And so, after this wickedly violent death of her fiancé, it seemed that Molly just said, "Okay, I've cleaved with the past and I've made a clean break with it, and now I'm going to move on and do my own thing and be courageous by continuing to resist my family."

DREYER: She never got married. I think she said at one point that her life—and I don't know if she was speaking to some people's perception or assumption or whatever—but she said that her life wasn't even so interesting that she was a lesbian. Something to that effect.

MINUTAGLIO: As she became well known, she was subject to so many rumors and innuendo and stories. As Kaye was saying earlier, she wanted to do something significant on planet earth and change things, make life better for people. She suffered consequences of this pop culture age we live in. People gossiped about her a lot.

Thorne, were you aware that Molly had once written for *The Militant* [a newsweekly associated with the Socialist Workers Party]?

DREYER: I read that in your book.

MINUTAGLIO: That blew my mind and that she had been doing some community organizing and, with her then boyfriend in Minnesota, Minneapolis, going door to door and even testifying in his behalf at a trial. So she had some radical inclinations, too.

DREYER: Kaye, before the *Observer*, you were editor of the *Daily Texan*, which was always a pretty powerful and often rebellious voice. Some called it the voice of conscience at UT.

NORTHCOTT: And the *Daily Texan* also provided the starting point for Ronnie Dugger, the founding publisher of the *Texas Observer*, and Willie Morris, who was also an editor of the *Texas Observer*—and I was very aware of that when I went to the *Observer*.

DREYER: Why don't you tell us about the editor that followed.

NORTHCOTT: Well, there was a backlash. My nickname was "Kaye Northcong," and I think the student body was ready for a different sort of editor, perhaps a conservative editor, which they got with John Economidy—who sort of majored in ROTC, I think.

DREYER: Didn't he campaign on, "Let's not have another one of these liberal girl editors"?

NORTHCOTT: He did. And then Charles Whitman got up on the Tower [in 1966] and blew a lot of people away, and that was on John Economidy's watch—so he started writing all these columns about how to fortify the Tower. And he wanted the top level set up with blinding bubble foam, you know, so if anybody got up there and pulled out a gun, they'd be just, you know, bubbled to death or something. Just bizarre stuff—and so that's what I wrote about in the first issue of *The Rag*.

And his first appearance at the *Texan*—he hadn't worked on it or anything—was to march into the copy room with this swagger stick and smash it on the desk and say, "General John is here."

DREYER: And everybody took note.

Bill, did you ever find anything that was too hot to handle in Molly's papers?

MINUTAGLIO: No, not really. She drank a lot and everybody knew that, and so we decided not to linger with that, or maybe did too much anyway. Molly—unlike a lot of the people she covered—wanted her life to be somewhat transparent and open.

I can't imagine why you would keep all that material unless you really wanted the public to see it at some point, and while she was alive she was donating it with the dictum that after she passed away it would be open, so anybody can go and really take a look at it. Her life was an open book.

It's interesting you mentioned the denim shirts. She decided to donate or put in there a shirt exactly like the one you're wearing, Thorne, and that Kaye used to wear—her old denim shirt, maybe, from the *Observer* days. It's actually in a box at the Briscoe Center for American History.

DREYER: So, with Molly, what you saw is what you got?

MINUTAGLIO: Well, yes and no. I think she compartmentalized some things because she wanted to be, I think, a lot of things to a lot of people.

DREYER: She repressed some stuff?

MINUTAGLIO: Like we all do.

Again, I think she wanted to genuinely be in the moment with people. She loved visiting people and hanging out with people, and I think she always had that great reporter's curiosity, no matter where she went. "I just want to get to know you." She could hardly sit still, it seemed, and some friends did say that they wished that she had more of an ability to find quiet time for herself.

I think she also was very generous. She gave away so much, you know, time, money, cosigned notes for people, mortgages and this and that; she was always giving, giving, and I think maybe at some point it did take a little bit of a toll on her, being so generous.

DREYER: Kaye, how will Molly Ivins be remembered by the world?

NORTHCOTT: By the world? Well, you know, it's too early to tell whether she is of the caliber of a Will Rogers or a Mark Twain. Her writing is very topical in ways that they weren't. But I think she's a major presence who will be remembered.

Texas Observer publisher Ronnie Dugger (*right*) is interviewed by Thorne Dreyer on *Rag Radio*, June 8, 2012. Photo by Alan Pogue.

RONNIE DUGGER

The rattlesnake rattled before he struck.

Ronnie talks about Texas Observer *history, the continuing threat of the bomb, and when LBJ tried to "bribe" him.*

Willie Morris called Ronnie Dugger "one of the great reporters of our time." Dugger, who was eighty-one at the time of our interview, was the founding editor of the Texas Observer *from 1954 to 1961 and later served as the* Observer's *publisher, spending more than forty years with the crusading Texas tabloid. At the* Observer, *Dugger mentored an all-star roster of writers and editors.*

Dugger was born in Chicago and educated at the University of Texas at Austin—where he edited the Daily Texan—*and at Oxford. His books include biographies of Lyndon Johnson and Ronald Reagan, and he also edited* Three Men in Texas: Bedichek, Webb, and Dobie *for University of Texas Press. Dugger, who has held fellowships from the National Endowment for the Humanities, the Rockefeller Foundation, and the Woodrow Wilson International Center for Scholars, received the George Polk Career Award in journalism in 2012.*

I first knew Ronnie Dugger during his years publishing the Texas Observer. *What tales he has to tell! Especially about Presidents Harry Truman and Lyndon Johnson and writers like Willie Morris and Billy Lee Brammer.*

JUNE 8, 2012

THORNE DREYER: Ronnie Dugger is an old friend and colleague and former editor and publisher of the *Texas Observer*. Brad Buchholz of the *Austin American-Statesman* called Ronnie "the godfather of progressive journalism in Texas." He influenced and mentored such progressive journalists as Willie Morris, Molly Ivins, Billy Lee Brammer, Bill Moyers, Lawrence Goodwyn, Kaye Northcott, and Jim Hightower.

RONNIE DUGGER: Actually, I didn't mentor Moyers; Moyers made a remark—when he was on a radio station here—that he used to read the *Texas Observer* but it was like "having to read a book under the covers with a flashlight."

DREYER: But he did say that you were a major influence.

DUGGER: Well, okay.

DREYER: So, you'll accept that?

DUGGER: If I'm going to be a godfather, I might as well be a major influence.

DREYER: You recently moved back to Austin from Cambridge, Massachusetts, where you were hanging out for the last—how long were you there?

DUGGER: I was gone for thirty years.

DREYER: You wrote biographies of Ronald Reagan and Lyndon Johnson, and you have a lot of wonderful stories to tell about Lyndon. There's an article you wrote titled "LBJ, the *Texas Observer* and Me," which was originally run in the *Texas Observer* in 2008, and then the next day at *The Rag Blog*.

DUGGER: By the way, you never can control headlines when you write for any place, and they changed it from "I" to "me" and made it ungrammatical. The subject was "I" wasn't it, not "me"? But anyway, it's uncorrectable.

DREYER: There's no accounting for editors, right?

DUGGER: That's right.

DREYER: In *North Toward Home*, Willie Morris's wonderful memoir of his life and times, he wrote that Ronnie Dugger "is not only one of the great reporters of our time in America; more than that, he had imbued an entire group of young and inexperienced colleagues with a feel for Texas, for commitment in the most human sense, and for writing."

Tell me how the *Texas Observer* came about. It came out of the progressive wing of the Democratic Party. [The wealthy Houstonian and liberal activist] Frankie Randolph actually initiated it, right?

DUGGER: She was actually the first publisher, although we had a group who were publishing it.

I was alienated. I was particularly alienated by McCarthyism at that time, and I was headed for a shrimp boat to go down to Mexico. And one weekend the liberals, that were then called "National Democrats"—they were the people who would be for [US senator from Tennessee Estes] Kefauver or somebody for president—decided they wanted to take over the *State Observer* that Paul Holcomb was running, which was more like an opinion newsletter. But good. And start a paper.

Well, they asked me to do it and we met that weekend. And I told them I would do it but I would do it only if they gave me total control of the content, exclusive control of the content. It was fine to have a party newspaper, but I wasn't going to work for it. And they agreed.

After I left—according to [then future US congressman] Bob Eckhardt, who was in the room when it happened—Mark Adams, who would become our printer, said, "If ever a rattlesnake rattled before he struck, Dugger rattled." Mark, incidentally, denied he ever said it.

DREYER: You did strike.

DUGGER: Yeah, I did. I did. And I didn't give a damn whether I took the job or not. I was sort of plus or minus. So that's how it started. And by the way, every editor that I appointed when I was publisher had the same right. That was the deal. You are free and I can fire you.

That was the deal I had with Frankie Randolph. She did fire me once. She was mad, I think, because I was for either Maury Maverick or Henry González for the Senate race [to fill the US Senate seat vacated by LBJ when he became vice president]. I don't remember which one I endorsed, but they were for the other, and she fired me. She was drunk,

I think. And she called me two hours later—she changed her mind. That's the way it goes.

DREYER: Tell me more about Frankie Randolph. Mrs. Randolph.

DUGGER: Well, she was one of four heirs of the Kirby Lumber fortune. One day, Mrs. Randolph—in 1952—walked into the Harris County Democratic Party office and laid down a thousand-dollar check and said, "Put me to work." And she went to work on the precincts.

She believed that the way to help the country and move it left and toward welfare programs and helping the poor was to organize the precincts, especially the precincts in the minority areas. And then form the liberal Harris County Democrats and take Houston. And that's what she did, and furthermore—in imitation and admiration of her—they did the same thing in San Antonio, and they were trying to in Dallas and Fort Worth. That's what was challenging the national impression of Johnson's control of Texas.

DREYER: Creating a grassroots footprint.

DUGGER: The idea was populism in political organization. And Mrs. Randolph was a radical, a liberal, she was—I don't know where she got her ideas—and she made the bargain with me that I'd have absolute control.

We drank very high-quality Scotch when I called on her in Houston. She was a fine woman. They did not have a pretentious house, though they were multimillionaires, I guess. I never knew how much money they had, but they had this low, quiet house in a better section, but not a big Turtle Creek kind of house like they have in Dallas. And she was a very quiet and modest person. Politicians got to where they were coming to her for support and she would try to figure out "whether," as she said, "they were *our* alligators or *theirs*." That's the way she looked at politics. She was a great influence.

DREYER: There's been some greats—so many incredible characters, personalities, figures—involved in the *Observer* over the years.

DUGGER: Still are. They've got a bunch of characters left, I think, I'm happy to say.

DREYER: Why don't you tell us about some of the people who edited and worked for the *Observer*. There's just a rogue's gallery of wonderful journalists.

DUGGER: I wonder if you could repair that metaphor?

DREYER: Repair that metaphor. Rogues can't be wonderful?
  Molly Ivins and Kaye Northcott, of course, were an editorial tandem and, I think—as Bill Minutaglio wrote in his book about Molly—probably the only two-woman editorial leadership team in the country.

DUGGER: I thought so. I couldn't think of anybody else who had two women running the paper, but now *Mother Jones* does.

DREYER: And Molly Ivins was like—I don't know how tall she was.

DUGGER: Eight and a half feet or something.

DREYER: Eight and a half feet tall. Well, then, Kaye Northcott seemed about four and a half. Anyway, they were such a contrast. Tell me about that first meeting with Molly Ivins, your interview with her.

DUGGER: We had thirty or forty applicants for editor at the time, and Billy Porterfield and Molly Ivins were, in my opinion, about equal. Billy was a wonderful writer, but when I interviewed him, he said he didn't like politics. Well, that's all right. I don't either. But if you don't like politics it might affect what kind of an editor you are.
  Molly was at least equally as qualified, and she had all these fine reports, front-page stuff out of the *Minneapolis Star*.

DREYER: And you thought that Ivins had more political grounding than Porterfield?

DUGGER: Molly didn't have a reputation as a writer yet—which she of course earned. She was a reporter, a good, tough, liberal reporter who was exactly right for the *Observer* model that was developing. So, finally I went with Molly.

DREYER: There was a wonderful exchange at one point, where you said to Molly, "When are you going to get serious?"

DUGGER: When I appointed an editor, they were in complete charge.

And so, I wasn't going around criticizing them or saying I don't agree with that or you should have written it this way. I never said anything to Molly. Gosh, she was good, and she was covering the legislature.

But one day at Spanish Village restaurant [in Houston], the only time in her years at the *Observer* that I asked her anything critical, I said, "Molly, when are you going to get serious?"

And she said—quick as a whip—"When we have a chance to win." And it was such a good answer, I didn't retort. I mean, that closed the discussion: "When we have a chance to win."

DREYER: Willie Morris wrote in *North Toward Home*, "When I had been in my third year at the University in 1955, the year the paper started, I recall Ronnie Dugger, then twenty-four years old, sitting in a small dark office in the old frame building on West Twenty-Fourth Street in Austin, surrounded by newspapers and magazines."

He said, "Brammer"—Billy Lee Brammer—"his associate, was out getting drunk with the lieutenant governor, and Dugger was writing the whole paper by himself in less than twenty-four hours." He said, "Once an issue was put to bed he [Dugger] would take out for somewhere in a woebegone 1948 Chevrolet, crowded with camping equipment, six-packs, notebooks, galley proofs, old loaves of bread, and sardine cans."

DUGGER: Willie could write.

DREYER: What an image. When you finally left the *Observer*, or maybe left as editor, he wrote that you took off to go camping and stayed for a while.

DUGGER: I figured out when I was there eight years that I was only home with my family about four hours a night. I counted how many hours I was working: 120 hours, and there are 168 in a week. Well, I think I lost my thyroid for it. I would have died in my forties if a smart doctor hadn't figured out that I had stopped putting out thyroid [hormones], but then for two cents a day I was able to survive.

DREYER: The *Observer* was an amazing phenomenon, but I don't think that it was always put together by you in twenty-four hours, writing everything.

DUGGER: No, of course not.

DREYER: But you did—or the editor always did—an awful lot of work. He or she wrote a whole lot of it.

DUGGER: Oh, yeah. Actually, what happened, I started alone on the editorial side and we had one business person, Bill Sackett. And I was putting it out alone for maybe a year—or half a year—something like that. Then Billy Lee Brammer came. Billy Lee's novel, *The Gay Place*, is one of the best novels ever written by anybody in Texas, I think. There was Katherine Anne Porter and maybe some others, although I haven't read enough of those novels to say, reliably.

I would have a long row of all the Texas newspapers stacked by days, and one night Billy Lee came in—though he was on the staff of the *Austin American-Statesman*—and started clipping the papers for me. And of course, we'd have a little beer and talk. And then he quit the *Statesman* and he was our first associate editor.

DREYER: His novel, *The Gay Place*, was actually three interconnected novellas.

DUGGER: It was about Governor Fenstemaker. But it was actually Lyndon.

DREYER: It's a great book.

DUGGER: Yeah.

DREYER: David Halberstam said there are two classic American political novels: one is *All the King's Men* by Robert Penn Warren and the other is *The Gay Place*. Billy Lee was in awe, and in some ways loved Lyndon Johnson. Unlike Willie Morris, who was elegant and erudite, Billy Lee Brammer was kind of a gonzo journalist in his own way.

DUGGER: There's a scene in *The Gay Place* where Governor Fenstemaker is in bed with his arms around two women, one on each side of him, and that, of course, reflects scandalously on President Johnson. And furthermore, there was this crusading editor of a liberal paper in Texas who used to go out and bed down with an English teacher in West Texas.

DREYER: Willie England. That was the name he used, and we thought it was a composite of Willie Morris and Ronnie Dugger.

DUGGER: Well, I asked Billy one time, I asked, "Did you say that the person who looks like me went out to West Texas and was making love with this English teacher?" And he says, "No, of course not. I wouldn't put you in my book, you're too inscrutable."

Absolutely a true story.

DREYER: The irony is that he writes this book that paints this incredibly larger-than-life picture of a larger-than-life character to start out with, Lyndon Johnson. Brammer, who worked on Johnson's staff, kind of loved him in many ways and admired him greatly. Even though Lyndon was, of course, on one hand a charmer and on the other hand a giant bully.

DUGGER: That's right.

DREYER: And an incredible manipulator. And I understand that Johnson hated the book.

DUGGER: I wouldn't say he was larger than life; I'd say, "included everything in life." He encompassed life.

DREYER: Johnson hated the book and wouldn't have anything to do with Billy Lee afterwards. And I understand that Billy Lee was just crushed.

DUGGER: That's right. I didn't know he was crushed.

DREYER: A lot of people thought it was one of the things that led to his downfall.

DUGGER: Well, he didn't have a downfall, exactly. He died of an overdose.

DREYER: Yes. But he died of an overdose that was kind of an extended overdose.

DUGGER: And it wasn't fair to Johnson. The last time I saw Billy Lee—I had to go see him in some house on West Twenty-Ninth Street and it was early in the morning, about nine o'clock—he came out of the bedroom, and then a young lady came out of the bedroom, and about five minutes later a second young lady came out. So maybe his imagination was fed by his own life. I wouldn't call that coming apart; I'd say that he just lived in the time.

DREYER: I believe he got terminal writer's block, too. I think that was one of the problems. He couldn't write that second novel.

DUGGER: I didn't know that, either.

DREYER: You turned down Lyndon's—and I want you to talk about this next—his sort of proposed quid pro quo for the *Observer*. I think he said, "Well, the *Observer* has—how big a circulation do you have?" And you said, "Six thousand." And he said, "Well, you want to make it sixty thousand?"

DUGGER: "Stick with me and make it sixty thousand."

DREYER: "And I'll take you there." And you basically said "no." And I want you to tell us about that incident. But you, unlike Billy Lee, ended up having continual interaction with him and wrote a biography of Johnson.

DUGGER: The reason I wrote it finally was because the editor asked me fifty years later to write about that relationship. And the reason I hadn't written it before is because it's sort of self-serving.

Johnson was trying to bribe me, basically. "I'm getting ready to run for president and you need to back me. You're trouble for me when the journalists come in from the Northeast. Sing my praises and we'll make the *Observer* a whamdinger."

Well, that's just a dime away from a bribe. But I didn't want to offend him. I was very shy in person—well, I'm not shy, but I mean I was polite. So, I just needed to get away from there. We were out at the ranch, and he said, "No, no, stay for dinner. Bird will have plenty."

So I was trapped and I stayed for dinner, and there was Bird and there was Mary Margaret Wiley, the managing editor of the *Brackenridge Times* in San Antonio, a high school paper that I was once editor of. And neither one of them said a word all night, I don't think. Johnson told his theory of what a young reporter like me ought to do, which is that you ought to pick out who you want to be president and then you make a book with him and go all out for him, as a journalist.

Well, of course he didn't believe that; he knew better than that. That's just the way he sucked a number of journalists in to write pieces about him—for example, in the *Saturday Evening Post*—about why he should be president. So I had to argue as though I believed he believed what he said he believed—and of course, we didn't get anywhere.

By the time I got away that night, we were at the ranch, out in front of his house. And maybe up to the knees, or just a little above the knees, was a very low fence—I mean, a *low* fence. And he was leaning at me so much that I remember I had to move back a step or two to avoid contact.

DREYER: You said that he put that "long face" right in yours. And he was hands-on, too.

DUGGER: Yeah, he was. And when the *Observer* ran that story about it, they had a photograph of Johnson leaning over [Supreme Court Justice] Abe Fortas. And Fortas was literally leaning back like a bow. That was the way you had to do with Johnson. He was something else.

DREYER: One of the things, I guess, that led to all of this was that you and the *Observer* were on the other side of a major split within the Democratic Party—or an insurgency within the Democratic Party.

DUGGER: And what Johnson was doing was siding with the conservatives because we weren't going to take orders from [Speaker of the House] Sam Rayburn and Johnson like the Democratic Party did in Texas. And therefore, he started calling us the "Red Hots." And that's why I got crosswise with him right away. Now, that's kind of ironic when he turns out to be the best liberal-policy president since Roosevelt.

But the fact is, in that context he was fighting for Price Daniel and the segregationists, and hell—excuse me, *heck*—he got Ben Ramsey appointed Democratic National Committeeman from Texas. And Ramsey was—I won't say Ramsey was corrupt, I don't know, but he was certainly the godfather of corruption in the Texas Senate, which he presided over. So, we had to fight him. Had to.

DREYER: He was such a mixed signal, it seemed like. I mean, he was a supporter of civil rights, but he was also an ultimate Machiavellian.

DUGGER: He wasn't always a supporter of civil rights. In the '40s he even voted against the bill to prohibit lynching Negroes in the South, like they were called at that time.

But I think deep down he was. I mean, when he said in a speech that "we shall overcome," I think deep down he was deeply satisfied to help Hispanics and Blacks. That's who he was, but I think it was [LBJ biographer Robert] Caro who said at one point that he always put his ambition first.

Well, I don't know about *always*, but certainly he was driven to be president. It was a dangerous and uncorrectable obsession. And therefore, I think he would do almost anything to sound like—whoever he was talking to—that he was on his side.

DREYER: And then he was brought down by Vietnam.

DUGGER: Definitely.

DREYER: And how did he struggle with all of that? Was the path just obvious to him?

DUGGER: I don't know. I did a lot of interviewing of him in the White House, and he'd walk up and down. One thing is, he saw Vietnam as a contest between Ho Chi Minh and himself, and it was a macho thing. Another thing that he talked about was, "We'll *make* him"—he used the verb "make" him, "make" them do this, "make" them do that. In other words, "force."

Also, when he was walking up and down, was he worrying about the two million Vietnamese who were dying or the fifty-eight thousand Americans? Well, yes, I guess, but what he talked about was "my boys." He was talking about the pilots doing the bombing; he wanted to be sure they'd get back. No, I'd say he was a very old-fashioned president. His job was to win the war and not imagine the opposition dying.

DREYER: Just sort of block that out.

DUGGER: Oh, sure. That's what presidents are supposed to do, isn't it? They're supposed to be nationally loyal, and to heck with the rest of the world. Well, that's the way he was, in my impression.

You know, it took me a while to more or less realize and acknowledge it, but if you look at Lyndon's presidency, I think it's perfectly and objectively true that it was the most progressive domestic-policy presidency since Roosevelt. After all, Truman was just following Clark Clifford on national health insurance to get the minorities out and get elected. But Johnson really did a whole lot in domestic policy, which is exactly what you would want the liberal to do.

And then, of course, the Vietnam War not only ruined that but killed two million people in Vietnam. I heard Robert McNamara admit to a Vietnamese general in a documentary that three million were killed. I guess he was including the French. So that was, of course, ruinous. And that was the problem with Johnson.

Kennedy came along, though, and he sounded like a lot more moderate man, domestically, than Johnson. Not nearly as liberal.

But in the longer run, I regard Kennedy and Khrushchev as two heroes of the human race. They saved us from nuclear war. Of course, Khrushchev knew very well that we were way ahead of them in our nuclear weapons buildup. They knew that we could first-strike and they couldn't retaliate strong enough to deter us.

In that case they put all their weapons—half their weapons—in Cuba. In retrospect, we realized they were loaded to fire. I just finished Sergei Khrushchev's memoir, where he says his father told him that if they had fired their weapons it would have killed eighty million of us. Well, imagine what we would have done then to the whole Communist orbit. Half the world would have been wiped out. It was that close. It was very close.

I remember Curtis LeMay, the member of the Joint Chiefs of Staff, was sitting there and he told Kennedy to his face—it's in the dialogues, in their transcripts—that what he was doing by refusing to bomb and invade at once, which the Joint Chiefs were unanimously for, was worse than what Chamberlain did at Munich.

Well, see, you can get me to talking about that and I won't quit. In other words, Khrushchev and Kennedy actually saved the human race. And history will show that in the long run. Just like it will show Truman as a mass murderer in the long run.

DREYER: You wrote that when you were at the White House, and you were talking to Johnson about the bomb and about Hiroshima, he said, "*I'm* the one who has to hit this button."

DUGGER: Yeah. There's a little more to it. I mean, it was impermissible to ask the president about nuclear weapons, and nobody ever did it, I don't think. But I had asked Harry Truman why we didn't have a "no first use" policy and—as I recall it—he sputtered with anger. I was about twenty or twenty-one, and his face went red and he didn't answer.

So later, I asked Johnson. I was interviewing him while we were at dinner with two other journalists over in Lafayette Square. You couldn't ask him, "Would you push the button, would you retaliate?" You just couldn't ask that question. I think you would have been thrown out of the White House, like I almost was at the press conference with Truman.

I asked him, "What are people like me supposed to say to our citizens out there when you tell us that in the first thirty minutes of a nuclear exchange four hundred million people will die?" And then he got mad at me because, of course, he and I were adversarial, more or less, and he didn't like me much, although I don't know why he was letting me in the White House then.

And he got into a work-up against "you liberals." He said, "I'm the one who has to know all the facts and I'm the one"—and he put his hand up and then ducked his thumb down in the air—"I'm the one who has to mash the button." That's what he said.

DREYER: Were you afraid that he would actually mash it?

DUGGER: I've been thinking about that for forty years. What does that mean? I think it meant he was psychologically prepared to mash the button. He would be the one who would have to do it, and he would have done it.

The question is, would we retaliate if we were struck? And the issue there—it's the one hidden in the deterrence theory—is that if we are the victims, we've got five or ten minutes that we know we are going to be committing mass murder. We're all going to die, or eighty million of us are going to die. Would we commit mass murder before it occurred?

And the answer is "yes." That's what the deterrence doctrine means. That's why the president, in my opinion—no, in my guess—meant that he was prepared to commit mass murder if somebody was going to mass-murder us. That's where we are now, instead of abolishing the damned thing—*dern* things.

DREYER: Ronnie, you wrote a book called *Dark Star: Hiroshima Reconsidered*, about a Texas pilot who helped bomb Hiroshima. I think he actually flew a reconnaissance mission.

DUGGER: He flew the weather mission over Hiroshima and sent back the words, "bomb primary," for which he was guilty the rest of his life.

DREYER: A fascinating story, and I know that the nuclear bomb was a moving issue for you throughout much of your life.

DUGGER: Still is.

DREYER: At that time, the bomb was on everybody's mind. Children would have nightmares. It was a great cause for all kinds of mental health problems among young people in this country. There was a sense of imminence about it.

DUGGER: And they were right.

DREYER: And they were right. Now it's receded as an issue. How much safer are we?

DUGGER: Worse off. We're worse off.

First, the thing about the Cold War, it was predictable. They knew we were going for first strike. But it nevertheless almost blew up three times. There was the Cuban Missile Crisis, which was just by a whisker. Then in 1979, when Brzezinski was national security adviser to Carter, he was being told by NORAD that twenty thousand Soviet missiles were in the air against us. And he's testified himself that he was five minutes from calling Carter to say we're about to be mass-murdered. What would Carter have done?

And then in the early '80s we were so strong, and Reagan was calling the Soviet Union the "Evil Empire." And Andropov and the Soviets—according to Khrushchev and other sources, especially from Richard Rhodes's book, *Arsenals of Folly*, about the illusion of our armaments—Andropov was getting ready to hit us first so we wouldn't hit him first. And then along came Gorbachev, thank God.

Gorbachev and Reagan. Reagan wanted to disarm, wanted to abandon nuclears. I think somebody lied to him at Reykjavik [the site of a summit between Reagan and Gorbachev in 1986]. We don't know who lied to him about Gorbachev's position, but then, of course, "Star Wars" [the Strategic Defense Initiative] became the hang-up that kept Reagan from going along with Gorbachev.

So that certainly makes Gorbachev one of the three great people on this issue, and I give Reagan a lot of credit. He just thought his way through it and said, "Hey, we can't kill all these people," and he was trying to prevent it. But it's still on the table.

Now we're getting nine nuclear nations, each one with a military-secrecy policy keeping us from knowing what they're doing. There's a guy named Rosenbaum who wrote a book where he basically says that the Israelis have five German-made submarines in the Mediterranean, armed with nuclear weapons, ready to retaliate if Iran strikes them. Who knows when they're going to use them? If they have them. I mean, we don't know. It's much more dangerous than it was in the Cold War.

DREYER: There also must be weapons out there that are unaccounted for, warheads that are unaccounted for, and who knows whose hands they're in?

DUGGER: Some of the guys have woken up—and one of those was McNamara before he died. But the fact is we've got to abolish them.

DREYER: Okay. Brad Buchholtz, in a feature story for the *Austin American-Statesman*, called Ronnie Dugger the "godfather of progressive journalism in Texas."

DUGGER: That piece was so complimentary. Brad did a really careful job. The trouble is it read like an obituary, and I'm not dead yet.

DREYER: In that story, you said, "I see myself as an eighty-one-year-old man with his life's work ahead of him."

DUGGER: That's right. That's right.

DREYER: So, you're just getting started, and you've got a lot of stuff going.

DUGGER: I figure on ten years, if I'm lucky.

DREYER: Our friend David McBryde just wrote in from Berlin. He said, "Why don't you ask him if he would tell some *Texas Observer* tales about courageous journalism in Texas and the fights about the oil depletion allowance?" And he also wrote that he remembers that the *Daily Texan* once ran a blank front page to protest the censorship of the report on the oil depletion allowance [a law that gives major tax breaks to oil producers].

DUGGER: Actually, that was Willie Morris. Willie was the editor of the *Daily Texan*, and he was raising all kinds of Cain.

DREYER: It was Willie Morris who did that, yes.

DUGGER: He was the editor there, and I needed an associate editor at the *Observer*, and when he graduated I hired him. But it wasn't on the front page, it was on the editorial page. They had put censors over him, the regents had, the Texas Board of Student Publications, at least temporarily, had. So, when they wouldn't let him run this editorial, he just ran a blank space—which is why I thought, "Hey, I'd better hire him over here."

DREYER: What was the issue about the oil depletion allowance?

DUGGER: I was just writing editorials about it—against the oil depletion allowance—and it's a complicated story. But it cost me, personally, like these things tend to. I was the university's nominee for the Rhodes Scholarship one year, and I got to the two judges who were in the regional—and it was a particular professor of law who hated my guts because of my editorials on the oil depletion allowance, and that's all we talked about. So I had to get to Oxford some other way.

DREYER: And you got there.

DUGGER: Yeah.

DREYER: And I think Willie Morris got there, too.

DUGGER: Thanks to the Austin Rotary Club, which sent me there. When I got back, though, I made a speech to the Austin Rotary Club. About a thousand people were there, and I got a standing ovation—except from the doctors present, who passed a resolution that the Rotary Club should stop sending students abroad because they were coming back infected with foreign ideologies. I was for national health insurance.

DREYER: You were for national health insurance way back when.

DUGGER: Oh, yeah, about '51, '52.

DREYER: What do you think about what's going on now?

DUGGER: Well, I think both political parties have descended pretty low.

The Republican Party, which used to have honorable conservatives of conspicuous power in it, seems to me has turned into a military phalanx to destroy government except for war, police, and enriching the rich. You just don't want any government for anything but that. And to commit wars around the world whenever we please.

Whereas the Democratic Party seems to have been hollowed out—I guess by the power of money that has now become uncontrollable. So we're in a vacuum situation. It begins to be comparable in my mind to the Weimar Republic.

So, along comes the Supreme Court and becomes a five-person dictatorship, first prohibiting the election of Albert Gore as president, but beyond that, opening corporate money vaults. Huge. We're talking Exxon, we're talking General Electric, we're talking all the banks; they can spend any amount of money for any candidate they want to because they're "persons."

Corporate personhood. Long history of absolute scandalous evolution into the idea that corporations have the full rights of citizens. I don't think the country can last five or ten years with open corporate vaults pouring into every election they choose. Now, you can still win some elections when you don't have as much money as your opponent. But in ten years? I don't know. I don't think so.

We used to have a guy at the *Observer* who went down to Mexico a lot and used to call Mexico an "imitation democracy." That's what *we* are now. We're now an imitation democracy governed by a corporate oligarchy in league with the billionaires, and a bought Congress. I think the Congress, with honorable exceptions, is now a whorehouse—pardon me, can I say that?

"We're now an imitation democracy governed by a corporate oligarchy in league with the billionaires, and a bought Congress. I think the Congress, with honorable exceptions, is now a whorehouse—pardon me, can I say that?"

DREYER: You can say it again if you want to.

DUGGER: All right, so you've got a whorehouse Congress, you've got presidents chosen by open corporate money vaults. And the other way you can look at it is that we're headed toward fascism. Now continue all the appearances of being a democracy, we'll continue to have elections, which—and I'm happy to have had a hand in establishing this fact—can now be stolen by counting them in computers.

DREYER: That was an issue that you've dealt with a lot.

DUGGER: Since 1988 in the *New Yorker*.

But Congress has not passed a bill yet because both Democrats and Republicans are elected by the same system. And you don't fix a system, like you don't fix the corporate money in politics, in the system which elected most of the members.

Maybe we should take some deep breaths and start thinking about a Social Democratic Party in the United States that isn't afraid of the word "socialism," that is willing to go into a much more active program of public ownership, that will not be segued or finessed out of facing corporate power. In other words, following the European model.

Now, the question is—and I'm not an optimist, but I think you have to continue to try—is American politics now so dominated by the rotgut imagery that has been promulgated? I always remember George Bush the First running his presidency about how horrible the L-word is, the word "liberal." Well, that was just a sort of symbol of what's happened to the whole political discourse.

I don't have any answers, but I think we ought to realize that we're in a very deep hole and may not get out. That our country may be ending as a free and a good place.

> **"I don't have any answers, but I think we ought to realize that we're in a very deep hole and may not get out. That our country may be ending as a free and a good place."**

DREYER: There's a lot of people who believe, for one thing, that we should start building alternative institutions, cooperatives, you know, that sort of thing.

DUGGER: Gar Alperovitz is a wonderful advocate of this, and he is arguing that we need a larger public sector—not so large as to jeopardize liberties like they did in the Communist countries. But he wrote a piece called "Not So Wild a Dream" published in *The Nation*, which I recommend to you. Alperovitz is saying that in some sectors we need more public ownership.

And in that connection, let me give you an example of how it gets lost. John Kenneth Galbraith advocated Democratic Socialism for the United States, but only in one book, in the '70s. And it was—it's a passage in this book, maybe eight or ten pages, that's very similar to what Alperovitz has written in *The Nation*.

Furthermore, both of them turned to Europe for all the models. I mean, my heavens—you remember Adlai Stevenson ran for president and he had a son who was a senator named Adlai Stevenson. He advocated a public oil company. We've got all this oil, why don't we produce it ourselves and find out how much it costs to produce it? Then you can compare it to what you're having to pay at the pump. Yardstick corporations, they're called.

Plenty of democratic nations have percentages, for example, of their airlines. Well then, the public airlines, they don't get tax advantages, if they're better than the private airlines—the private airlines have to get better.

What's actually happened, if I may say so, is the whole theme of free enterprise has been replaced as a reality by what I think of as a second system, which is essentially gigantic corporations that are transnational.

First, if you can't get the banks, the big banks that are "too big to fail," to break down, as Alperovitz says—then the logic is the country should take them over. Because then you can go back to a competitive banking system.

DREYER: But the public sector has been so demonized.

DUGGER: I know it has. That's what I'm asking. Have we gotten so propagandized that we can't think any more in our own interest?

Paul Krassner at City Lights Bookstore in San Francisco. Photo by Heidi De Vries/Creative Commons.

PAUL KRASSNER

A raving, unconfined nut.

Satirist Paul Krassner talks about his legendary publication, The Realist, *his collaboration with Lenny Bruce, and his acid trip with Groucho Marx.*

According to the New York Times, *Paul Krassner was "an expert at ferreting out hypocrisy and absurdism from the more solemn crannies of the American culture." On the other hand, the FBI claimed that Krassner "purported to be humorous" but was in fact "a nut, a raving, unconfined nut." Krassner in turn titled his autobiography* Confessions of a Raving, Unconfined Nut: Misadventures in the Counter-Culture.

Paul Krassner was one of our most important social critics: a stand-up comic, an author, a journalist, the editor of The Realist—*one of the most significant satirical publications in this country's history—a radio personality (named "Rumpleforeskin"), a countercultural icon, a founder of the yippies, a collaborator with comedian Lenny Bruce, and a member of Ken Kesey's Merry Pranksters.*

I would run into Paul Krassner in the '60s and '70s at underground press gatherings and other national events. When I was working at KPFT radio and Guru Maharaj Ji came to Houston to levitate the Astrodome, Krassner helped anchor our "bliss-to-bliss" coverage. But I got to know him better when he became a regular contributor to The Rag Blog *and we started having conversations on* Rag Radio.

Paul Krassner, who joined us on this show four times, died on July 21, 2019, in Desert Hot Springs, California, at the age of eighty-seven.

AUGUST 3, 2010, AND AUGUST 10, 2010

THORNE DREYER: Social satirist, *Realist* editor, *Rag Blog* contributor, and longtime friend and colleague Paul Krassner was a major inspiration for those of us involved in the early days of the '60s underground press.

Hey, Paul. How are things in Desert Hot Springs?

PAUL KRASSNER: Hot.

I appreciate your introduction because when I was going to perform at the Just for Laughs comedy festival in Montreal, it was like a whole conveyor belt of stand-up performers and the emcee just came in and said, "Okay, what do you want me to say about you?" And I said, "Oh, just say I'm a social satirist"—what *you* called me, Thorne. But when I got up onstage, he said, "Our next performer is Paul Krassner, a sociopath."

DREYER: So, you went by both, you acknowledged both?

KRASSNER: Yes. Yes. Two sides of the same coin.

DREYER: I know you've called yourself an investigative satirist.

KRASSNER: That's true. I do research before I make up stuff.

DREYER: You once said that when you took Spiro Agnew's name and rejumbled the letters, it said, "Grow a Penis." And you pointed out that you could actually say that in the underground press.

KRASSNER: But you know, about the Spiro Agnew anagram that you just mentioned: When I was on *60 Minutes* and Mike Wallace said to me, "Well, now, what's the difference between the underground press and the mainstream press?" I said, "Because I can point out that when you mix around Agnew's name, it comes out 'Grow a Penis.'"

And of course, that was edited out of the show, proving my point.

DREYER: So, tell us how *The Realist* came about.

KRASSNER: I had been working for Lyle Stuart, who put out a paper called *The Independent*, and it was in the anticensorship tradition of

I. F. Stone's paper and George Seldes's *In Fact*—and going all the way back, in that tradition, to Tom Paine during the American Revolution.

At that time Lyle Stuart was the general manager of EC Comics, which included *Mad* magazine. And so they became friends, Lyle and Bill Gaines, who was the publisher of *Mad* and all those comic books—and even though he was an atheist, Gaines also published what his father had left him, which was the *Illustrated Bible*.

So, we all became friends and we moved our office onto the same floor as their office in downtown New York, in what was then known as the Mad Building. And so I submitted a few things to *Mad*. I would write the script and then they would assign it to an artist.

But there were certain things that were too adult for them. They had a circulation of a million and a quarter, and they were mostly teenagers or even preteens. And at that point there was no adult satire magazine. This was before *Spy* magazine, it was before *National Lampoon*, and it was before *Doonesbury* and before *Saturday Night Live*. I had an open field of taboos that I could explode one at a time.

"And my personal goal was to communicate without compromise."

And so, what *The Realist* was going to do was combine both what I had gleaned from *Mad* and from *The Independent*; it was going to be a combination of entertainment and the First Amendment. And my personal goal was to communicate without compromise.

DREYER: I was just recently reading Frank Jacobs's biography of William Gaines and also revisiting Paul Buhle and Denis Kitchen's wonderful book, *The Art of Harvey Kurtzman*. You know, *Mad* magazine, even though it wasn't adult, was in many ways—especially during Harvey Kurtzman's reign—was really pretty subversive. And I think it had an impact that affected us all.

KRASSNER: Oh, no question. No question. It triggered the irreverence gland in young kids, and once that was triggered it was hard to go back to believing all the piety that came out in misinformation, disinformation propaganda.

DREYER: And that's a major gland and potentially very active.

KRASSNER: Yes, exactly. So, what I was just trying to do with *The Realist* [founded in 1958] was a *Mad* magazine for grown-ups.

DREYER: I remember, every time it came out, just reading every word in the thing from front to back. You know, its impact was profound on a lot of people.

There are two things, I guess, that *The Realist* is most known for. One is the feature on the parts that were left out of the Kennedy book, and the other is the wonderful Disneyland Memorial Orgy poster. You're probably better at telling about the things that were left out of the Kennedy book in a way that can be said on radio.

KRASSNER: Let me give you the context first. It was in 1967, four years after the assassination of John Kennedy, that a book was going to be published called *The Death of a President* [by William Manchester]. And this was a book authorized by Jacqueline Kennedy and Robert Kennedy, about the assassination, what led up to it, and the aftermath.

Suddenly, in January of that year, there was a big splash in the media that Jackie and Bobby didn't want the book to come out, and their contract meant that they had final say.

So, parts had to be burglarized from the manuscript.

I did my best with contacts in the publishing industry to get the original manuscript, but I failed, so I was forced to write the parts myself, in Manchester's style—and it started out with a seduction. I didn't know then, but there was a literary category called "apocrypha"—and what I wanted to do was to nurture the incredible in the credible by starting off with, you know, the outside layer of peeling an onion.

In this case it was that during the 1960 primaries, Lyndon Johnson and Jack Kennedy were vying to win the primary. And during that campaign Lyndon Johnson said that John Kennedy's father, Joseph Kennedy, when he was an ambassador to England, was a Nazi sympathizer. Now, this was a true story. He did say things that would indicate that with total clarity. And so, it was really just pure pragmatism that

Kennedy had Johnson as his running mate because, you know, he could get that Southern vote. There were no ideals attached to it, or loyalty.

So, I would take things like the affair with Marilyn Monroe that reporters knew about, but it was just not known to the public except by gossip. And so, I printed that—again, in Manchester style. And then I got some stuff that was half true—like there was a movie magazine called *Photoplay* which asked the readers, "Should Jackie Kennedy start dating again, or is it too soon?"

And so, I had Jackie Kennedy—quoting her—saying, "What else do they want to know? Do I use birth control, do I use a diaphragm, or do I take the pill? Do I keep it in my nightstand or in the medicine cabinet?"

So, it has a ring of truth to it.

When I finally got to the climactic paragraph about when Kennedy's body was being brought back from Dallas to Bethesda where the hospital was, Jackie described a scene in which she walked in on Lyndon Johnson leaning over the casket with Kennedy in it. And she said—and this is my euphemism for what she said—but she described that Lyndon Johnson was performing an act of necrophilia on the corpse.

And, you know, I'm not judging necrophilia, by the way, as long as it's between consenting adults.

DREYER: One adult in that instance wouldn't be able to consent.

KRASSNER: Well, that's true, but, you know, I'll sacrifice facts for a good punch line.

So, then it continued on with the Warren Commission, discussing what the purpose of it was: to change the entrance hole from the grassy knoll so that it would look like an exit wound from the Texas [School Book] Depository. A lot of people believed it—if only for a moment—because they had been seduced into it, and they were in an acceptance mode.

DREYER: Ready to believe anything.

KRASSNER: If only for a moment, because they, at that moment, they believed that the leader of the Western world, LBJ, was what the FBI called *me*: "a raving, unconfined nut."

DREYER: And it wasn't real hard to convince people of that. I think there are those of us who will never again think of that event, especially of that plane flight, without that image coming into our minds.

KRASSNER: I published it because it blew my own mind. That particular scene was suggested by writer Marvin Garson [later editor of the underground newspaper the *San Francisco Express Times*], who was an unheralded genius. My mind was blown in the writing of that, and I wanted to share that with my invisible community of readers. And since I was relatively jaded, there was no doubt in my mind that it would blow the minds of the readers.

So, there was that spark and that image that really woke a lot of people up, you know—among them George Carlin and Lewis Black and Elayne Boosler. A lot of comedians, budding comedians, read *The Realist*. And the feedback I got was that it inspired them to speak as freely as they thought rather than hold back for fear of offending the audience. And that was my purpose, you know, to do what the mainstream press didn't do.

"And that was my purpose, you know, to do what the mainstream press didn't do."

DREYER: The other thing that became pretty famous—that had legs that carried it beyond *The Realist*—was the Disneyland Memorial Orgy centerfold. Which was quite a day in the park. And was done by Wally Wood, right?

KRASSNER: I'll tell you how that came about. I think it was in December 1966 that Walt Disney died. And I remember that he had been the intelligent designer of all these imaginary characters—who felt real. You had seen them so many times, and you could identify with them in certain situations. Except that they had no libido, you know; it was repressed by the Disney empire.

DREYER: Terminally wholesome.

KRASSNER: Yeah. A good description.

So, I imagined that there would be a funeral. And I thought that Disney's casket should be carried by the Seven Dwarfs and the eulogy could be given by Goofy. But then I thought, well, there would be an old-fashioned Roman binge with all this repressed sexual energy that had built up over the decades.

DREYER: The witch is dead.

KRASSNER: Yeah, that energy can go in any direction.

Wally Wood had illustrated the first piece that I sold to *Mad* magazine, and it was a thing called "If Comic Book Characters Answered Those Little Ads in the Back of Magazines." And his style was so good, and I knew he could capture those figures, so I described to him what I just described to you about this orgy in Disneyland. And he liked the idea right away.

So, he sent back this magnificent montage of all these characters, you know. Goofy and Minnie Mouse doing it in the park. Tinker Bell doing a striptease as Pinocchio's nose got longer. It was in black and white and I published it as the centerfold in *The Realist*. In the same issue, by the way, that had the cover story of the parts left out of the Kennedy book.

There were some communities that wanted to censor it. They thought it really showed how decadent *The Realist* was. It was so popular that I published it as a poster, also in black and white. But then a couple of years later there was a pirate edition in Day-Glo colors and Disney went after them—but didn't go after me.

DREYER: Who would dare?

KRASSNER: They certainly discussed it, from my sources there. But they figured it would only increase awareness of it and backfire on them. Then the statute of limitations passed, and just five years ago I published a new edition that was digitally colored by a former employee of Disney and on better paper, and people can see it on my website. It really captured the spirit of what I had wanted Wally Wood to convey.

And there were kids who grew up on that. Whenever an order comes in, I always say, "How did you learn of our website?" And usually the answer is, "Well, when I was a kid my mother tore the Disney poster off the wall and I've missed it all these years and I just googled you and there it was."

DREYER: You talked about the characters—that they were sort of *in* character—but you just took it a step further. That's kind of the basis of a lot of satire isn't it? You tell the truth by telling a little more than the truth.

KRASSNER: Yeah, you just exaggerate it. But, as things get more and more bizarre in the real world, it's becoming more and more of a challenge to satirize it, to present a metaphorical extension of the truth.

DREYER: Because it's all so crazy as it is.

KRASSNER: Oh, it is. There's so much information coming in that the attention span has gone from Play-Doh to MTV. A recent example of that was when John McCain denied that he ever said he was a "maverick." You know, being blinded to the fact that there are video records of his saying it. Not only that, but the title of his autobiography included him calling himself a maverick.

DREYER: When we look back on it now, what kind of impact did you have? And, for that matter, what impact did the underground press have? Because there was a new kind of media that got created in that day and time; it grew out of the counterculture and the radical political movement and was made possible by the ready availability of the offset press. Right now, when you look back, what's the legacy?

KRASSNER: Well, you know, it developed organically. The *Berkeley Barb* and the *San Francisco Oracle* were two of the early ones; the *Barb* was mostly political, and the *Oracle* was mostly psychedelic. And then—on October 6, 1966, I think it was—LSD became illegal. At 2 p.m. on that date everybody was standing around in San Francisco—at intersections and the Panhandle and Golden Gate Park—holding a tab of acid in their hands. And there were cops there—cops were around. Then at 2 p.m. promptly everybody ingested their tab of acid and the cops could do nothing; there was no law against internal possession.

It was that event that kind of made the *Berkeley Barb* realize that taking illegal drugs was political. And arresting people for it was a form of making them political prisoners. And the psychedelic *Oracle* editors realized that they couldn't separate freedom to ingest or smoke any drug that you wanted to—couldn't separate that from the political, like the war in Vietnam and civil rights. They were different aspects of freedom.

DREYER: *The Rag* in Austin was like the sixth underground paper, and it was started with the premise that they were both interrelated, the political and the cultural. That was part of what was happening in Austin, anyway; it was all tied together.

KRASSNER: Each paper—and each community—had its own personality. But what they all had in common—and I'm sure this was true of Austin—there was an instant readership for this kind of publication. Because these readers saw the difference between what they experienced on the streets and how it was reported in the mainstream media.

DREYER: Absolutely. The underground press reported it differently—and I think the underground press had an impact on the mainstream media. What's the relationship between what's happening on the internet now and what we were doing in the '60s?

KRASSNER: I think it's important because the internet has changed the nature of demonstrations, for example. You know, young people today, they don't even know what a mimeograph machine was, but we used to get our hands all full of ink turning out these leaflets, which would then be folded and sent out in the mail. And on the web, there's no postage, it's essentially free—and you can reach more people, more quickly, by just hitting a send button.

As the editor of *The Realist*, my ultimate goal was to see myself put out of business, which would mean that communication had been liberated—not by me, but by cyberspace. Anybody could say anything now. It's not like the old saying, "We have a free press as long as you can afford to buy a printing press." That no longer holds. And so, you know, it's like any tool. A hammer can be used to build a house or to hit you on the head.

DREYER: There is a difference, though. There's an alienating aspect that wasn't there: you sit in your living room and you don't interact with other people. I remember the underground papers were community institutions, and we'd have hundreds of people get involved by coming to the *Rag* office or the *Space City!* office in Houston. It became a community center and got people involved, then, in the larger activities. There's no question that the internet can mobilize people instantly, but we also become sort of isolated at the same time.

KRASSNER: There's that element of it, but that's one end of the spectrum. The other element is that it brings people together, you know, and in different ways. It brings people together only electronically if it's something like the important task of getting Betty White on *Saturday Night Live*. But it has brought people together literally. The first one that comes to mind is these things that they call freeze actions.

DREYER: Like at Grand Central Station.

KRASSNER: Grand Central Station, where people broke out singing opera and others joined in, and you could just see a smile on people's faces. At some point they realized that it was planned, it wasn't spontaneous, but they nevertheless enjoyed it. And, you know, that's what Emma Goldman said: "I don't want to be in a revolution if I can't dance." If you can make people feel good, that's a start.

DREYER: And then Facebook and all the incredible contacts that get created, you know.

KRASSNER: It's a strange phenomenon, because I was a loner: I was a kid being a martian trying to learn how to fake being an earthling. I essentially had no friends through high school and through college. Lyle Stuart at *The Independent* became my first real intimate friend as well as mentor and severest critic.

And then, as I got into publishing, I would meet friends in all of the things I got into. If I was covering a conspiracy convention, I would meet people there. When I was covering a swingers' convention or going to the cannabis club in Amsterdam, I would meet more and more people.

"I was a kid being a martian trying to learn how to fake being an earthling."

And now it's ironic because I have almost five thousand Facebook friends, which I think is the limit. And I would say 99 percent of them I've never met. But sometimes I'll mention something there and information will come right away from somebody who had a similar experience. Or I'll just say something, and then I watch the Facebook friends get into arguments about it. It's like throwing a pebble into the stream and then watching the ripples that the pebble created. It has nothing to do with me anymore.

DREYER: Yeah, it's a lot of fun.

A friend, I think a mutual friend, David McQueen, contacted me when he saw that you were going to be on the show, and he said, "Have Paul tell the folks how he was banned from the KSAN airways in San Francisco." He says it's quite a story.

KRASSNER: Then you know what a sweet guy Dave was, but if you looked up in the dictionary "radio voice," it would be his picture next to it.

DREYER: Booming, eloquent.

KRASSNER: I had been on a radio station in San Francisco. I had my own show.

DREYER: Were you "Rumpleforeskin"?

KRASSNER: That was my name. At first the telephone book didn't want to list it. They said, "We can put 'Foreskin, Rumple.'" I said, "No, no, it's not the same." There was a call-in show and one guy called in very flustered and angry and said, "Let me talk to Rumpleforeskin"—and saying it, you know, it just loosened him up.

Eugene Schoenfeld—who was known as "Dr. HipPocrates"—had a syndicated column in the underground press. And he had a radio show on this station, and his guest that afternoon was going to be Margo St. James, who was the founder of COYOTE, an acronym for Call Off Your Old Tired Ethics. It was essentially an organization to fight for prostitutes' rights.

And so she was going to be his guest. But they got there early and came into the studio where I was, and Margo started unzipping my pants—and I said "no." I said, "Be careful, the zipper is held on by a safety pin"—which it was. I didn't want her to stick herself, bleed on my jeans.

DREYER: Certainly not.

KRASSNER: And so I did the station break, and I said, "This is KSAN, the station that blows your mind in San Francisco." It was innuendo, but nothing that would account for being fired. But I wasn't fired, I was just banned from the station for a while.

DREYER: So, tell us about your acid trip with Groucho Marx.

KRASSNER: Oh, well, this was when—I guess it was '67—when Otto Preminger was directing a movie called *Skidoo*, and it was about a Mafia family. Well, one of them got into this prison where there was a hippie who got in the mail a letter that had been soaked in LSD. And he put it into the water supply of the prison. And, so, you know, everybody drank the water and was tripping. It was kind of simplistic. It showed one prisoner saying, "Oh, I see it all now. I'll never rape anybody again."

They originally wanted George Raft to play a gangster, a leader of the gangsters, but they got Groucho Marx to do it—and his name was "God." When I met him, I said that now he would be typecast. He could put it on his resume: "I played God." But anyway, Groucho was a reader of *The Realist*. I had interviewed Otto Preminger for *Playboy*, so I was able to get on the set. Groucho and I had dinner, and now, since this was essentially a pro-acid movie, he wanted—well, he had always been curious about LSD.

DREYER: And being a known method actor, he needed to experience it, right?

KRASSNER: Right. And then he turned on Stanislavski, would you believe it?

DREYER: No.

KRASSNER: He had never taken LSD, but he had read about my exploits and asked me if I could get some pure stuff for him—because there were all these rumors that it had arsenic in it—and would I care to accompany him on his trip? So I did not play hard to get. We met at the home of a Beverly Hills actress. I didn't drive—[folk singer and yippie activist] Phil Ochs drove me there—and it was a nice apartment.

I was used to taking acid and listening to rock music, but the only albums there were Broadway show tunes and classical music. I remember there was Bach's Cantata no. 7, and we were listening to that, and Groucho suddenly said, "Hey, I'm supposed to be Jewish, how come I'm seeing visions of beautiful Gothic cathedrals?" And I said, "I don't know, I was seeing beehives myself. Moving beehives."

There was a lot of quiet time. At one point, Groucho went to urinate and he came back and he said, "The whole human body is a miracle," and he went on like that for a little bit.

We talked about his show, *You Bet Your Life*, the quiz show. He said his favorite contestant was a guy who was just very joyous, and Groucho said to him, "You know, you seem like a happy guy; how do you do that?" And this was an elderly gentleman, Groucho described him, and he said, "Well, every morning I get up and I decide I'm going to be happy that day."

And Groucho was just—it just remained in his memory because he hadn't thought of happiness as something that you could decide that you would have until it became a habit.

DREYER: Tuli Kupferberg, who recently passed away, was a poet, an actor, just an amazing character. He was one of the founders, along with Ed Sanders, of the Fugs, one of the most important, outrageous rock bands that came up out of the '60s. You and Tuli were good friends. Give us a little sense of what we've lost.

KRASSNER: You know, I just finished writing my *High Times* column, "Brain Damage Control," this morning, so I want to read to you just a couple of quick paragraphs from it. I want to get the language exactly right.

DREYER: And we'll hear it here first.

KRASSNER: That's true. And okay, here it is: "In 1966 I published an article by John Wilcock called 'Who Do the Fugs Think They Are?' Tuli talked about the importance of sexual liberation. He said, 'Americans like to kill or be killed. Aggression is reaction for frustration. Sexual frustration is still the major problem to be solved, and, in my opinion, the appearance of sexual humor is a healthy sign, and if we can put some joy, some real sexy warmth into the revolution, we will have really achieved something.'"

And then one other little paragraph: "In 1968, at the counter-convention in Chicago, hash oil and honey was the drug of choice. Ed Sanders and Tuli Kupferberg sampled it. This was strong stuff and they got completely fugged up. Sanders described the grass he was walking on as, quote, 'a giant frothing trough of mutant spinach egg noodles.' Tuli's friends had to carry him by the armpits back to the apartment where he was staying. 'They're delivering me,' he explained."

So, anyway, what people miss about him was how genuine he was. I met him in the early '60s at the Paperback Gallery, a bookstore in Greenwich Village, and I was delivering copies of *The Realist* and he was delivering copies of this booklet he had called *Birds*. And there was an electricity immediately because there was no small talk. I remember we were talking about the relationship between tragedy and absurdity. And when one becomes the other.

He just had a really thoughtful mind and a gentle quality about him, so that people who knew him have a personal loss. And the culture at large has a loss because he was so true to himself and his views. Audiences loved him because they trusted him not to hold back because he was afraid he would offend them.

DREYER: It is an incredible loss and the Fugs were just very important. When you talk about sexual humor, they certainly dealt with that. And they were very political. Tuli and Ed Sanders were the primary forces; they were different kinds of people, but they were both incredible artists and they melded very well together.

KRASSNER: I talked with Ed a couple of weeks ago and he said that when he visited Tuli in the hospital in New York, Tuli said to him he knew he was going to die but he didn't know how long he was going to have. But he said, "From now on I'm going to see everything as absurd." And, you know, of course he had been doing that all along. But there were some things he felt he must have not included.

And I just realized now, talking to you, that that's the other shoe dropping about the very first conversation I had with Tuli about tragedy and absurdity. Kind of brings it full cycle.

DREYER: I think there's a lot of people who didn't know that much about his legacy before, but hopefully that word is being spread a little bit now.

KRASSNER: Oh, yeah, yeah. I got back a lot of emails, actually, and incorporated a few of them into my piece for *High Times*. You know, it's like the names of the songs became part of the condolences. So, one, for example, was "Dear Tuli, I hope you see boobs a lot in heaven." That kind of thing, you know. It's like returning the spark.

DREYER: "Boobs a Lot" was a Fugs song. For people who weren't familiar with the Fugs, the Mothers of Invention took some of the same approach, but they didn't have the kind of heart and the soul that the Fugs had.

KRASSNER: The Fugs made the Mothers of Invention look a little bit more pristine.

DREYER: When I was working with KPFT, with Pacifica radio in Houston, the Guru Maharaj Ji, the thirteen-year-old perfect master, came to town—the Divine Light Mission, you know—and they tried to levitate the Astrodome. I guess you and I were both involved in two levitations, the Astrodome and the Pentagon.

KRASSNER: Right. The copycats, those guys.

DREYER: Anyway, KPFT had nonstop "bliss-to-bliss" coverage of this event, and Paul Krassner was one of our live correspondents on the scene.

I want to talk about Lenny Bruce. You edited his autobiography, which was serialized in *Playboy*, as I remember. And spent a lot of time with him. I think Steve Allen [the first host of *The Tonight Show*] hooked you up with Lenny Bruce, is that true?

KRASSNER: Steve sent some *Realist* subscription gifts to several people, including Lenny. And then Lenny sent a bunch of subscription gifts out, and that was how—with no advertising, just word of mouth—it got started.

DREYER: And I think you said that Steve Allen was your first subscriber.

KRASSNER: Yes, he was, and right after that came Tom Lehrer, the singing mathematician. But, yeah, Steve Allen was the first. You know, it was strange about Steve's death. He got hit by a car on his way from an interview to a Thanksgiving party. He took a nap on the sofa at the party, but he had had a concussion, and so the thing they do is try to keep you awake.

The thing is, Steve was being interviewed about *me* by a guy from NPR who had been given the go-ahead to do an advance obituary of me so that they'd have it ready in case I just left the planet and hung around with Tuli.

So, even though I had nothing to do with his death, I couldn't help thinking that if the interviewer had said, "One more question, Steve," and Steve had said, "Okay," it would have changed his whole existence. He wouldn't have come in contact with the car that crashed into him, and he wouldn't have fallen asleep on the sofa and not awakened. So, it's very strange how the timing of something can have so many repercussions.

DREYER: There's a whole generation of people who never heard of Steve Allen, who never heard of [the early television comic] Ernie Kovacs.

KRASSNER: They were pioneers in that field. I mean, forget about that time. There are people now who hear Abbie Hoffman's name and think that it's the congresswoman from upstate.

DREYER: You wrote for Steve Allen some, didn't you?

KRASSNER: A couple of things, yeah, on a freelance basis. One was a sketch on unknown heroes of television—and it would be like the guy who dropped the duck when somebody said the secret word, like on Groucho Marx. [A toy duck that looked like Groucho would drop down with a hundred dollar bill.] Or the guy who pushed—on one of those quiz shows—who pushed the isolation booth forward. You'd never see him, but he pushed the isolation booth with contestants in it. And so, it was just a whole bunch of unsung heroes. And then I wrote a song that he put to bossa nova music and sang it—my lyrics—and it was called "Cosa Nostra, Our Thing." It had lyrics like, "I give you the kiss of death."

DREYER: This was very early television, really.

KRASSNER: Oh, yeah, it was still—I think it was all live.

DREYER: And these guys were oddball. I mean, the humor was a very oddball kind of absurdist humor, and you lost a lot of that once television started having to reach more of a mass audience and started dealing with demographics.

KRASSNER: There was a kind of freedom then, partly because it was live and so you had to check on whether your impulses were right or not, whereas, when they can do several takes of a scene—it could be bleeped out or it could be edited. So it was really like walking on an electronic tightrope without any net.

So, anyway, Lenny Bruce, when he came to New York after I saw him perform on *The Steve Allen Show*, he gave me a call and we met. And the thing I remember was that he was still using euphemisms for the f-bombs. I gave him an advance copy of the issue of *The Realist* with an interview with Dr. Albert Ellis, who at one point started talking about the semantics of profanity. He said that whenever somebody was angry, they might say, you know, "eff you."

And he said, but "effing" is a *good* thing, so if you really want to insult somebody say "un-eff you"—except I didn't just use the initial letter. I mean, magazines in those days were still using asterisks. Or dashes. But the Supreme Court ruled that to be considered obscene, material had to result in prurient interest. And nobody was going to get aroused just seeing the word itself. If that were true, then they would get aroused when they would see the asterisks or the dashes.

DREYER: Maybe even more so because it leaves more to the imagination.

KRASSNER: Exactly. Yes.

So, Lenny said, "You can get away with printing this?" I said, "Yes, it's on the newsstands, it's in the bookstores, it goes through the mail." And I gave him that Supreme Court ruling, and he said, "Prurient interest." His suitcase was on his bed in the hotel room—and he opens up this case and took out a huge unabridged dictionary and looked up the word "prurient"—and he says, "'To itch.' Is that like they give you the itching powder from the novelty store? And that's prurient?"

I said, "No, there's other definitions," and then he read the rest of it and we translated it to our own jargon—which was that if it was "prurient," it meant it got you horny.

Around that time there was a lot of "positive thinking" and there was a book by a guy named Dale Carnegie called *How to Win Friends and Influence People*—and so Lenny called his autobiography *How to Talk Dirty and Influence People*. He worked on it a little bit at a time, and it was going to be serialized in *Playboy* and they hired me to edit it. But it was all written by him. I would make a suggestion and we would talk about it and then he would either write it or dictate it into a tape recorder.

It was a kind of bonding experience, you know. We both stayed at the YMCA—no fancy hotels—and we'd eat in a Chinese restaurant.

DREYER: Lenny Bruce was out there first. I mean, he was naked in a lot of ways. Tell us about the impact he had on the culture and about the government's response to him.

KRASSNER: What he did onstage was to articulate the consciousness of his audience and take it a step further—because he challenged *his own* beliefs and then would challenge the audience, assuming that they had similar beliefs.

And so he—like George Carlin and Richard Pryor—were self-taught semanticists, you know, parsing the meaning of words. Lenny did a whole bit on the meaning of the phrase "to come"—a simple four-letter word. The difference between Carlin and Lenny was of methodology. Lenny didn't have a script or notes. You might see an occasional news clipping on his desk or something, but he would just absorb.

He was a good listener, and he would ask questions and learn from that process. And his modus operandi was to try and have the same freedom onstage that he had in his living room. Without having to compromise either his language or his point of view. And George Carlin was the same, except that he wrote everything down and then rewrote it, edited it, and then memorized it.

DREYER: They cracked down on both Lenny Bruce and George Carlin.

KRASSNER: Oh, yeah. When Lenny got arrested in Chicago at the Gate of Horn, George Carlin was in the audience. They put Lenny in the police wagon and the cops went around asking for the IDs of the people who were in the club. Carlin refused to show any ID, and so they busted him and threw him in the paddy wagon, too. And Lenny says, "What are you doing here?" Carlin says, "Well, I refused to show them my ID," and Lenny says, "You schmuck."

DREYER: Lenny Bruce was a tragic figure, and his story was also a tragic story.

KRASSNER: He got busted fifteen times in one year. In fact, one time he was opening up at a club in LA, and *Variety*, the bible of show biz, had a little news item about it, saying that Lenny Bruce performed at such and such a place last night and *he did not get arrested*. You know, it was news.

DREYER: A difference, too, wasn't it, that audiences didn't always laugh at Lenny Bruce? Sometimes he made people feel uneasy.

KRASSNER: Oh, yeah. Well, you know, the more he got arrested, the more serious he got. And Lenny also was blacklisted, in the sense that a local district attorney would threaten a club owner and say, "If you let him perform, we're going to see that you lose your liquor license."

In Chicago I remember Lenny saying, "It's so corrupt, it's thrilling."

DREYER: You wrote not too long ago about politically correct comedy, and you pointed out, for instance, that David Letterman, although he apologized to Sarah Palin for his remarks about her daughter, that he did not apologize for referring to her as a slutty flight attendant. And you also pointed out that Jon Stewart and Stephen Colbert referred to her as a generic librarian in a porn flick who takes off her glasses and lets down her hair.

There's a lot of material out there. Is everything fair game?

KRASSNER: Well, fair game as opposed to legal. Because if there's libel in there, I mean, it's fair game to try it, but there are different consequences.

DREYER: Your life has been rich and full. At age six, you played in Carnegie Hall. You were a violinist, a child prodigy, is that true? And then you became a political activist with the yippies. Do you deal with all of that stuff in your latest book?

KRASSNER: Absolutely, yeah. "Yippie" came out of the acronym of YIP, which stood for Youth International Party. They were active in the demonstrations in Chicago in 1968 at the Democratic Convention to protest the Vietnam War.

Anyway, Phil Ochs was among the yippie founders, and he expressed the spirit that a demonstration should turn you on, not turn you off. So I invented the "yippie" name; just as a journalist, I knew you have to have a who, what, when, where, and why—so that was the who. And it worked.

DREYER: You had a couple of very theatrical people who were the public face of it, of course: Abbie Hoffman and Jerry Rubin.

KRASSNER: Oh, yeah, it was street theater. You know, and if that were happening today it would be on YouTube.

DREYER: I recently saw something that you had written: that you actually felt like some positive things are happening again. I mean, it's very easy to be depressed about what's going on in the world right now, in this country.

KRASSNER: It's a challenge to be happy and yet not become numb to your sensitivity of what's happening outside. You know, outside your own little universe. And we're more and more aware of it—and yet, you know, you don't want to feel gloomy. You do what you can and that's all you can do.

DREYER: Do you feel that there's some rebirth of some of the energy?

KRASSNER: Lenny Bruce, fifty years ago, said that someday pot will be legal. In ten years, he said, because there are a lot of law students who smoke and they would become legislators. It was a premature ejaculation on Lenny's part because it's fifty years later now—but he was ahead of his time as a performer and as an idealist. And now it's possible, at least in the state of California.

DREYER: Jonah Raskin was on with us and talking especially about the California marijuana initiative [Proposition 19]. What's your feeling about it right now?

KRASSNER: Well, there were two things. One is that it's interesting to see people who are against it because, as they say, "Well, if this becomes law, why doesn't the wording of the initiative call for a mass amnesty for those in prison on nonviolent marijuana charges?"

I interviewed the author of Prop 19, California legislator Tom Ammiano, and he said we have to do these things step by step, which I think was comparable to Obama's plan with health care. You know, we would have liked to have single-payer, we would have liked to have a public option, but with what he has done, those things are likely to happen. I think we have something to build on.

And then the other aspect is the growers. The growers in Humboldt—some of them have bumper stickers that say, "Keep Pot Illegal."

DREYER: Yeah, there are anarchists who say that there will be too many controls.

KRASSNER: Right. Right. So, you know, *que será kazoo.*

Filmmaker and two-time Academy Award nominee Al Reinert (*right*) with Thorne Dreyer. Al was interviewed on *Rag Radio* on March 14, 2014. Photo by Roger Baker.

AL REINERT

Take me to the moon.

Texas journalist, screenwriter, and two-time Oscar nominee Al Reinert discusses a range of topics, including the birth of Texas Monthly, *his years in Hollywood, and his brush with the Ku Klux Klan.*

Reinert won major awards in a career that included newspapers, magazines, and film. He was nominated for two Academy Awards—one for producing the documentary film For All Mankind, *which won the Grand Jury Prize at the Sundance Film Festival, and one for cowriting (with William Broyles) the screenplay for the major motion picture* Apollo 13, *directed by Ron Howard and starring Tom Hanks.*

Before turning to the screen, Al worked as a reporter at the Houston Chronicle *and as development director for KPFT, Houston's Pacifica radio station. Also a political junkie early in life, he served as press secretary to Texas Congressman Charlie Wilson.*

Al Reinert was my colleague in the early days of Texas Monthly *magazine in the 1970s and a frequent coconspirator and running buddy through the years. We both lived at the Plaza Hotel on Montrose in Houston for a time. Chaucer's—downstairs at the Plaza—was an artists' and writers' hangout.*

Born in 1947 in Tokyo, Al died of lung cancer in Wimberley, Texas, on December 31, 2018, four years after he and I reunited for this interview.

In an obituary in Texas Monthly, *John Nova Lomax called the multitalented Reinert a "modern-day Renaissance man" (Texas A&M had even offered him a baseball scholarship), and the* New Yorker *called Al's* For All Mankind *"a head-spinning revelation."*

MARCH 14, 2014

THORNE DREYER: Al Reinert, my old friend and collaborator, thank you so much for being with us on *Rag Radio*. It certainly has been a while since we've done this.

AL REINERT: It's probably been forty years since we were on the radio together.

DREYER: Okay. Your first job was at the *Houston Chronicle* way back in 1970. What was that like?

REINERT: I started out as the night police reporter, which was the lowest-ranking job you could have as a reporter at the *Chronicle*, or at any newspaper. It meant that I came to work about eight o'clock at night and covered the police station all night long.

And that was journalism school for me. I mean, you've got to figure out what the facts are—who, what, where, when, why—in the middle of the night at crime scenes where people are all going nuts. It was a great training ground for me. Then I rapidly got promoted to cover politics, where I had all the wrong politics for the *Houston Chronicle* and got myself fired within a year.

DREYER: Then *Texas Monthly* started, and you were also a freelance contributor to *Rolling Stone*, *Esquire*, *The Atlantic*, and a number of other publications. But *Texas Monthly* was an amazing phenomenon.

REINERT: Well, they were just getting started. The timing for me was perfect. I got fired from the *Chronicle* just about a month before *Texas Monthly* got started. I just folded one right into the other. Nobody at the *Monthly* really knew what they were doing then. Hired a whole bunch of people who had never worked at a magazine before.

DREYER: But Bill Broyles turned out to be just a brilliant choice for editor. And *Texas Monthly* became a place where writers could write.

"The great thing about being a Texas journalist is that Texas grows these incredible ridiculous characters all the time. And they're always doing this crazy stuff. How could you go wrong? It's just a great place to be a journalist."

REINERT: Well, it covered Texas. The great thing about being a Texas journalist is that Texas grows these incredible ridiculous characters all the time. And they're always doing this crazy stuff. How could you go wrong? It's just a great place to be a journalist.

DREYER: I worked at Pacifica radio's KPFT in Houston in the early '70s for several years. You were actually the original development director for KPFT, were you not?

REINERT: For a while. My first day on the payroll was the day they got blown up the first time. This is a station that by Texas standards was considered too radical at the time. This crazy man from the Ku Klux Klan dynamited our transmitter.

DREYER: And it was the first of two times that the station was blown off the air.

REINERT: Exactly, yeah. But it actually made it much easier to raise money.

DREYER: It gave you a hook.

REINERT: Exactly. "Put us back on the air!"

DREYER: It was the first—and only—radio station in the history of this country to be blown off the air. Arlo Guthrie's "Alice's Restaurant" was playing when the station went down the second time, and when it came back, Arlo Guthrie was there in person, singing "Alice's Restaurant."

We should also mention that the Klan at that time was extremely active in Houston. Houston was a wide-open city; it wasn't progressive, it wasn't really reactionary, but it was open enough that the Klan could function, especially since the Klan and the Houston Police Department at that time were very interconnected.

REINERT: Very interesting time.

DREYER: You also worked in politics, Al; you've had a multifaceted career. You were talking earlier about larger-than-life characters in Texas, and you worked for one. You were press secretary for Charlie Wilson, who was a congressman from Lufkin.

Charlie Wilson, of course, was depicted in a major motion picture.

REINERT: Tom Hanks played him in the movie *Charlie Wilson's War*. And I thought he did a really good job.

I was really into politics when I was younger, and I knew a lot of people in politics. I covered it as a reporter, was personally involved in a lot of campaigns, and Wilson asked me if I wanted to go to Washington. And I thought, well, that might be fun.

So I went to Washington and discovered that I didn't like it, and the truth of the matter is that I've been much less involved in politics ever since then. I think politics is personally corrupting. It just turns good people into bad people.

DREYER: When you look at what things were like when we were sort of young and perky and hopeful—and thought we could change the world—and then you see the way things are now.

REINERT: Politics wasn't as angry as it is now. You could actually have a debate with somebody that you didn't agree with and not end up getting in a fistfight.

DREYER: How did you make the transition into film? Did you make a conscious decision, or did *For All Mankind* just happen to you?

REINERT: I'd always been interested in film, and I'd always sort of been an on-the-job-training kind of a guy. I'd been a geology major in college. I didn't know anything about journalism. I didn't know anything about newspapers, I didn't know anything about magazines. Those both worked out okay. I figured, how complicated can the movie business be?

DREYER: And you found out?

REINERT: Well, the on-the-job training took a long time. It took me eight years to make my first documentary.

DREYER: And you didn't have to shoot it.

REINERT: But, you know, there was a lot to learn.

DREYER: Tell us about *For All Mankind* and how that evolved.

REINERT: When I was working at the *Chronicle*, I was covering NASA; it was part of my beat. And so I started meeting these guys who had been to the moon—this was several years after they had been to the moon—and everybody had sort of forgotten about them.

Like Jim Lovell, for instance, the commander of Apollo 13. At the time I met him he was running a tugboat company on the Houston Ship Channel. And people were not exactly beating down his door to do interviews. So these guys were sitting around with stories to tell, and that interested me.

And at the same time access to NASA was a lot easier in those days. Nowadays, you've got to have all these security clearances and you park five miles away and you've got to go through four checkpoints just to get close to the place. But in those days, I could drive my car right onto the base, and I started looking at film footage. I mean, we sent these guys into outer space with movie cameras and they shot up a storm. They shot film constantly, I mean, and I thought it was pretty remarkable film.

DREYER: Incredibly high tech, right? For the time.

REINERT: They were shooting sixteen millimeter, pretty low tech today, but at the time it was pretty high tech.

And we'd never seen it on a big screen. I mean, we'd see little tiny clips on TV. You know, they're out there on the biggest location in cinema history, and we're seeing it on this tiny little screen, and I thought, "Well, somebody ought to take this and put it on a big screen."

And, not knowing anything about the movie business, I thought that was going to be easy to do. But it wasn't. That's part of why it took years to do this, to transform that sixteen-millimeter film.

They came back from the moon, they landed in the ocean, aircraft carrier drives up, picks them up, the guys get out, and then they reach in and they get these film magazines that they fly back to the Johnson Space Center, where it's developed and processed and they'd store it in zero-degree refrigerated storage to preserve the film.

Nobody had ever taken that film and blown it up to wide-screen thirty-five millimeter. And I learned very slowly the hard way why nobody had done it before: because it's very challenging and difficult and you're dealing with film that you can't risk harming.

DREYER: Yeah.

REINERT: Anyway, the movie got made. Just took a while.

DREYER: There was incredible footage.

REINERT: Yes. In the course of the project I became the world-record holder for research in the NASA film archive.

DREYER: Right. And nobody had done much with that stuff. It was all just in the archives.

REINERT: Yeah.

DREYER: I wanted to mention that *For All Mankind* won many awards. It was not just nominated for the Oscar, but it won the Grand Jury Prize at Sundance and won awards in a number of other festivals.

REINERT: Turned out pretty well.

DREYER: Turned out very well, and folks might have seen it on PBS over the years, and other outlets.

So, Al. You were in Los Angeles for the last fifteen years and you came back to Texas what, six months ago? You spent ten years or more just trying to get back to Texas, right?

REINERT: We were out there fifteen years. I mean, yes, about ten years longer than I thought we were ever going to be.

DREYER: Okay, you spent a year in Japan working on *Final Fantasy*, which was a video game.

REINERT: I was hired to write the movie version of the video game.

DREYER: How do you do that? How does that work?

REINERT: It probably works differently from game to game and movie to movie. In my case, I was hired by this genius Japanese video [game] programmer. At the time, *Final Fantasy* was the number one video game in the world. It had been through seven sequels, and I think *Final Fantasy VII* was the top-selling video game at the time I was hired to adapt it into a movie.

And I basically did what I was told to do. I mean, it's a Japanese company and I'm an employee and I'm writing a script in English that then goes to a translator and gets translated to Japanese. And Sakaguchi, who was the guy who ran the company and invented the video game, would then read it.

He'd write notes in Japanese that would get translated by another translator before I could read it. Which means that basically you have these two translators writing the movie.

It was absurd and ridiculous. These guys were geniuses visually, but they didn't have a clue how to tell a story. Video games don't tell a story; in a video game you want the central character to be exactly the same person at the end of the game as he was at the beginning of the game. And that doesn't make for a very compelling story.

DREYER: Because you want the people playing the game to come back and play it some more.

REINERT: Exactly. It's a role-playing game. You're playing this character and the character really doesn't change. That's a tricky transition to make, if you're trying to do a narrative film.

DREYER: Did you find that difficult to do? It certainly had to have been challenging.

REINERT: I found it impossible to do because they didn't want to change the character or any of the characters. They had made billions of dollars off of these characters in the video game, you know. They weren't going to screw with something that was working.

DREYER: It's interesting. We're in Austin, Texas, which is a video game production center.

REINERT: Oh, yeah, and they have not turned any of those into successful movies, despite many attempts.

DREYER: But they've tried.

REINERT: Oh, sure. I mean, they figure there's a big audience out there—and those are the most disappointed people of them all when they finally see the movie.

DREYER: I guess they'll be able to make them work as movies once they can be more interactive.

REINERT: I don't know why they would want to. The video game business is bigger than the movie business today.

DREYER: Your latest film is a documentary about Michael Morton called *An Unreal Dream*. And Michael Morton, for those who don't know about him, spent twenty-five years in a Texas prison for a murder that he did not commit. It was a wrongful conviction. Folks may have seen the movie on CNN.

REINERT: Yeah. Well, it was on CNN, and then the rights shifted over to the Discovery Channel.

DREYER: How did you decide to make that movie and how did you put it together?

REINERT: I had been looking for a project that would bring me back to Texas. I was homesick, I was tired of Los Angeles, and some friends had been sending me stuff about this case. So I was paying attention, and I was watching television on the day that he was released from prison. And when I saw him for the first time, I thought, "This guy's got some charisma." I wanted to know more about him.

I thought he was very well spoken, that he could tell his own story, which is what you want if you're trying to make a documentary. You want a central character; you want the person who's at the heart of the film to be able to carry the film. And I thought he could. I came to Houston, met him, liked him, thought he was terrific, and it sort of took on its own life.

DREYER: With the exonerations that are happening all over the country—that are happening consistently on death rows—people realize more and more how arbitrary our criminal justice system is.

REINERT: A lot of wrongful convictions in this country. One estimate I saw is that 20 percent of the people in prison today are wrongful convictions.

DREYER: And the rest of them were arrested for simple drug charges.

REINERT: That's another 30 percent, probably.

DREYER: So you're studying birds, now?

REINERT: I'm doing birds these days. We're making a documentary about John James Audubon, the great and early American painter of birds.

DREYER: What are you doing? How do you go about researching something like that?

REINERT: It's interesting and challenging because there was no photography in those days. I mean, visually, you've got very little to work with, which is part of the challenge of trying to do the film.

Partly, it's the Ken Burns approach, where you've got a lot of talking heads and still images. And we're trying to combine that with the Terry Malick film approach of just beautiful natural scenery—because Audubon was celebrating pristine America.

In the 1820s when Audubon was doing this, when he was painting his birds, America was raw material. We had not yet destroyed our natural environment like we have now. We're going to a lot of trouble to take great cameras and great camera people to the last vestiges of that America.

We have found some really beautiful places where we're shooting some really beautiful film. And there's still survivors of the birds that he painted. There's not as many of them as there were then, but we're trying to re-create the world that he was trying to capture then as best we can.

DREYER: Austin is, of course, a thriving independent movie center. Is it more interesting to be in Austin at this point in time?

REINERT: For me personally it has less to do with the business than just the people that you deal with. Southern California is a really tough place to live and work. Sports teams, I think, are the best metaphor for it. They pay outrageous prices to bring in somebody else's stars and they all hate each other, and they play terrible together. It's a culture that encourages all your insecurities.

And Texas, in general—and Austin, specifically—is a culture that encourages you to be who you are. No matter how nutty you are. And the people are so much nicer, they're so much easier to work with. The hardest thing to reconcile for me is how nice the people are and how awful their politics are. I just don't understand it, really, but that's what Texas is. It's full of contradictions. But it's just a better place to live and be and deal with other people. And the filmmaking business is just one aspect of that.

"And Texas, in general—and Austin, specifically—is a culture that encourages you to be who you are. No matter how nutty you are."

DREYER: The filmmaking business is certainly thriving. Of course, Austin is known as a music center and a tech center.

REINERT: Austin has been the Greenwich Village of Texas for a hundred years. I mean, if you grew up in some little town in Texas and you were a little bit out of sync with your neighbors, Austin is where you went. And that's always been true. It's been the creative center of Texas since literally the days of O. Henry a hundred years ago. It's always been a creative mecca, it's always been a town where people were encouraged to be creative and tolerated for being weird. I don't think that's changed at all. I mean, it's gotten kind of bigger—with better advertising—but that's the heart of Austin and always has been.

In Los Angeles, in the movie business, there's a lot of jealousy and resentment that you don't feel here at all. People here really help each other, they encourage each other. If you've got a question, they'll be happy to answer it. You root for each other and you never see that in Los Angeles, you really don't. I mean, it's sad.

DREYER: People talk about how Austin is changing so much—and how it's not like the good old days.

REINERT: Well, it's a bigger pain in the ass than it used to be, you know. But every place is.

DREYER: You did a lot of magazine writing—you did major feature stories for major publications—and one of the things about doing that, it's almost like writing a book, you have to do so much research.

Even writing a feature for *Texas Monthly*, you have to get into that subject matter to such an extent. How different is that from working on screenplays, where you're working on one project for a whole long time?

REINERT: Well, it's using the same muscles. You're still storytelling, and for me, as an old journalist, I'm only good at telling believable stories about realistic people. I don't have the imagination to do vampires, you know, which is really what the studio business is built around these days.

It was really difficult; it was a challenge for me to try to be part of that world because it's all about make believe—the Hollywood big movie business is literally about make believe. They don't want to be realistic; they resent realism.

And that's not me. Fundamentally, I'm a true-story guy. And that really limited me in terms of the kinds of things I could do well. But in terms of execution, it's a lot the same. Writing a screenplay is not all that different from writing a cops-and-robbers story on the night police beat for the *Houston Chronicle*. You still want to have a beginning and a middle and an end. You want your characters to go through changes so that they're compelling and interesting characters.

DREYER: But you have to think in terms of pictures and action as opposed to words, don't you? When screenwriter Stephen Harrigan was on *Rag Radio*, he said that virtually nothing he ever wrote actually ended up in the finished project like he wrote it. He said that when he worked on a project with Robert Altman, it was so much fun; Altman was exciting and there was all this spontaneity about it.

But he said Altman would sit with him and say, "Let's do this." So he would write something for Altman, and then Altman would do something totally different. Altman was a unique figure, and in some of what you've done you've actually had some control over the whole process.

REINERT: Well, some of it. I worked with some pretty interesting people; I spent two years working with Jim Cameron on a project that was one of the best things that I've ever written, and I'm sorry that it never got made. I mean, the best things that I did in my fifteen years in Hollywood never got made, and the worst things did—*Final Fantasy* being one of them. It's very frustrating—or it was frustrating for me.

DREYER: Is that part of the story of working in that business?

REINERT: I don't think it's unusual at all. I've known plenty of other screenwriters who have the same complaint as I have.

DREYER: What that you've done is out there for people? *For All Mankind* is available on Blu-ray, right?

REINERT: The Criterion Collection. That documentary's been in print for twenty-five years, which is close to a record.

DREYER: That doesn't happen very often, does it?

REINERT: Well, and the Michael Morton film is out there. When it was airing on CNN, they had a blockade on the DVD; that's up now, so it's available on DVD.

DREYER: So, they keep exclusive rights when they're showing it.

REINERT: Exactly. As long as they've got the TV rights, you can't be selling DVDs.

DREYER: Well, what else do you want to do in the future? Do you have any other plans?

REINERT: Documentary films are kind of my comfort zone. They're true stories, they are manageable, they're doable. I don't have to sell it to a bunch of studio executives who are half my age.

Journalist and Trump biographer Harry Hurt III.

HARRY HURT III

The country, however, might go out of print.

Harry Hurt III riffs on topics around his book about Donald Trump, including Trump's "scalp reduction" operation (ouch) and his ex-wife Ivana's allegation of rape.

An award-winning magazine journalist and nonfiction author—and Donald Trump's "most-hated biographer"—my old friend Harry Hurt joined us on Rag Radio *two months before Donald Trump was elected president of the United States. Harry's unauthorized biography,* Lost Tycoon: The Many Lives of Donald J. Trump, *originally published in 1993 and reissued in July 2016, was listed by the* New York Times *as one of its top books of 2017. Hurt, who traveled in some of the same circles as Trump and occasionally played golf with him, was privy to much inside information.*

A native Houstonian who graduated magna cum laude from Harvard, Harry is the son of Harry Hurt Jr., president of Hurt Oil Company. Harry was a senior editor at Texas Monthly *from 1975 to 1986 and has been a business columnist for the* New York Times, *a correspondent for* Newsweek, *and an editor at* Travel + Leisure Golf. *He has also contributed to* Esquire, Fortune, Sports Illustrated, *and* Playboy, *among other publications, and served as a correspondent for ABC News and ESPN Radio. Harry, who also authored* Texas Rich: The Hunt Dynasty from the Early Oil Days Through the Silver Crash, *lives on Long Island in New York.*

Harry Hurt has been a close friend through the years; he, Al Reinert, and I all wrote for the early Texas Monthly, *and I was in Harry's first wedding.*

SEPTEMBER 17, 2016

THORNE DREYER: Harry Hurt III, according to Tim Mak at the *Daily Beast*, is Donald Trump's "most-hated biographer." Harry is the author of *Lost Tycoon: The Many Lives of Donald J. Trump*, originally published by W. W. Norton in 1993. After more than two decades, the controversial book that Norton deemed, quote, "too dangerous to reprint," is finally seeing the light of day again in a new release by Echo Point.

Mak called the book the Rosetta Stone for all things Trump, while Michael Barbaro of the *New York Times* has labeled it the bible for Trump reporting. Among other things, the book revealed the bombshell that Trump's ex-wife, Ivana, accused him of rape in a sworn deposition during their divorce—something she has since said she didn't mean in the, quote, "criminal sense."

Harry Hurt, a longtime friend and colleague, is with us on the phone. Where are you exactly?

HARRY HURT III: I'm at the far eastern end of Long Island—what's known as the South Fork. Not to be confused with the ranch in Dallas where J. R. Ewing once resided [in the television series *Dallas*]. I live in a town called East Hampton.

DREYER: I am holding in my hand a first edition of the 1993 version of *Lost Tycoon: The Many Lives of Donald J. Trump* with a pasted-in disclaimer, a "notice to the reader." Should I be holding this, or should it be in a vault somewhere?

HURT: You probably should have sold it about four or five months ago. At one point, bidding for the kind of copy that you now have in your hands started at $120 and went up to $3,880—of which, of course, I would get zero. Somebody is asking $3,880 for a copy of your book. I guess that's cool.

In the financial realm, I'm suffering something of a conflict of interest. If Donald Trump is elected president of the United States, *Lost Tycoon: The Many Lives of Donald J. Trump* will never go out of print. The *country*, however, might go out of print—that's the problem. And

I think that Donald Trump, much like this radio station, should be converted to solar power and community management.

DREYER: Don't you think it's time he got cut off?

HURT: I'm pretty sure it's time his hair got cut off.

DREYER: Well, there's that. What's under there?

HURT: That's an interesting story.

DREYER: Mr. Reporter?

HURT: Earlier, you mentioned the statement by Ivana Trump [Donald's first wife] during a deposition in their divorce about being raped. Well, let me put that in context which relates directly to Donald's head and his hair. Donald and Ivana had been living separately for about eighteen months, in the sense that they had not had conjugal relations. This is a period in 1989 and 1990, but they were both still occupying the principal residence in Trump Tower, which is quite roomy, as it covers three floors.

DREYER: They had not had such relations—at least with each other, right?

HURT: At least with each other, yes. That's a good point. Donald had probably had sexual relations with Marla Maples, who would become his second wife. Again, we're talking 1989 to 1990—and the book is basically a cinema verité snapshot of that picture, with some historical background on all the principal characters.

Donald decided that he wanted to cover a bald spot in the back of his head, and so he got an operation, improbably but actually called "scalp reduction." So, you're asking what's under his hair? A reduced scalp, and this scalp-reduction operation was performed by a doctor named Steven Hoefflin who had previously done plastic surgery work on Ivana Trump. So, in a sense, he regarded this doctor as *her* plastic surgeon.

He came into the residence at Trump Tower one night in 1989 in a rage. In pain over this operation, he began pulling Ivana's hair in the corresponding spot on her head to which he'd had the operation on *his* head, the scalp-reduction operation. And it was then that, according to her testimony, "he raped me."

At that point, Ivana ran down the hall to the room that was assigned normally to her mother, who happened not to be present at the time. She goes in, locks the door, cries all night, and when she gets up the next morning, the first thing Donald says to her is, "Did it hurt?" Now, was that the hair pulling, the rape, or what?

But this is a man who is really unhinged and unbalanced, and I think that this story and many, many others in *Lost Tycoon* bring out this point. That he really is not to be trusted with the nuclear codes, the so-called nuclear football. He is a very, very, very volatile personality; he is quite deeply disturbed, psychologically.

And this notion that this seventy-year-old man is going to somehow quote, unquote, "pivot," as they keep saying—become more presidential in a turn, in a period of weeks—it is absolutely absurd. It defies anything about human nature. I would say that a seventy-year-old leopard doesn't change its spots, and similarly a seventy-year-old skunk doesn't lose his stink.

DREYER: Okay. Let me go back to the book for a second.

HURT: Yeah, anything else you need to know?

DREYER: Yes, I do want to know everything, and you're my fount of valuable information here.

About the first book when it came out: in their prepublication review, *Kirkus* wrote, "A deliciously wicked take on casino / real estate mogul Donald J. Trump. Drawing on a wealth of sources, Hurt offers an exhaustive, gossipy run-down on a golden boy of the so-called greed decade who lost his touch—and way—in the hard realities of the 1990s."

And then Echo Point, at their site, the publishing house that's now published the new version of this book—I guess it's basically the same book—wrote, "*Lost Tycoon* presents an unvarnished in-depth portrayal of the man who vows to 'Make America Great Again.' Although it was first published in 1993, *Lost Tycoon* shows us that The Donald's personal character, political philosophy, business ethics, and attitude towards women haven't changed much in the past two decades. Trump is a man of many lives, and many wives. He is arguably the greatest self-promoter in the annals of American business."

Okay, this was in the '90s, and at that point everybody thought he had kind of caved, he had bottomed out, and I'm not going to ask you the stupid question that interviewers ask: "Did you ever think that he might become president?"

HURT: Well, no, I didn't—and if I did, I probably would be able to cash in on stuff. But no, not in my wildest nightmare did I think that he would . . .

DREYER: . . . That he would even recover?

HURT: No, I gave him—and I give him at the end of that book—even there, I give a chance that he could recover. I mean, the resilience of Satan is amazing. I thought perhaps he might run for president of the United States as a kind of a marketing gambit, but the idea that any reasonable party would nominate him for president and that he might have a chance of getting elected was beyond my wildest dreams.

I will say that I didn't think until probably sometime around April or May of this year that Donald Trump himself thought that he would be nominated—you know, that he actually had a chance to win the presidency. I think that he began this whole thing as yet another marketing ploy to raise the profile of his hotels and his golf courses and his other properties.

Because I know the person who most realizes on this earth that Donald Trump is not fit to be president of the United States, and not fit to actually do the job of being president of the United States, is Donald J. Trump himself.

DREYER: Do you think that it scared him for a minute when he realized that maybe he was going to have to live in that sort of dingy house in Washington, that he might have to deal with all of this stuff, that he might actually become president? Don't you think that was kind of a sobering thing?

HURT: I think it probably did send something—some sort of a chill or reality check—through him. Because clearly, he can't run the country. I mean, the president is the chief executive of the United States; he cannot be the chief executive of a country unless it's like, you know, a country that consists of two golf courses and a couple of hotels. I mean, he's just not capable of doing that. He doesn't have the experience; he doesn't have the background.

There are certain things, of course, anyone must delegate in running the country, but you can't delegate the ABC knowledge of the names of the countries in the world and the history. And the idea that somebody who goes around singing the praises of a Russian dictator like Vladimir Putin is really qualified to run . . . But, you know, like the hydra, you cut off one head and he grows another.

The recent trip to Mexico is a good example. He went to see the president, and that resulted in a backlash of negative publicity for the Mexican president; then he comes right back to the US and starts bad-mouthing Mexicans again. There is a conflict within his campaign that's been talked about in the media a lot and is transparent, quite frankly, in the operation of the campaign even to an outsider.

And that is the conflict between Donald trying to be quote, unquote, "more presidential" and then Donald Trump being Donald Trump. And the sheer fact of the matter is that what got Donald Trump where he is today, god forbid, is him being Donald Trump. Being presidential isn't something you can learn in six months or six weeks during the presidential campaign. You know, it's the sum of all your life experiences and being up to that time—and good gosh . . .

DREYER: But the bar has been set so low that suddenly—because he's able to read off the teleprompter and he's able to stand next to the president of Mexico and not throw up on himself—then that means he's a diplomat.

HURT: But, you know, these two candidates have the highest negatives of any two presidential candidates in history. I think his is 70 percent and Hillary Clinton's is 69 percent. There's your dead heat.

DREYER: *Lost Tycoon: The Many Lives of Donald J. Trump* is now back in print for the first time—in how many years?

HURT: In twenty-three years. It was originally published in 1993. And, you know, Thorne, actually the longevity of its availability is salient to the ridiculous struggle that I've gone through this year—and also it reflects quite a bit on how Trump is perceived.

And that is simply this: the book was originally published in 1993 by W. W. Norton and Company, a prestigious old-line New York publisher that also had published my book *Texas Rich: The Hunt Dynasty from the Early Oil Days through the Silver Crash.*

DREYER: Which I also have.

HURT: Well, hold on to that, baby. Everybody's hanging around cheering for me to die so their book prices go up, you know.

But, anyway, Norton is very meticulous in their publishing; twenty-three years ago, this book was thoroughly vetted by their in-house lawyer at the time, a woman named Renee Schwartz, who is still alive and practicing at the age of eighty-something. So back then she was already around sixty.

She's a petite woman. One day prior to publication, Donald Trump, all six foot three of him and blubber—and his also tall but more lean lawyer Jay Goldberg—came for a little sit-down at Norton with Renee Schwartz, my editor Starling Lawrence, and me. And they were basically trying to fish for information about what the book might contain. And of course, you know, I'm like now pitching little questions back at them, some of which cover this rape allegation by Ivana.

And finally, Donald jumps up from his chair and pulls a tape recorder out of the pocket of his suit coat and goes, "I've been taping this the whole time." Well, you know, his own lawyer, Jay Goldberg, goes napkin white on that. And little Renee Schwartz says, "Oh, you've been taping this the whole time and you didn't tell us? That's not right."

At this point, Goldberg has no choice but to give his client the hook, and so they go storming off down the hall. And it was as an upshot of that that a couple of weeks later, while the book was already physically at the printers being printed, we were sent this statement by Ivana Trump that we pasted in the front of the book.

DREYER: I'm looking at it. I'm looking at it right now. When you open the book and you see it, it makes you feel a little naughty.

HURT: To me it was like manna from heaven. I mean—"Oh, you can read about a rape in this thing. What page is that on?"

I'll get back to that issue in a second, but I just wanted to tie up this thing about when back in the spring I contacted Starling Lawrence about reissuing the book. They were going to reissue it as an e-book, and

I in fact signed a contract and at his request I wrote a brief introduction, which is contained in the new issue. Just, you know, 1,200 words or so, not substantively adding, but connecting some of the themes of the book and how they relate to Trump today.

There was a delay of ten days or so, and I called and asked, "What gives?" He said, "Well, our current in-house lawyer deems the book too dangerous to publish." And I replied that—how to phrase this on the radio—that that was chicken excrement. And even Star himself agreed, but that left me to find another publisher.

I put a scan of my book up briefly; it was a down-and-dirty scan that I had made myself of the original edition, and along comes Echo Point Books, which is a reissuing specialist based in the Bernie Sanders stronghold of Brattleboro, Vermont. And they said, "Well, we'll publish it as an actual physical book—paperback and hardcover."

The process of printing the thing, from start of discussions, was really only about five weeks, and we're back in. And we had a Kickstarter campaign; we raised about $5,000 for that, and merrily we go along.

And then there's a delay on their part, and finally I go, "What gives, what gives?" And I talked to the editor, and he says, "Well, you know, we think that we're not going to get sued, but we thought we could get libel insurance, and we were told by the lawyers who had read it before for us that that wouldn't be a problem. But we couldn't get it. No carrier would take it."

DREYER: You were too hot; you were too hot for libel insurance.

HURT: Too hot for libel insurance. But, Thorne, I mean, look, the book has been available for twenty-three years. I've added an introduction, but nothing in the introduction is libelous or defamatory; it's just reviews, some things like that. If you haven't sued me for twenty-three years, how come you're suing me now? And what are you suing me over? What's incorrect or false? Yes, the book went out of print officially, but it's been available on Amazon.com for all these years.

My point is that Trump has bullied and scared people so that they think he's going to sue even when he's not. And by the way, Trump never threatened to sue me back in '93, in 2016, this year, or at any other time. So, all this is just this sort of paranoid fantasy, but his saber-rattling and his presentation of a litigious persona has obviously had an effect. And it's a chilling effect on the First Amendment—and that thing's already about ice cold, so I don't think we need too much more. But should we look at the statement, do you like the statement?

DREYER: I loved the statement. I'll read the first of it just so people will know it's really there.

HURT: Okay.

DREYER: It begins, "Notice to the reader." And at the end, it says, "This statement can only be released and used in its entirety. Approved: Ivana M. Trump. Date: April 6, 1993." So it says, "On April 7, 1993, when *Lost Tycoon* had already been printed and was awaiting shipment, the publisher, who had met with Donald Trump and his lawyers on March 3, received the following communication from Donald Trump's lawyers. The statement by Ivana Trump does not contradict or invalidate any information contained in this book, and it is included here only to give full expression to differing points of view on an important event." And then she describes the deposition situation.

HURT: I can do that.

DREYER: Do that.

HURT: "During a deposition given by me in connection with my matrimonial case, I stated that my husband had raped me. I wish to say that on one occasion during 1989, Mr. Trump and I had marital relations in which he behaved very differently toward me than he had during our marriage. As a woman, I felt violated, as the love and tenderness which he normally exhibited to me was absent. I refer to this as a 'rape,'" quote, unquote, "but I do not want my words to be interpreted in a literal or criminal sense. Any contrary conclusion would be an incorrect and most unfortunate interpretation of my statement which I do not want to be interpreted in a speculative fashion and I do not want the press or media to misconstrue any of the facts set forth above." Which is the longest run-on sentence in the history of Czechoslovakian literature. "All I wish is for this matter to be put to rest."

Well, I believe that last comment.

At any event, Ivana's statement is really classic. It is one of the greatest nondenial denials I've ever seen.

But here again—and this is somewhat ironic, but perhaps maybe just simply predictable—people will say, "Oh, she's denied it." Denied what? If you look at it, she says, "Yeah, I swore in my deposition that he'd raped me, and yeah, I felt violated as a woman, but I don't want the word 'rape' to be used in a literal or criminal sense." Well, with respect, ma'am, how you want it to be used has got to derive from how it is used and the fact that you used it. I mean, if it looks like a duck and it quacks like a duck, it's a duck.

And, you know, I was on [then Fox News host] Megyn Kelly's show a little over a year ago, and she's referring to this, and she says, "She denied it." And I said, "Well, no, not exactly. She didn't deny it. What she said is, 'It's without merit.'" Well, what do you mean the story is without merit? That means that you don't like it? And you don't get a merit badge for it?

"It's without merit" doesn't mean "it's not true." It may not be a happy recollection for her. It may not be how she wants to now present herself and her husband if she and the other ex-wife angle for bedrooms in the Trump White House.

But the fact is that the story's true, and yet much of the news media, in their cursory reading of everything, not just my book, entirely misses that. And, indeed, the reporting has been so atrocious. One of the *New York Times* reporters calls me up and says that they've read through the book but they couldn't see anything about the rape thing that's mentioned in Ivana's statement. And I have to go and point out to them that the incident that's described—that I described earlier here on your show, Thorne, about the pulling of the hair and all that—it's on page 55 through 56.

Guys, all you've got to read is the first sixty pages and you get it. You don't even have to read the whole four-hundred-page book. So, I mean, it's just incredible, you know, that they can't even do their own homework.

Another incident related to that. A couple of months ago the *New York Times* did a big front-page piece called "Crossing the Line" about Donald Trump's treatment of women. It was a front page on the Sunday edition. And the lead anecdote about Donald Trump and his treatment of women—or really mistreatment of women—involved a woman whose name is now Rowanne Brewer Lane. And the thrust of the *Times* story was that within minutes after Donald Trump met Rowanne Brewer, he asked her to take off her clothes. And he asked her then to put on a bikini and then come model the bikini out by the pool at Mar-a-Lago.

And the *Times* went on to say that this was very denigrating to Rowanne Brewer and how it showed he was a sexist and blah, blah, blah. The next day Rowanne Brewer, now Lane, Rowanne Brewer Lane, comes out and says, "Well, you know, the incident happened," but she didn't say any of the stuff that she felt demeaned or any of this or denigrated in any way.

So that kind of triggered something. I went back to the index of my book, Thorne, and sure enough, there it was in the index: Rowanne Brewer. Rowanne Brewer.

So, I go back, and I look up the passage there—it's in the latter chapters of the book—and you know what Rowanne's job was when she met Donald Trump? Her job was swimsuit model. So Donald Trump was guilty of asking a swimsuit model to model a swimsuit. That's point number one. So why would the *Times* use that—of all the anecdotes available—as their lead anecdote to show that he mistreats women? Because they're stupid and they don't do their homework.

Then, ironically, I read on in the passage and indeed, back at the same time, Donald Trump was denigrating Rowanne Brewer behind her back, making remarks about her sexual prowess and her intellectual capabilities that I will not repeat on family radio here. The point is that they didn't bring that up in the *Times*; they didn't say, according to Harry Hurt's book, this is what was going on at the time. And then she basically calls them out the next day.

"So, the reporters, they can't really get it right. They can't really nail down the facts, and it's part and parcel of the overall decline in reporting and investigative journalism that's occurred, especially over the last fifteen years with the rise of the internet..."

So, the reporters, they can't really get it right. They can't really nail down the facts, and it's part and parcel of the overall decline in reporting and investigative journalism that's occurred, especially over the last fifteen years with the rise of the internet and the decline and shrinking of some of the major magazines. But it would be comical if it wasn't such an important issue. Megyn Kelly says, "Oh, she denies it." No, Megyn, you're a lawyer, she didn't deny it. You know, why can't they just be accurate? They're doing a disservice to the American people.

DREYER: I read somewhere that—in terms of Trump's treatment of women—you didn't really think he was a misogynist because you thought he was abusive of *everybody*.

HURT: Well, yeah. And that's true. He's a pretty much equal-opportunity offender.

DREYER: Let's venture into something else. You and I both wrote for *Texas Monthly* magazine in its very early days, when it was a pretty dynamic, innovative, and in some ways daring publication. And it offered a forum for writers and artists in Texas that wasn't there. I think you might agree with me on that, and that's certainly not the case anymore.

HURT: Look, *Texas Monthly* is almost a metaphor for that thing that you're talking about. It was a homegrown, Texas-born magazine that had national reach. Now it's let itself devolve into basically a regional that gives you for the umpteenth time the best barbecue in Texas and the best Mexican food, with the occasional article of interest.

But there was a period there that if you lived in Texas and were of any circles above dogcatcher—if you hadn't read *Texas Monthly* you couldn't participate in the conversation. And also, if there was some person of high stature that you wrote about, you better be right because you are likely to run into that person at some event or gathering—be it social or political or businesswise—so you had to stick to your guns.

But there has been this evolution towards the internet and towards social media in which the average length of a communication gets shorter and shorter, less and less grammatically correct. And people's attention span and so forth declines. The advertiser migration has certainly happened there. People just don't read books or lengthy magazines in the way they did thirty years ago, and it's sad.

"People just don't read books or lengthy magazines in the way they did thirty years ago, and it's sad."

I don't really write anymore, Thorne, except occasionally for a little summer throw-out here—if I can do the piece in an hour or less. I tutor mainly overprivileged white kids in high school and college in writing, English, history, sociology, economics, and life.

DREYER: So you're basically sharing your great gift.

One of the things that's happening is that staffs are getting cut back at newspapers all over the country. It's one thing when we talk about Fox News or the *New York Times*, but all of the newspapers, they're going to online versions, and then they keep cutting back on content. There are no bureaus anymore; there are fewer reporters who can be dedicated to spending time developing a story or researching a story.

But I personally have this ultimate faith in the fact that people like to hold books and like to have a newspaper in the morning that they can spill their coffee on.

HURT: Yeah, some still do, but you know what? It's going to phase out very, very rapidly. I have an eighteen-year-old son who has just entered Georgetown University's elite School of Foreign Service, a school within the school. He's in Bill Clinton's old dorm there, and my son and his debate partner in high school were ranked number one in the nation.

My son does not read newspapers; my son is very well informed, and especially because the debate topics were quite topical, covering real serious issues. One was about Putin and Crimea. Another was about mass incarceration in the United States.

My son gets his news online and is updated, and never does he get a newspaper in his hands. Now, there is something lost. There's something gained there—you can get information immediately from a variety of sources—but, you know, there's breadth but there's not depth.

He provides his own depth because he has to argue and research debate topics, but the general reader doesn't get any depth nor, you know, do they seem to long for it or to miss it. The problem is you end up with a population that is ill informed, even those that are well intentioned, not the—what did Hillary call them?—the "deplorables." Even the 'plorables, Thorne, can't get the information they need. And at a certain point they stop realizing what they're missing because they don't really *know* what they're missing.

In the early days, *Texas Monthly* did a really great job of that: they were entertaining as well as informative, and so you got a good story as well as a bunch of facts that were relevant to your daily life. And more than just your daily life, your sort of long-term decision-making and understanding of what's going on in the world around you.

All that's missing. The *Wall Street Journal*, on the left column on the front page, used to run in-depth investigative pieces and even if you don't call them investigative, just in-depth pieces about important subjects.

DREYER: When we talk about the ill-informed public in this country, is Donald Trump going to be the president of the deplorables and the 'plorables? Is he going to win?

HURT: I don't know. I think all them 'plorables are going to move to Canada. But look—without sort of sounding like Hillary Clinton—I think you could phrase this election: "Are there going to be more smart white people that go to the polls than there are dumb white people that go to the polls?" Because the Black people and the brown people are going to probably vote for Hillary and, I mean, duh!

But there are a lot of dumb and angry white people out there, and I will certainly respect anyone's choice to vote with their conscience. And I don't say that Hillary Clinton is the be-all, end-all; in fact, far from it. Years ago, when Edwin Edwards, the corrupt governor of Louisiana, was running for reelection, the bumper stickers said, "Vote for the Crook, It's Important." So, in this thing I say, "Vote for the crook, not for the psycho."

Although someone then came back to me and said, "Yep. But Harry, which one is which? Or aren't they both *both*?"

DREYER: Yeah, well, there are facts out there. Oh, but wait. Facts?

We've become such a country of misinformation; the fact-checkers are going out of business because nobody will read them.

HURT: Because nobody cares, and it's like the drunken uncle on *Saturday Night Live*: "Why, I heard that Hillary Clinton had spinal meningitis." "Oh, no, no, she had pneumonia." "That's just what I said: *spinal meninonia*."

I mean, it's just crazy pass-around information, and people don't want to know. Certainly, the audience for my book is not people who are thinking of voting for Donald Trump. They're the undecideds—but *really* undecided—and Hillary Clinton supporters. People who support Donald Trump do not want to be confused with the facts about Donald Trump. That's for sure.

DREYER: There's even people now who are saying, "I don't agree with anything he says—but somehow, he'll shake things up." So, yeah, he will. He'll do that.

HURT: He will. So will a bull in a china shop.

VISUAL ARTISTS

Art historian and author Pete Gershon on *Rag Radio*, June 7, 2019. Photo by Roger Baker.

PETE GERSHON

Fistfights, food fights, fires, and floods.

Pete Gershon discusses the food fight at Houston's Contemporary Arts Museum, skinny-dipping on the roof of the Lawndale Art Center, and the larger-than-life figures who changed the face of Houston art.

Pete Gershon is a Houston-based art historian, curator, archivist, music journalist, and author. He curates projects for the Orange Show Center for Visionary Art and directs the Houston Art History Interview Project, which collects and makes accessible oral history videos from significant members of the city's arts community, an endeavor funded by the City of Houston through the Houston Arts Alliance. He is also the former program coordinator for the Core Residency Program at the Glassell School of Art at the Museum of Fine Arts, Houston.

Gershon's latest book, Collision: The Contemporary Art Scene in Houston, 1972-1985, *is a comprehensive narrative of the years when contemporary art took Houston by storm. Kealey Boyd wrote in* Hyperallergic *that* Collision *"meticulously traces the craggy rise of Houston's art community" and added, "I wish every city a Pete Gershon to document its art scene." Pete is also the author of* Painting the Town Orange: The Stories behind Houston's Visionary Art Environments. *He is working on a book about the golden era ('60s-'80s) of Houston's Montrose neighborhood, often known as the "Greenwich Village of Houston."*

Pete Gershon and I became friends after he was on Rag Radio, *and he has since interviewed me for a video project about Houston artists. I knew personally many of the colorful characters in his excellent book about Houston's contemporary art scene, and he really brought them to life. It was a wild and woolly time in the Houston art world.*

JUNE 7, 2019

THORNE DREYER: I have a book here that could be a weapon.

PETE GERSHON: Or a doorstop.

DREYER: But it's much more. It's a beautiful book, very ambitious, and somewhat overwhelming—especially because I remember well so many of the people you write about.

My guest is Pete Gershon. Pete is the author of *Collision: The Contemporary Art Scene in Houston, 1972-1985*, which is, according to Texas A&M University Press, "the raucous, delightful, no-holds-barred story of how contemporary art came to Houston." Clue: It was a *collision*! And I would have to say that it included fistfights and food fights and floods.

GERSHON: Fires.

DREYER: And fires. It's an adventure story as much as a story about art and change.

Again, from the publisher: "In his expansive and vigorous survey of the Houston art scene, Gershon describes the city's emergence as a locus for the arts."

So, Cheech Marin—is Cheech your buddy?

GERSHON: That might be a little bit of an overstatement, but we had some tacos one time for lunch.

DREYER: Well, that does it for me.

GERSHON: He was very nice.

DREYER: Did he pay?

GERSHON: I'm not sure who paid; neither of us paid. But he is as quick with a joke as you might imagine.

DREYER: According to comedian and art collector Cheech Marin, "Pete Gershon puts you in the middle of this wild, dynamic scene, which is exactly what you want from this kind of book."

And, to quote Bill Arning, director of Houston's Contemporary Arts Museum [2009-2018], "Gershon is not afraid of big personalities and their grand mythologies. In tackling the history of art, artists, and nascent institutions in Houston, Gershon has found clear narrative lines in the cast of thousands that built the culture here. . . . *Collision* also functions as a case study and how-to guide for building sustainable cultures outside the glare of New York."

It's also got great photography, great art in it—and it's 8½ × 11, 440 pages. And it's full of some of the most colorful characters that you'll ever meet. It's got both the crazy Wild West edge and the sophistication of fine arts. It's a great trip and I enjoyed it immensely.

Okay, the book covers the years 1972 to 1985. I'm tempted to ask, well, what happened before 1972 in the Houston art world? And we can obviously cover that, but why did you pick that specific span of years?

GERSHON: Well, I guess I will answer the subquestion first and talk a little bit about the fact that before the 1970s, there certainly was a thriving art culture in Houston, but the city was still very much on the cultural frontier. There were artists working in a modernist vein here, for sure, as early as 1900, and then the arrival of Emma Richardson Cherry, who set up an organization called the Houston Art League— nothing to do with the current Art League Houston—it actually evolved into the Museum of Fine Arts Houston.

And there were several successive generations of artists who worked and taught younger artists, and of course the arrival of [famed art patrons] John and Dominique de Menil in the 1940s was really transformational and the work that they did at the Contemporary Arts Association, Museum of Fine Arts, St. Thomas University, Rice University.

But I feel it was really in the '70s that things took off. And 1972— I picked that opening date since that is the year that the current Contemporary Arts Museum [CAM] building opened, in March of 1972. And the building opened with a very avant-garde exhibition called *Exhibition Ten*. Perhaps you were even there, Thorne.

DREYER: Yes, I believe I was.

GERSHON: The director at the time, this guy Lefty Adler, went out and found ten contemporary artists that he convinced to come to Houston to create these site-specific works for the new museum. And some of these were somewhat conventional works, you know—a minimalist sculpture by Robert Grosvenor, for example—but some of the work really confused people in Houston.

One was an indoor farm with plants growing on these vertical panels and different fruits and a worm farm. But the thing that really upset people was a piece by an artist named Ellen Van Fleet named *New York City Animal Levels* that consisted of these tiered cages of rats, cats, doves, pigeons. There were cockroaches in jars. And the people who showed up for this opening, many of whom had given a lot of money for this new building, were very confused and actually very upset. A lot of them did cut their ties with the museum.

DREYER: Especially when there started being deaths.

GERSHON: Yeah.

DREYER: Kitties started dying.

GERSHON: Yeah, cats were surrounded on all sides by disease-carrying animals, and some of them did start to die during the show, and it was somebody's responsibility to go in there at the beginning of the day and clean things up.

DREYER: And were there—did some escape, some critters?

GERSHON: Yeah, cats escaped, a lot of the mice escaped, cockroaches escaped—they started turning up in the desk drawers of the museum's administrative people. It was a little bit of a mess; the whole museum smelled terrible for months.

DREYER: This wasn't all of the show. There was other stuff that was not *as* controversial.

GERSHON: It certainly was all very cutting edge. William Wegman is maybe one of the most famous of the artists—although he was just getting going at the time—but he had an early video piece with one of his Weimaraners in the show. There was sculpture and installation work and some video.

There was a trench that was dug, an actual piece of land art, where the Noguchi sculpture garden is now. It used to just be an empty lot on that corner, and the one Houston-based artist in that show, Vera Simons, planned for a trench that would have a wave in it—a machine would push this wave back and forth—but it didn't really work.

DREYER: Why don't you give us just a little bit of background about what was so significant about this new CAM building and a little bit of its history. I remember when the CAM was in front of the Prudential Building.

GERSHON: Yes. Well, the CAM had started off in this very simple—very modern but very simple—A-frame building designed by an architect named Karl Kamrath. This building had been constructed on property up near the park downtown [on Dallas, adjacent to Sam Houston Park], but at some point the building was sawn in half and loaded on flatbed trucks and brought down to the Prudential Building on Holcombe Boulevard [in the Texas Medical Center].

But by the late '60s it was leaking, it was falling apart. They really had to find something new, so they hired an architect named Gunnar Birkerts, who had done some really important work in other parts of the country. He was from Michigan. He came down and he devised this incredible building—very advanced for its time—this large parallelogram that would provide this really huge open space for any kind of installation work they might want to show at the museum.

He called it "Envelope"—for whatever the emerging cultural forms were going to be—with this really incredible metal corrugated skin on the outside. You know, Houston had never seen anything like this, and they certainly had never seen anything like the art that was shown in that first exhibition.

DREYER: And one thing, too, should the Museum of Fine Arts, Houston ever get complacent: this was hovering across the street.

GERSHON: Yeah. Directly across the street.

DREYER: This stainless steel wonder.

GERSHON: Yes. And throughout the '70s there were these periods where it seemed like the CAM was always on the edge of disaster. And there was always this idea that it was going to have to be folded into the Museum of Fine Arts, Houston.

And there is precedent for that. [In 1963, the failing Dallas Museum of Contemporary Art merged with the Dallas Museum of Fine Art.] But every time that threat came up, the CAM found its way out of it. It really operated very much like an alternative art space and not like a museum during that era.

DREYER: Okay, so another dynamic that we have at play through all of this is the crazy artists and curators and directors and the patrons—the people who support, come up with the money, and make the final decisions. And so what was the reaction to this CAM show?

GERSHON: The people who were the patrons, who gave the money for this, were very upset. I think a lot of the artists liked [the first exhibition], but the people that the museum was depending on for support were not into this at all, and director Lefty Adler was gone within a year.

DREYER: So, what else? Why '72? What about this stretch of '72 through '85?

GERSHON: Well, this is where things really took off. Jim Harithas was the director who succeeded Lefty Adler, and he came from Syracuse, New York, where he had been the director of the Everson Museum, and he had been at the Corcoran in DC before that. So he was a very serious museum person. Very well educated, coming down here to Houston despite all the advice of his friends saying, "Don't go to Texas, you'll never be heard from again."

But I think there was something that appealed to Jim—not only about the proximity to Mexico, which he was interested in exploring—but he already knew Vera Simons, the artist that I just mentioned, and Dorothy Hood. He'd done some work with them in New York. Had written for their catalogs. So he had a point of access.

He arrived in 1974 with his family, really ready to go—but also, walking in the door and finding a pretty impoverished institution that had spent what money it did have on a new building. So he really had to reinvent the CAM—and what he did was to organize a series of shows of work by Texas artists, which nobody had done in Houston before.

DREYER: Amazingly enough.

GERSHON: It is kind of incredible, and he was particularly rankled by the fact that he came down to Houston and then found that Latino and Chicano artists weren't being shown anywhere in town. So that was one of the things he wanted to remedy the most.

He got in his truck with Mark Lombardi, who was a student of his from Syracuse who followed him down, showed up at the museum ready to work. They got in Jim's truck and they drove all over the state and they found what artists they could, and many of these people were invited to do solo shows at the CAM during the mid-'70s.

And we are talking about Luis Jiménez, we are talking about James Surls—who didn't live in Houston yet—John Alexander, Terry Allen, Forrest Prince, Richard Stout. Julian Schnabel, of all people, was a University of Houston student, and he came into the museum to bother and bother and bother Jim until he gave him a modest little show in the basement. [Schnabel would gain fame as a painter and an independent filmmaker.]

So this was a new thing for Houston. Previous to that, it was very difficult for Houston artists to have their work shown, but here was a context in which it was really celebrated and made very central to the cultural fabric.

DREYER: Harithas, along with two or three other characters, including John Alexander and Marilyn Lubetkin, who was a board member but also sort of strode both sides of the fence because she was always close with the artists, too. These people run through the book and through different institutions—and they were a very rowdy bunch.

GERSHON: Yes.

DREYER: James Surls—I mean, I left out James Surls, who was a central character in this play.

GERSHON: That's very true, and it was a macho scene and it was a pretty rowdy scene—but from what I understand, that was just the nature of life in Houston at the time. You went out to a bar, there was a fight. That's just what happened, and I think, really, it's this sort of personality and this kind of mythmaking that makes this an interesting story, every bit as much as the art.

DREYER: I also want to talk about the great flood.

GERSHON: In June of 1976, there was a—it wasn't even a hurricane, it was just a torrential summer rainstorm that pretty much filled the entire first floor of the CAM, which is the basement floor. Most people wouldn't put a basement in a building in Houston, but this architect from Michigan sure did.

And the water just ran down the loading dock in back and filled the entire first floor. You eventually had Jim Harithas and John Alexander putting on scuba suits and dropping through a trapdoor on the first floor to go dive for art. It's where all the museum storage was. More than a million dollars' worth of art was destroyed—they were holding a lot of art for a dealer in town—and, in addition, all of the museum's records as well. So, all of that was lost; a lot of it went down the drain, some of it went to NASA to be dried out in these freeze-drying chambers.

And the museum was closed for a year. It wasn't at all obvious that they were going to be able to reopen, but Jim leveraged all of his art-world connections, got artists from all over the country, including very prominent ones, to donate work for an auction. And he raised enough money to get the museum back together.

DREYER: I think there were other artists diving, too, as I recall. I remember getting a call from someone saying, "Hey, they're diving for art over at the CAM."

GERSHON: It could have been you.

DREYER: I could have gone over there.
Okay, we were just listening to some music. Who was that, Pete?

GERSHON: That was Terry Allen. He's an artist who came from Lubbock and then went to school in LA, but Jim encountered him like we were just talking about, on these statewide treks, and invited him to come to the CAM. And I think this was 1975 when he did his show. He debuted his *Juarez* album at the museum—actually did a concert that was broadcast live on the radio—and featured all of his sort of collage wall relief work that related to that cycle of songs.

DREYER: Remarkable performer and artist.

GERSHON: Still is.

DREYER: Houston had always been a pretty lively art center. But this period in the '70s to the mid-'80s was also a rollicking time politically, in all kinds of ways, and a lot of the people involved in this story, a lot of the artists, were also very political. Harithas was politically radical, I would say. It was just a wild time.

Tell us a little bit more. Tell us about the incident with the bread. Tell us about that event.

GERSHON: Well, sure. This is kind of everybody's favorite story from the era. This is about a show after the CAM reopened following the flood.

It was closed for about a year. They reopened a couple of times briefly for some shows and things, but I think the building wasn't really ready to reopen for another year. And I believe it was your mom's paintings—I think the first thing after the museum reopened was that posthumous show of Margaret Webb Dreyer's work.

DREYER: Right.

GERSHON: So, following that—I guess this would have been September of 1977—Jim invited this Spanish conceptual artist named Antoni Miralda to do a show at the museum. And Miralda was an artist who worked primarily with food, making these elaborate sculptures, photography, all different kinds of media, but all dealing with food—and thinking about its linkage with sustenance and energy.

And what he devised for the CAM was really a performance piece. What he was going to do was divide the gallery with a long bench, and then he brought in the Kilgore [College] Rangerettes drill team, and they started off with their own performance.

DREYER: To get the scene all hyped up in the first place.

GERSHON: Yeah. I mean, if you can just picture these incredible silk red-white-and-blue outfits. I mean, if people don't know who the Kilgore Rangerettes are, they're just sort of a drill team that was there for the purpose of egging on a football team and the fans and the stadium and just getting everybody crazy and wild.

DREYER: And they were nationally famous.

GERSHON: Yeah, yeah. So they did their routine, and then there was a break—and then the Kilgore Rangerettes would come up one by one from the basement of the CAM with these trays of bread—loaves of bread that had been made with food coloring, so they're orange and green and purple, red and blue. And they stacked these loaves of bread on this long wall bisecting the space, and it kind of created this strange us-versus-them situation where you had people on either side of this long wall of bread.

". . . people start tearing off little chunks of bread and tossing it around the room at each other. And then eventually this one guy picks up a loaf of bread, throws it across the room like a football, knocks over this little girl."

They're serving wine, the air-conditioning goes out, so it's very hot in the room and people are getting all riled up with the Kilgore Rangerettes, and people start tearing off little chunks of bread and tossing it around the room at each other. And then eventually this one guy picks up a loaf of bread, throws it across the room like a football, knocks over this little girl. And one of the artists there sees this happen, grabs the culprit, and drags him out back to deal with him. The whole room just erupted, and it's just a brawl, just a complete free-for-all at this point.

DREYER: All the names are in the book, by the way.

GERSHON: All the names are in the book, indeed. I will even tell you, this artist was John Alexander, who was well known for being ready to throw a punch when the situation called for it.

DREYER: As was Jim Harithas.

GERSHON: Yeah, well, this is also true. And there's a lot of discussion between people about how calculated this was. Did Jim and Miralda really know what they were getting into? And a lot of people thought they knew exactly what they were doing, and they knew exactly what the result was going to be. So, there was just a huge donnybrook, a Texas-style donnybrook.

DREYER: In an art museum.

GERSHON: In an art museum. The police came, cleared out the whole museum, everybody went home. Jim and Marilyn mopped up the blood. Subsequently, there were articles in the paper—and it did not really impress the art critics in town at all. But it's a cherished story now thirty, forty years later, however long it's been.

DREYER: When we started out, Houston—before the CAM—had the Museum of Fine Arts and that was pretty much it. There were art departments—U of H didn't have much of an art department.

GERSHON: It was pretty weak until the mid-'70s.

DREYER: St. Thomas had an art department, I believe, and Rice University.

GERSHON: True.

DREYER: But there weren't any other institutions other than art galleries.

GERSHON: Yeah, that's pretty accurate, I think.

DREYER: And as a result of this energy and all of this activity, there ended up being multiple institutions, and we'll talk about that. So, the CAM moved into an absolutely empty space—not just their new building, but in terms that nobody was showing that kind of contemporary art, that kind of edgy contemporary art in Houston, except in a few galleries. But how did that affect the Museum of Fine Arts?

GERSHON: I think it took some of the pressure off of the Museum of Fine Arts—as far as people who were saying that they should be showing more contemporary work. Now all they had to say was, "There's a museum right across the street that's showing that work, so that's their terrain."

I think what the Museum of Fine Arts was interested in showing—

I mean, obviously they are meant to be an encyclopedic collection—and they are interested in showing many, many centuries' worth of the best art that can come to Houston. And they always said, "Well, this is how we serve our community, and this is how we serve the artists of Houston: not by showing their work, but by showing them the work that comes from around the world and giving them that information and that inspiration."

And it is certainly true that the museum employed many of these artists through what was then called the Museum School—now it's the Glassell School of Art. So, they made a significant contribution, and depending on the director, the focus may have varied a little.

When James Johnson Sweeney was there—backed up by the largesse of the de Menils, who were on the board at that point—he brought in a lot of de Koonings and Pollocks and abstract expressionist work from midcentury. He had a very good eye for it. Sweeney came to Houston from the Guggenheim; he was also a very accomplished museum man, and he knew exactly what he was doing.

His successor—not his immediate successor, but following Sweeney—was a director named Bill Agee, and I think he was interested in a set of early-century American abstractionists. But they also showed a lot of color field painting during his time, and that's kind of what Houston became known for as far as the museum and what the galleries were showing.

But the work that the artists in Houston were doing was just something completely different, like a more personal, more human kind of art and very authentic and not trying to fit into any particular national trends at all.

"But the work that the artists in Houston were doing was just something completely different, like a more personal, more human kind of art and very authentic and not trying to fit into any particular national trends at all."

DREYER: Another dynamic that happened was the alternative institutions started.

GERSHON: Yes.

DREYER: Tell us about Lawndale. Another crazy story.

GERSHON: So, what happened in December of 1978 is James Surls was working with one of his students, one of his protégés named Robert Graham, and they were working in the building that served the art and architecture departments at the University of Houston. And there was a thunderstorm, and a lightning strike started a fire in the building. They actually had to get the very large sculpture that they were working on out in time with a winch.

DREYER: Was there some question whether it really was lightning that caused the fire?

GERSHON: Bob Graham kind of assumed that a stray spark from his welding torch might have landed in some rags. And there had been fires already at this building; this was a different time, and things were a little loose. So there's a little bit of disagreement about exactly how this fire might have started. But the upshot was the building was destroyed, the art department had to move into a new space, and the head of the department, George Bunker, took the faculty over to a large former Schlumberger [oil-field services] cable factory out in the East End of town.

DREYER: Massive, massive.

GERSHON: Absolutely huge and pretty much empty except for some trash at this point—and offered it to the art department. And, very apologetically, Bunker said, "I'm sorry, but this is really all we have to offer you."

And somebody like James Surls could look around at this completely empty space, where his students would be able to work with absolutely no supervision whatsoever, and really recognize the possibilities there. And they were very happy to settle into this building. Not only to make art but to build out some gallery spaces and present art. And this was happening at a time—this is 1979 we're up to.

DREYER: And also to have studios upstairs.

GERSHON: Studios upstairs.

DREYER: Some of which were lived in.

GERSHON: Yes, indeed. People lived there.

DREYER: And nobody fell through the big air vents.

GERSHON: Yeah, miraculously nobody fell through the vents. There were some mishaps there and people who got hurt.

DREYER: It was a very anarchic time and place.

GERSHON: Yeah, you could never get away with something like that today. But it was a really meaningful place, and Houston had not really had a viable alternative art space before that. The CAM sort of operated that way; there was this Houston Museum of Modern Art that Sandra Stevens ran, and that was certainly an alternative space, but Lawndale was really the first durable alternative space in Houston, I think. And whole successive generations of artists have come up through the original Lawndale, which no longer exists. [The name came from its original address on Lawndale Avenue.]

DREYER: Okay. We assume a lot here. Let's tell people who James Surls is and what his art is like.

GERSHON: James Surls is kind of the Paul Bunyon figure of the Houston art world, just this big, burly guy who came out of the East Texas woods with his hatchet and his chain saw. He lived in Dallas for some time, teaching up at SMU, but after he had his first opportunity to show his work at the CAM in 1975, he really fell in love with Houston. His friend John Alexander got him a job at the University of Houston, so James moved with his wife, the sculptor Charmaine Locke.

DREYER: And his chain saw.

GERSHON: And his chain saw. They actually found some property up north of Houston in Splendora, just this beautiful, off-the-map kind of space up there. They had a lot of wild parties up in Spendora, for sure. But he was just a great inspiration for the whole community. He really led by example, and when he was in charge of Lawndale, he said "yes" to absolutely everything people wanted to do, often whether he thought it was a good idea or not.

DREYER: Tell us about his art.

GERSHON: At the time he was doing these very totemic-looking figures—you wouldn't quite call it minimalistic—but these very organic wood figures that had been roughly chopped with an axe. But at the same time, they projected so much character and personality; sometimes they were almost humanoid figures, sometimes not. You might see some commonalities between the tribal art of the Pacific Northwest in some cases. Work he is doing now is a lot more refined, I think, but I just loved those early sculptures so much.

DREYER: Right, right. And very totemic, very totemic.

GERSHON: Yeah.

DREYER: When we were talking about Lawndale—the students who were living there and working there tried to build a swimming pool on the roof.

GERSHON: They did. Yeah, there was a sort of a depression on the roof where all the rain rolled down. They noticed this happening, so they brought some hoses up there and filled it up, which worked pretty good for skinny-dipping—until the water started leaking through the ceiling.

DREYER: And some neighbors complained, too.

GERSHON: Exactly, yeah. The neighbors didn't like it.

DREYER: Probably not a very wise plan. What other alternative institutions grew up?

GERSHON: There were a bunch that emerged in the early '80s. One was a place called Midtown Art Center, which still exists in some form, although it's gone through a lot of changes over the years. But this was an idea to put something right in the middle of Midtown that would help rejuvenate the neighborhood. Where have we heard this before? Put an art institution somewhere to drive up real estate values.

There is also a place called Center for Art and Performance, which is something that Michael Peranteau organized when he was first in Houston. Maybe the most durable would be this place called DiverseWorks, and I'm sure a lot of your listeners have been to DiverseWorks in Houston. It's been in a few different physical spaces over the years, but it was established in 1982.

DREYER: Wasn't it at Market Square?

GERSHON: Yeah, it sure was. And if you want to talk about the impact of DiverseWorks, cleaning up Market Square was a DiverseWorks project. At the time that DiverseWorks moved downtown, Market Square was a garbage-strewn empty lot. And it really took the investment of the artists to clean it up, fill it with sculptures, make an organized plan for it to be a center of activity downtown. And you know, it would not be an exaggeration to say that these artists were responsible for the rejuvenation of downtown Houston. It's really true.

DREYER: Pete, what was the music we were just listening to?

GERSHON: That was Herschel Berry and the Natives.

DREYER: They were very much a part of that Houston art scene.

GERSHON: Absolutely, they played countless concerts around Houston at the time, and Herschel was also a visual artist. In the early '70s he was part of the collective—as a very young artist—called Daucus Carota [named for the flowering plant known as wild carrot or Queen Anne's lace]. And they would do these absurd poster campaigns. They put posters up all around.

The first thing they did was to make this huge, man-sized cement carrot, and they would place it in the middle of the night on the front of the CAM or on the lawn of the Museum of Fine Arts. It would get carted away, and then they would try and get their carrot back and have to fight to get the carrot. As a result of this they made a poster campaign all over the city with a picture of the Museum of Fine Arts director, warning people that he was an enemy of Daucus Carota. So, it was this real sort of juvenile Dada.

DREYER: Now, we've talked about the book—I mean, there are 440 pages of incredibly rich information and art in this book. Tell us how you did it, why you decided to do this book, how you got started on it.

GERSHON: I moved to Houston in 2005. I had been living in Vermont, and I'd been publishing this avant-garde jazz magazine called *Signal to Noise*. I came down here to Houston, and I was raising my two babies and working from home and just very isolated.

And at a certain point I really realized that I needed to get out there and get involved with the community. I did some volunteer work at the Menil Collection. I had been doing a Sunday jazz show on the Rice University radio station. And one of my fellow DJs there heard that I had been transferring my collection of rare jazz recordings on cassette onto CD, and she said, "Well, if you know how to do that, you should volunteer in the archives at the Menil Collection. They could really use your help."

And I said, "Heather, they do not want some bozo like me walking in off the streets and getting my grubby hands on their archives." But she made an introduction, and they were very happy to have my help.

DREYER: They wanted your grubby hands.

GERSHON: I transferred all of their audio and video cassettes over the span of about a year and a half. And in the process of doing that I met an artist who was also working there, volunteering there, who was setting up a program through DiverseWorks to put young artists and young artist professionals together with older regional artists to help them document their work and to preserve their archives and get things organized.

So, she put me together with this artist named Bert Long [founder of the Houston community art space Project Row Houses], who was just an amazing guy—incredible painter, sculptor, printmaker, photographer. He also made these enormous, monumental, multicolored ice sculptures with a chain saw—that would melt away in the Texas sun. Really great guy, really great storyteller—talk, talk, talk, all the time.

And I worked for him for a little over a year before he died. And when he died it really made me understand that somebody needs to be preserving these stories and getting them down, because this information is just not going to be around forever. I had also been—after writing about music for over a decade, I wanted to do something different.

When I first got to Houston, I started hearing about places like the Orange Show, the Beer Can House, the Flower Man's House, these so-called visionary art environments that are sort of our version of the Watts Towers in LA [the outsider artist Simon Rodia's interconnected sculptural towers]. These handmade spaces by usually untrained artists, just looking for something to do in their retirement usually, although oftentimes they have a very serious purpose.

DREYER: Sometimes obsessive.

GERSHON: Actually, usually obsessive. And I was really interested in these places and wanted to find out why somebody would make something like the Orange Show. The Orange Show is a space on the East End of Houston that was built over a period of decades by a retired mail carrier named Jeff McKissick, starting in the late '60s. First, he wanted it to be a beauty shop, and then it was going to be a plant shop—and then he had this sort of epiphany that he was going to make this a tribute to the orange and to steam power.

So, with his own two hands he built out this nutty space, with a little steamboat that goes around in a pond and a little amphitheater, and a little museum with these costumed mannequins—and all of these handmade signs with little slogans encouraging you to be healthy and drink orange juice. And this is just how you are going to be healthy and happy as a human being.

And he thought this was going to be as big as the Astrodome; he thought people were going to be coming from all over the country. And now people do. But in his lifetime, when he opened the space to the public, he did no advertising; he really did nothing at all to get the word out about it.

It was really just the artists in town who had accidentally stumbled across the space that showed up—and he died six months later. Many of his friends think he died of a broken heart because he wanted to share this with the community so much and he just didn't really have the right way to do it.

Now Marilyn Lubetkin, who is Marilyn Oshman since her divorce, was a friend of Jeff's and bought the property after his death. She rounded up a bunch of patrons to split the cost and started the foundation that not only does programming of the space throughout the year but also is responsible for our annual Art Car Parade.

So, I think Jeff would be very pleased now to know the impact that his space has had on the cultural life in Houston.

DREYER: And there's other things in Houston that are somewhat similar.

GERSHON: Yeah, the other really prominent one is called the Beer Can House.

DREYER: Right. Which is amazing.

GERSHON: It's great. It's a little bungalow on Malone Street just north of Memorial Drive, and this is where an upholsterer for the railroad named John Milkovich lived. He came from a family of old-world craftsmen, and he lived in that house for almost his entire life. And somewhere along the line, he decided, "Well, I don't want to mow the yard anymore," so he covered it in concrete and put marbles and beads and all kinds of little things pressed into the concrete.

And when he ran out of yard to cover, he started covering the house with flattened beer cans, one strip at a time—because he wasn't sure what his wife was going to think about all this. So he did it very slowly until the whole house was covered. These amazing dangling garlands of can tops just sort of glitter in the sun and make this amazing, delicate chimelike sound. If you're ever in Houston and if you haven't been to the Beer Can House and you haven't been to the Orange Show, you should totally go. You will not regret it, I promise you.

DREYER: How did all of this get you into this book?

GERSHON: Writing about the Orange Show, that's how I met Marilyn and that's how I met Jim Harithas. This was a place that people like Jim or John Alexander—and there's a lot of argument over who discovered this place first—but they would bring board members there. They would bring girlfriends there; they would bring visiting artists.

Jim brought Willem de Kooning there when he came to do a show at the Blaffer Museum at the University of Houston in the late '70s. He brought de Kooning over there to meet Jeff McKissick, and they talked for a long time. These two men were a similar age. And of course Jeff McKissick had no idea who Willem de Kooning was; he just didn't know anything about the art world, didn't care anything about the art world.

When it came up in conversation that de Kooning was a painter, McKissick said, "Well, you should really think about moving to Houston. You can see all this new construction here—you'd probably find a job really easily."

DREYER: Paint these buildings for us. Okay, so through all of that you started gathering all this material.

GERSHON: Meeting all those people and doing those interviews for that book, I really understood that a place like the Orange Show was only one component of an incredibly rich cultural environment that was happening in Houston at the time—in the thick of the oil boom, all this money flowing into the city.

It was the first time that you could buy alcohol by the drink in restaurants, just everything was loosening up in Houston. And coming from somebody with a background as a journalist, when you hear stories like that that haven't already been collected into a book, it's just like a gold mine.

And I'm really lucky, as I've gotten to know these people better and better, I've made a lot of really incredible friends in this scene. And I will say about Houston, it's an incredibly welcoming scene. If you want to get involved in the arts in Houston, there are a million ways to do it, and people are really happy to have you there.

DREYER: Yeah, I know. All the way dating back to when I basically grew up in an art gallery.

GERSHON: The research continues. Even with a very long book with 160,000 words, I feel like I've barely scratched the surface; there's a lot of people that I didn't interview for the book, or didn't have the proper way to include them in the book, or I wanted to go deeper. So now I'm working on a grant from the City of Houston to collect some interviews on video.

I'm going to put lightly edited versions on the book's website, so people can use those interviews for further research of their own. But the endgame is to take these collected interviews and edit down to some tighter programs about various figures or various themes. So, this is what I'm working on over the course of the next year or two. And, indeed, I'm actually collecting some interviews here in Austin this weekend with Bob Wade [creator of monumental sculptures] and some other people—and with Thorne Dreyer.

DREYER: With Thorne Dreyer? How about that. I hear he's a tough interview.

GERSHON: Well, we'll see how it goes. Seems like he might be okay, actually.

DREYER: Okay, what else?

GERSHON: I have a show that I'm organizing at the Glassell School of Art. This is a show of prints and ceramics from a printshop in Houston called Little Egypt Enterprises that was run by a Tamarind [Institute]-trained master printer named David Folkman, who passed away quite some time ago.

But in the '70s and the first half of the '80s, he worked with almost every prominent artist in Houston to make prints, and he was a beloved figure and really just produced an incredibly diverse and rich body of artwork. All collaboratively produced with the artists.

DREYER: One other thing to mention is the show *Fresh Paint: The Houston School*, which was in some ways a downer, in the end. But on the other hand, it had expectations that probably were not realistic.

GERSHON: I think that's true, and that's why this book goes up to 1985.

This was a show that was curated at the Museum of Fine Arts by Barbara Rose and Susie Kalil, *Fresh Paint: The Houston School*. It was really the first time that the museum had taken on the idea of a local art scene and, you know, a categorical approach to who was painting in Houston. This was all painters in the show. And Houston was a painting town at the time. And it was very meaningful to the artists to get that recognition from their own home museum that they had not had before.

But there was this idea that the show was going to go on to New York and LA and Europe and everybody was going to get a gallery [show] in New York, and this was going to place Houston alongside New York and Chicago and LA as a major art-producing city in the country. And the show did go to MoMA's PS1 in New York [a nonprofit arts center devoted to contemporary art].

But around the time that the tour was being arranged, Barbara Rose left the museum, and she really was the person with the clout to carry this through and get the show moving around the globe. And without her behind it, it went back home through an art space in Oklahoma City and then back to Houston, and that was really it.

There are some people from the era who have gotten out of Houston and done well. James Surls, John Alexander, Mel Chin, certainly. But as the economy in Houston collapsed in the mid-'80s, it kind of sapped the scene of some of its energy.

And maybe it was for the best, because the reason the art is so good in Houston is because people are really making it for the right reasons. They're making it for themselves, not to sell, not to make money, although they would like to sell work. So, the fact that the scene didn't explode maybe even saved the scene in a way.

DREYER: Houston is still a pretty important art scene.

GERSHON: It really is. There's been a lot of growth over the past couple of decades. And I think all the seeds were planted during this time that I cover in the book, where we're very lucky to have had these inspirational catalyzing figures to open things up for us.

Artist and art professor Margo Sawyer (*left*) with Thorne Dreyer on *Rag Radio*, April 20, 2018. Photo by Roger Baker.

MARGO SAWYER

Prepared to answer the universe's call.

Margo Sawyer talks about synchronicity in her work, being alone in King Tut's tomb, and the role of women in the arts.

Margo Sawyer is professor of sculpture and extended media in the Department of Art and Art History at the University of Texas at Austin. Most recently Sawyer was awarded the 2018 John Simon Guggenheim Memorial Foundation Fellowship. Sawyer combines art and architecture into "sacred spaces," emphasizing "the ways in which the architectural and ritual converge to create a forum for contemplation and reflection."

Sawyer, who was born in the United States and brought up in England, was Texas State Artist of the Year in 2015. In addition to the Guggenheim Fellowship, she has received two Fulbright grants and a National Endowment for the Arts grant. She has exhibited throughout the United States and internationally in the United Kingdom, Italy, India, and Japan, and at the US embassy in Pristina, Kosovo.

She is best known for her large public artworks in such cities as London, New York, and Indianapolis. Her most celebrated work is Synchronicity of Color, Red and Blue (2008) at Discovery Green in Houston. The park, which she helped design, and her sculpture installations have become iconic Houston spaces.

APRIL 20, 2018

THORNE DREYER: According to her bio, Margo Sawyer "has created installations which translate the notion of an ancient sacred space into a contemporary vocabulary.... Recently Sawyer's practice has focused on creating large-scale—often public—installations that combine her parallel interests in art and architecture."

Michael Barnes noted in the *Austin American-Statesman* that Sawyer "is the niece of Harlem Renaissance painter Aaron Douglas and her father was one of the first African Americans to serve in the US Diplomatic Corps during the 1950s. He met her British mother in Accra, Ghana. Her grandfather founded the NAACP in Topeka, Kansas, and helped initiate the legal action that became *Brown v. Board of Education*."

Which of course led to the Supreme Court decision that struck down school segregation.

MARGO SAWYER: Just a small lineage.

DREYER: Sawyer's art not only "intersects sculpture and architecture," it also involves mindfulness—which we will talk about.

"Synchronicity" has been defined as the "simultaneous occurrence of events that appear significantly related but have no discernable causal connection." You use the term "synchronicity" in some of your work.

> "... I really use color in terms of collisions, of unexpected meetings in the ways that colors can collide and have a conversation."

SAWYER: I use it a lot. I've had many synchronistic events over my life—with friends, with relatives, with encounters that have no explanation. I work with color, and color is a very complex thing. And rather than composing, I really use color in terms of collisions, of unexpected meetings in the ways that colors can collide and have a conversation.

We might feel uncomfortable or we might not notice that in that field of blue—that blue field is so blue because there's this vibrant pink and there's this acid yellow and there's this purple that's making that whole field speak.

DREYER: You let the colors make their own decisions?

SAWYER: It's a little bit like jazz in that I work very vigorously. I work with a lot of precision metal fabrication, or I work with precision painting, or at the moment, I'm working with glass, very precision glass, hand glass painting. Yet when I bring those things together it's really like the impromptu-ness of a jazz musician.

I have all my bricks and my parts and I'm sort of in the moment, and my Zen practice comes to the fore. Maybe I have three days or a week to install an exhibition, or I have three weeks to install a big public sculpture—and there's often changes that happen right in the moment, and I'm very much okay with making those changes and being fluid in a way.

DREYER: Let me ask about the importance of public art.

SAWYER: I'm a professor; I teach at the University of Texas at Austin. I've been sort of on campus for thirty years, so it's an honor to be able to teach multiple generations over the years. But most of us go to museums and we look at artwork, and we're lucky in some places, where it's free, and [there are] other places where you have to pay money. With public art you can walk by it and not really notice it—and then be held and forced to sort of stop still and love the thing that you're looking at, or be curious about the thing that you're looking at.

So, here in Austin I have a work called *Index for Contemplation*—one of my earlier public art projects—which is in the Austin Convention Center. It's the northwest wing of that building and it's forty feet high and four hundred feet long. And I love people-watching; I love spying on people walking down the corridor, and then all of a sudden they come to a screeching halt and look up.

And, you know, they're kind of in awe and they're trying to make sense of what they're seeing—and then they will like *that* passage and they point to *that* passage. And for me, as the artist, that is the joy of making. Somebody unexpectedly came along and was kind of wild for a moment. Maybe just for a moment, but it was enough to kind of charge their day.

DREYER: But then it's something that they maybe see a lot and aren't consciously thinking about it, but it brings back that initial response.

SAWYER: Yeah. And you know, one of my most celebrated works in Texas—because I've lived here thirty-odd years—is the work that is housed at Discovery Green in Houston, and it's called *Synchronicity of Color, Red and Blue*. And unbeknownst to me, when I was on the initial phases of designing the park and designing that work, I had no idea I was creating a monument. And I had no idea I was creating an iconic sculpture.

DREYER: We should give people just a little background on this. Discovery Green is a miraculous urban park in Houston that was designed specifically for the space, and it's over in an area of town where, basically, there wasn't anything not very long ago. It's by the George R. Brown Convention Center and near the ballpark, Minute Maid Park. And I guess a lot of it is your work.

SAWYER: I was on the design team. So, that particular project was opposite the Convention Center, right next to the Hilton, in downtown Houston.

DREYER: When I said there was nothing there, I didn't mean there was *literally* nothing there.

SAWYER: There was just parking lots—so you would look out from the Convention Center and just see parked cars, and it was not the beautiful space that you see today. I was part of the team. For the team, they wanted a national artist and a Texas artist. So, we were chosen, and we worked with the architect Larry Speck, and we also worked with the landscape architect Hargreaves—with Mary Margaret Jones, and her team—and we really influenced the palette and the avenues of that particular park.

And my particular project wanted to knit the parking garage. So, my artwork actually houses the stairwells that go down to the underground parking garage. And they don't look like parking garage exits; they are these wonderful fake boxes that people peek in and kids don't really know what's inside—"What is this?"

DREYER: Space can be beautiful; space can be fun. It doesn't have to just be, you know, a way to get from one place to another.

SAWYER: Yeah. And people love it; they get married, they've gotten engaged, they have their quinceañera pictures in front of it.

DREYER: Why don't you describe the primary piece.

SAWYER: There are two rectangular buildings, and they're about fifty feet long and about twelve feet high and about twelve feet wide, and right next to them is a big, huge wooden structure, which is a vent for the parking garage. And there's a door, kind of *Alice in Wonderland* door—"Where are you going?" But one building is hues of blues, and one building is hues of reds; part of that was because when you leave the parking garage, you need to remember where your cars are.

DREYER: So you do it by color.

SAWYER: I did this large installation many years ago for the Austin Museum of Art—which is now the Contemporary—called *Blue*. And it's a large floor installation made of thousands of pieces of wooden blocks. I was coming up empty as to what to do, and I was in my studio and I was looking down from my balcony onto the ground—and there were some boxes on the ground in color and I think maybe the catalog was open, and I went, "Ah! I'll make a floor installation of wood." And, you know, it was just like this aha moment.

And Houston's George R. Brown Convention Center back then was a complicated building, because it's not the most beautiful. It's big—red, white, and blue—and you veer completely away from it or you embrace it and go towards it. I made this giant work called *Blue*, and so I thought, "Well, I'll make a blue building and then I'll make its counter, I'll make a red building."

From the ground, you don't know that the roof is also clad in this artwork. But I knew that there would be skyscrapers that would be built and Google Earth would look down, and you would actually be able to see this artwork from the sky and from tall buildings, and indeed that is exactly what happened. They're blocks and they have two different depths so that a lot of people think it looks like *Tetris* or some sort of a game, and of course children love it.

DREYER: All of us children love it.

SAWYER: So, they're able to get their hands all sticky. "I can climb this." So, now I have to think about interactive, really embrace the interaction.

There's another project that I did which is called *Austin Ranch* in Dallas. I was asked by a developer in Dallas called Lucy Billingsley to design a monument, like a classic sculpture. Which I was not so thrilled about, you know, just a big monument sitting in a park. I just wasn't that interested. So, I came up with a pool and a plaza design and a roadway design. She looked at it—and her team was around her, and she's this very petite woman—and she goes, "I want to do all of it." I was like, "Well, gosh." So we did, and the pool is there—it's this wading pool.

DREYER: Yes, I've only seen pictures, but the pool looks wonderful.

SAWYER: You wade out—sort of calf high—and then you can wade into these inverted tile pyramids: one is red, one is blue, one is green. And she named it "Sawyer Pool," so it's named after yours truly and my predecessors. But it is a loved pool and people hang out in this space. I mean, I've not seen it with my eyes, you know, filled with people, but photographs show that this space is just loved. I mean, this is probably what an architect feels when they walk through the buildings that they've made that people really love and enjoy and linger and live with.

DREYER: Sometimes it feels like the artist loves it, and that comes across.

I wonder what you think of the Rothko Chapel in Houston? Since a lot of what you do is meditative, and also some of your painting is actually reflective a little bit of Mark Rothko. And we've got Barnett Newman, too, to create the monumental aspect of it.

SAWYER: Oh, I love the Rothko Chapel. You know, as a student in London I remember vividly, as you go into the Tate Gallery—I must have been seven or eight times with my high school class—and I remember going to this room and feeling incredibly depressed. I was just very, like, I didn't want to be there. And then years later I realized that it was the Seagram project that Rothko made for the Seagram Building and almost immediately after that, he committed suicide [in 1970].

And I think as a kid I kind of got it. I had this knowledge. I didn't know what that knowledge was, and I think all of us have this ability to read people, to read spaces and places, and to read auras. So, actually the Rothko Chapel was one of the first things I saw the first time I came to Texas, when I was a student at Yale.

But I made a pilgrimage because it is such an iconic and important place, and it's one of my talismans. When I go to Houston, the Menil and the Rothko Chapel are my places that I love to be in and go to.

DREYER: I had the very, very special pleasure of working for a short period of time as a gallery attendant at both the Menil Collection and the Contemporary Arts Museum in Houston.

SAWYER: Oh, fantastic.

DREYER: You know, when my mother [Margaret Webb Dreyer] died, we had the ceremony at the Rothko Chapel.

SAWYER: Wow.

DREYER: And it was all these Houston artists—and family and friends— and it was just such a moving thing.

Speaking about the meditative, it's like those paintings just infuse the space. And I've known people who don't get that, who it doesn't happen to.

SAWYER: Well, I think you have to be still and quiet, and you have to be slow. Particularly nowadays, where we're very rushed and we're distracted by our devices and the importance of that text or that appointment or this phone call. Just to be still and quiet is a treasured thing. And maybe the counter to what's happening now, maybe there will be

> "Well, I think you have to be still and quiet, and you have to be slow. Particularly nowadays, where we're very rushed and we're distracted by our devices and the importance of that text or that appointment or this phone call. Just to be still and quiet is a treasured thing."

a flip and people will begin to really embrace the quiet, really embrace the contemplative. Because our world is so not that.

DREYER: The Rothko Chapel was actually designed with Mark Rothko's paintings in mind. I don't know how much he was involved in the actual design of the structure.

SAWYER: Well, I believe he had a studio and the building is actually designed by Philip Johnson.

DREYER: Johnson did a number of important works in Houston.

SAWYER: He did the chapel very close to there.

DREYER: At St. Thomas University.

SAWYER: But he also was a precursor to a lot of mindful, contemplative work by artists of the next generation. So, whether it's James Turrell or Robert Irwin, Donald Judd—maybe the only other kind of one would be the *Water Lilies* of Monet. But sort of a sense of being enclosed and circled by just one work.

DREYER: So, take us to Egypt.

SAWYER: One of my big teachers in life has been the opportunity to go to Egypt a number of times—and looking at the monuments there. And the very first time I went, I was about twelve or thirteen. My mother never liked Christmas, so we would go anywhere that avoided Christmas. So that would mean that we would go to many Islamic countries, like Tunisia, and all these different places where Christianity was not the main thing—and to Greece.

And so we went during the 1973 war, and all my mother's friends were like, "You're mad. What are you doing? Your only child, and just you and her, you're going to a war zone?" My mother was—"Oh, it'll be fine." Anyway, so we were the first seventeen that were allowed into the country; we were the *only* seventeen tourists in the country. And so, as this kid, I got to go to the Valley of the Kings and I got to be in Tutankhamun's tomb, on my own, for like half an hour—and just look and look and look at it—just maybe fourteen, fifteen, very impressionable age.

And what I came away with was that a lot of the main temples, like Tutankhamun's tomb, are carved out of living rock. The sculpture—

the faces and the hieroglyphs—are carved out of the living stone and then they are painted. And so, it's this embrace of sculpture, architecture, and painting, and they're all one.

In a way, that's been my call to arms—like it's a unification of those disciplines. It's not a fracturing of those disciplines. So, I'm fascinated by architecture, I'm fascinated by landscape, I'm fascinated by color, I'm fascinated by the contemplative.

I went back many years later and it was not quite the same. Maybe one should not return to places that you remember—because it was packs of tourists, and you realize the fragility. You go into some of these tombs and it's sweaty and hot and too many people.

DREYER: That's not what they were made for.

SAWYER: No. You worry about the fragility of those objects, those spaces.

But it was a monumental moment for me. And, maybe it's because of my upbringing, but I really have to see with own eyes and experience with my body, places and spaces. And so, I've traveled. I've lived in India. I've lived in Japan. I've lived in Africa. I've lived in Rome. I've been fortunate to get grants to go do all these things.

To be able to live and work in a country like Japan and begin to learn about Buddhism, begin to learn about tea ceremonies and the meditative gardens and the temples, and really let it soak into your being, as opposed to looking at a book. You know, it's really about the experiential learning.

So, as a teacher I try to encourage that it's really the experience of learning. But learning the history is really important: going out and seeing, going out and experiencing, and making your own interpretations. Because every generation comes to it with a very different set of information.

DREYER: When you talk about the mindfulness—and how much it's not only what you create, what you want the effect of your creation to be, but of your process in creating it. Tell us a little more about your creative process.

SAWYER: Well, I've had various spiritual teachers along the way, and most recently, Reb Anderson at the San Francisco Zen Center has been a great teacher. And locally, Flint Sparks has been just an incredible teacher. Over the years I have done three-day retreats or one-day retreats and tried to engage with that practice and then daily try to spend some time in reflection, in meditation. I wouldn't say it's a lot, but like five minutes. But five minutes is better than no minutes.

DREYER: And it might be just what you need.

SAWYER: But I also think the act of making—as an artist or as a writer, or as a composer, or maybe as a chef, maybe as a gardener, maybe if you're in the gym and you're working out. I think there's a meditative quality, and that's when we're in the zone and we become free of worry.

I think, you know, the meditative becomes the lived. And as an artist, I get to do that. I mean, there's also a huge amount of mundane in this. Eighteen thousand pieces of glass have to be polished and dusted and, you know, put back.

DREYER: What about the economics of the art world and of your work? Because you've been involved in some massive projects. If we're looking at it from the economy of the art world—you're putting lots of bucks to work out there in the community in various ways, hopefully in positive ways.

SAWYER: I think the global art market is like a $3 trillion business, and in America it's now like $20 billion. It is huge—and that's the visual arts, that's music, that's fashion, that's architecture, it's design. There's this huge cultural impact.

And how important the arts are to education. And the whole thing about STEM—science, technology, engineering, and math—well, I advocate for STEAM, which is science, technology, engineering, *art*, and mathematics. And it's the art that really changes how we problem solve and how we look at things.

But back to the economy, specifically to my work on Discovery Green in Houston. It was a three-year project. I hired a number of my former students, and in total I hired about 139 people—maybe it's 132. There were two factories making my work, and one was a precision metal fabrication company called EVS Metals in Pflugerville. And that particular year, I was their third-best client: it was the US government, Motorola, and myself, as a female, minority, single-owned business.

So, initially two-thirds of this place was just packed full of my boxes. It was like Christmas every day when I went to look at all these boxes and boxes. It was astounding. And then, obviously, Discovery Green—that twenty-acre park has made downtown Houston explode. There's been development and all these skyscrapers—and at the time when we were designing it, it was a ghost town around there. And now it is a magnet for culture.

DREYER: You mean that area, that immediate area.

SAWYER: And it was just empty during the weekends.

DREYER: But it's affected the whole city. As someone who grew up in Houston, I remember when—and this was true in Austin, too—you'd go downtown at night and there was nothing happening, no energy. And I then remember when things started happening. Houston started becoming a night city. Artists working on Market Square helped rejuvenate that part of downtown. Something like this affects the energy of the whole region.

SAWYER: And here in Austin, you know, Waller Creek Conservancy. I did a number of tours of the park when this was in its inception, and I think city leaders have come and gone and looked at Discovery Green. But Waller Creek also has the potential to be this finger of renewal and beauty—which, of course, the Contemporary Austin has been—a big advocate for and partner in putting art in the public realm.

DREYER: And what they were doing with Buffalo Bayou, too, in Houston.

SAWYER: I know some of the founders of Discovery Green and Buffalo Bayou were similar people who were partnering. It takes a few families in a community to really be the conduit to create art patronage, which of course in Houston was started by Mrs. de Menil [Dominique de Menil, the art patron and collector].

Big patrons for the arts at the University of Texas are Jeanne and Mickey Klein. And Jeanne Klein—Mrs. de Menil was her mentor—and Suzanne Deal Booth is also somebody who Mrs. de Menil sort of shepherded. It's legacy building and its one generation teaching the patronage to another and then to another and to another. And hopefully, the young entrepreneurs out there will be encouraged to see that art is really important, and it really makes a difference.

DREYER: We were talking about the art world. What about the role of women? I think women have always played an important role in the art world, but maybe not at the top, where the money flows. What about that? Are changes happening? How does it look?

SAWYER: Here in Austin the Blanton Museum has a leader [Simone Wicha] who is a woman and it's a huge organization. And in their work, they support women artists and also the art community in a number of different ways. As a professor, it's interesting that probably over two-thirds of our student body in the fine arts are female.

DREYER: I'm not surprised.

SAWYER: And probably the same would be true of our graduate students.

There have been articles recently that the art world is really remiss in its upper-level management, whether it be museum curators or art critics, with the dollar amount that artists are getting for their work. I mean, women are in the majority of creators, but yet we make less money and we're underrepresented. But I think it's changing.

Years ago, I brought the Guerrilla Girls to campus—and those of you who don't know the Guerrilla Girls, they're a group of women who are anonymous.

DREYER: These were not zoo escapees, folks.

SAWYER: They wear gorilla masks and would do actions and make posters—and they had facts and figures about, you know, the number of naked women at the Metropolitan Museum versus the number of actual women artists showing. And it would be like point one percent of women artists represented in the museum. It's constantly being questioned and challenged, but I think it's improving. But it really needs to improve a lot more. And I often find, if I'm on a jobsite, or if I'm in a situation where there's two artists and somebody who doesn't know either of us . . .

DREYER: . . . Gravitates toward the man?

SAWYER: Yes. And if it's a technical issue, they will immediately go to the man. And I'm the one with the most expertise, and I'm the one with the pocketbook, and, you know, I'm being overlooked and not respected. I'm shocked and amused, but it's also so endemic that people don't even know that they're doing it. I might be guilty; I might look to talk to a guy first before talking to—I think it's endemic. I think the paradigm really has to change, and I think ultimately it has to change within. The only ones we can change are ourselves.

DREYER: The paradigm has sure changed a lot, wouldn't you say?

SAWYER: Broadly speaking.

DREYER: Broadly speaking, in terms of women having major roles in the art world. That's happened in a lot of places, but once you look at the facts and figures and once you look at the numbers, it's nowhere near where it should be.

SAWYER: So, one of my great stories from being at Discovery Green in Houston. The big George R. Brown Convention Center, their largest client, their largest convention—it isn't the helicopters association, it isn't the architects association, it isn't the arts fair—it is quilters of America [the International Quilt Festival]. And quilters of America pack that entire building, they pack all the hotels—there may be five to a room—and they're 99 percent women.

It's this incredible industry, and it's a sleeper, and it's generating hundreds and thousands of millions of dollars. And it's primarily run by women.

I suppose also women are the pocketbooks, you know. We're the ones who go out and get the groceries and we buy the shoes and we—"I want that house. I want that car." And we're big drivers, and I suppose, you know, if we did not drive and if we did not—if we used our pocketbook in a different way—it would be an incredible financial loss.

DREYER: So, what are you working on now? What can we look forward to?

SAWYER: I have most recently been doing a lot of work in Munich, Germany, and I'm working with a company called Franz Mayer of Munich, and they are a glass and mosaic company. It's a fifth-generation company, and they work with artists all over the world—but I think primarily in Austin. They just did the glass for the Ellsworth Kelly chapel [the artist's monumental work *Austin*, located at the Blanton Museum of Art], and there's a really beautiful work by Clifford Ross in the courthouse in Austin that's hand-painted glasswork, and I particularly am working with hand-painted glass.

So, I just completed a chapel in a small town between here and Houston, a privately owned chapel where I designed windows, and I've yet to actually see it with my own eyes. I've seen it in pictures, but I was flying to Munich when it was being installed—so the joys of getting too busy. And the other thing I'm working with is a large atrium project: these panels will be suspended on a three-story atrium of glass for the University of Houston at Victoria. And then the last piece I'm working on is a giant spiral room made out of glass that will be for the new US embassy in Kosovo.

With every project, I love to find out new techniques and learn. And color changes, you know—painted color versus silk or wood. I mean, the material of it, it changes.

DREYER: Like chameleon colors?

SAWYER: Like chameleon colors. So, hand-painted glass casts the light and it's also, it's forever. The ceramic frit [a component of ceramic glazes] that is fired, it never fades, it never goes away. And it's about translation: a little bit like maybe a composer. The musicians are playing the music and interpreting the music. My work is being interpreted by the craftspeople in Munich.

DREYER: When I was looking at the pictures, the photographs of work of yours, there's a certain sort of commonality, especially with the Discovery Green and the stuff with the blocks. My mother was a painter, primarily a painter and a teacher and a gallery owner, but she also worked with mosaics—and did mosaic murals—and when I was a little kid, she'd get out these wonderful tiles and we'd play with them and make things. She worked with a factory and had like Italian Byzantine smalti [colored-glass] mosaics.

SAWYER: That's fantastic.

DREYER: That memory just came to my mind.

SAWYER: I have a picture that was in *Austin Woman* magazine. It is a picture of me as a kid, and I'm out in my back garden and we've got all these bricks and I've made this brick kind of doll's house—and my pussycat is inside my little fortress that I made. And you know, that's still what I do today. I haven't stepped too far away from that. And I feel fortunate that I'm able to do the thing that I love and do the thing that I was always really good at. And I was encouraged to follow my passion.

And then I had great teachers along the way who really encouraged me. And as a teacher myself, I love to see the growth and development of my former students or my current students. And sort of nurture ambition, nurture fearlessness, nurture inquisitiveness. You know, I'm risk taking, and I think as a young creator, you have to create your own way and that has to evolve. But I can nurture out of people, you know, what might be part of them. And it's just fantastic to see.

DREYER: Does the current Guggenheim grant money go to a specific project?

SAWYER: Some academics have very specific, you know—"I'm going to photograph in the North Pole." Mine was very broad. Mine was really about looking at immersive spaces and also with particular interest in looking at gardens and garden artists who've made immersive gardens—to potentially design my own immersive garden space.

So, where will that take me? I'm already there, kind of, but it will take me further. There are only three individuals in all of Texas that were given a Guggenheim this year, that reside in Texas. There were a number—maybe five—that were either born in Texas or studied at a university, particularly the University of Texas. But three of us: a writer from the Michener Center [UT's graduate creative-writing center], myself—the only visual artist—and a mathematician.

Like many people, I've applied many times. When I got this email, the text said, "Please hit the link below," and it was a little pdf. And I was like, I'm not going to do that, that looks like a virus 101. So I deleted it, and then I saw that it said Gug dot org—and I thought, well, somebody could have hijacked that thing. And then I got this other email a week later, and it said, "Congratulations," and I screamed. And my poor assistant thought, you know—"What happened, what happened?"

And I cried. Anyway, so I'm still pinching myself. It's really a dream come true.

DREYER: It's such an honor. Undeniable. You said that—and I think this may have been also in Michael Barnes's piece in the *Austin American-Statesman*—that "this year feels transformative and the recognition is monumental, a testament to the personal commitment and belief in the vision I have created." What is the transformative thing that's happening, and where is your vision taking you?

SAWYER: I think, in working with this hand-painted glass, I'm trafficking sort of in Isis painters' territory—but as a sculptor, and with a very different visual phenomenon. And so that feels very new, and I think working in the scales that I'm working at—I mean, I'm used to working large, but I almost feel like the universe is calling on me to take on larger and bigger projects. And I have the skill set to be able to do that.

DREYER: You're prepared to answer the universe's call.

SAWYER: I am, yes, in whichever way it may be. For better or for worse. So, yeah, I feel a shift and a change—and also because I'm learning new techniques. I'm learning new skills.

Iconic Texas artist Bob "Daddy-O" Wade (*left*) is joined by cultural historian Jason Mellard (*right*) on *Rag Radio*, November 18, 2016. Photo by Roger Baker.

BOB "DADDY-O" WADE AND JASON MELLARD

Straddling more than one side of the fence.

Sculptor, performance artist, and cultural icon Bob "Daddy-O" Wade regales us with larger-than-life tales of his unique journey and monumental art.

Bob Wade is a native of Austin who is best known for his Texas- and southwestern-themed sculptures. His massive iguana long resided atop the Lone Star Café on Fifth Avenue in New York City, and his giant cowboy boots set the Guinness record for world's tallest cowboy boot sculpture (and had a homeless person living in them, to boot). An ambassador for Texas culture, Wade had one foot in fine arts and the other in the "Cosmic Cowboy" movement.

Wade received three National Endowment for the Arts (NEA) grants, and his work is held in major collections, including the Menil Collection in Houston and the Contemporary Austin. A retrospective of his work took place in 2009 at the Austin Museum of Popular Culture (nicknamed AusPop).

Wade's collaborator Jason Mellard, who also joins in the discussion, teaches at Texas State University in San Marcos and is a historian of the modern South and Southwest. His book, Progressive Country: How the 1970s Transformed the Texan in Popular Culture, *explores the intersections of political change and pop culture in Texas.*

Bob "Daddy-O" Wade died of heart failure in Austin on December 23,

2019. He was seventy-six. In an obituary, the New York Times wrote, "For more than 40 years, Mr. Wade ... built whimsical, outsize public art that nodded to Texas's culture of bigness, gaining renown for his uninhibited style but also drawing attention as a serious artist."

NOVEMBER 18, 2016

THORNE DREYER: This comes from Jason Mellard's 2013 book, *Progressive Country: How the 1970s Transformed the Texan in Popular Culture*: "In the Austin, New York, Houston, Nashville, and Dallas of the 1970s, Willie Nelson, Waylon Jennings, Eddie Wilson and Doug Sahm, Bud Shrake, Larry L. King, Aaron Latham, and Bob Wade; and *Texas Monthly* and *The Whole Shootin' Match* all tackled 'the Texan' in this troubled and exhilarating moment and, through progressive revisions and conservative salvages, created a body of work, songs, institutions, and ideas whose legacy continues to delight and frustrate, entertain and intrigue, instruct and inform."

Artist Bob "Daddy-O" Wade is with us today, and also joining us is Jason Mellard, historian of popular culture.

Bob, "Daddy-O" is not just a name you picked up, it's something you lived. If I understand, you had the slicked-back hair and hopped-up cars.

BOB "DADDY-O" WADE: I was born here and moved around. My dad was a hotel manager and at one point we were living in El Paso—and in fact I went through middle school and into high school there. And El Paso was kind of a little offshoot of LA. Had the hot rod clubs and had a lot of cool stuff going.

And being a border-town kid, you take on all the trappings of that. Like, I had the long hair, and when I got back to Austin I had a customized '51 Ford. A lot of people had their daddy's Pontiac, or whatever. And they said, "We're just going to call you 'Daddy-O.'" And it stuck. A lot of people still call me "Daddy-O."

DREYER: So how did Daddy-O first get interested in art?

WADE: I was one of those kids in class who could draw better than the other kids, and so I was always part of that art thing and my parents always encouraged it. My dad was very good—kind of got it from him.

And when I was ready to come off to school here, I said, "I'm going to major in art." And they said, "Go—go do your thing."

And I went straight to the old University of Texas art department. We were in World War II barracks. So I was part of that early crowd of kind of ruffians. You can imagine going to art school when you're twenty years old—in barracks, and everybody else on campus was in these nice buildings. So I said, "Well, this is not a bad gig at all."

So here we were in art school, and they're teaching us, you know, classical training, which I'm very happy I went through because I can draw pretty well. And then I became an art professor for many years, and I used to say, "I can make you draw like Leonardo in one semester."

Besides having all that kind of education going on, you had guys like Gilbert Shelton—Tony Bell, I think, was another one—a lot of these guys that drew for the *Texas Ranger*, and I just loved those drawings.

And it sure lightened things up. You'd see these guys like Gilbert down at Scholz Garten, and I'd try to hang out there a little bit, even though I was not really part of the *Ranger* group; it was a breath of fresh air compared to the real straight academic art school.

DREYER: Shelton, of course, became world famous for his comix art. And then there was Jim Franklin. He's a wonderful classically trained surrealist artist and he's still going. And he developed the armadillo as an icon for Texas.

WADE: Now, that guy knows his stuff, he knows his history. But the first time I ever saw a great image of his, I think it was actually on a T-shirt, and it had a picture of the armadillo humping the state capitol. And underneath, it said, "Crossbreeding."

DREYER: Yeah, I've got that on my wall.

WADE: That's all you need right there.

I went straight from here to Berkeley. I come from a border town to Austin and then to Berkeley—and what an eye-opening thing. I showed up with a buddy of mine wearing madras shirts, clean shaven. I mean, there was not—except maybe for some of the Janis Joplin crowd—there really wasn't what you would call a hippie in Austin, Texas, when I left in '65. Maybe the next year, the year *The Rag* started.

DREYER: Okay, I don't want to leave Jason Mellard out of this. You've worked with, studied, interacted with this gentleman here for many years. Written for his catalogs, and maybe been his sort of interpreter to the world.

JASON MELLARD: I've been lucky to have been a part of Daddy-O's circus for some time.

How I got into this whole story—and the Cosmic Cowboy thing and this countercultural stuff that was swirling around—is thinking about what it means to be a Texan. As someone who grew up to be taught that that was an important part of who I was—and then, in my own political and cultural coming of age, finding that I didn't always line up with how things are classically framed as Texan.

And I saw this counterculture of the 1960s—not only in Austin, but Houston and Dallas, and elsewhere in the state. Well, I wanted to try to become both, you know: to be Texan but also have this expanded view at the same time when other movements—Mexican Americans and African Americans—were making that same claim for this more fluid sense of Texanist.

And so, it was larger than life, you know. Like the way that Jim Franklin uses the armadillo is just this very subversive project about these underground, undervalued critters that nonetheless—they are a part of this place.

DREYER: Austin has always been the center, with the confluence of all these different genres, different influences.

MELLARD: And I appreciate this about Daddy-O's past, too. Growing up, your father was a hotel manager, and so you have a foot in every part of this state. And so, when you talk about Texas and you reflect on this place, there are so many different corners of it.

I think you are probably the first artist to come out of Marfa, right Bob?

WADE: I love to tell people that I was the first contemporary artist to have lived in Marfa, Texas. So, I've got sculptor Donald Judd and a bunch of my other buddies beat by quite a few years.

I remember as a little kid seeing the Marfa lights [mysterious "ghost" lights, often attributed to paranormal phenomena]. I really did.

I remember going out there and sitting in lawn chairs before there was a building and a specific place where everybody goes.

DREYER: But for people who don't know, Marfa, of all places in the world, has become a major art center.

WADE: Big-time art center. I lived in the Paisano Hotel when I was a little kid, and we'd go back there a couple of times a year. I'd wander around and see all the stuff, and I said, "Boy, what a deal." And of course when Judd came there, it was just this kind of sleepy little town and he was trying to be off by himself, and he would roll over if he saw what was there today.

DREYER: You studied art and could draw a little better than everybody else in the class—and that gave you a leg up. But how did you get into combining the art and the cultural icons, the cultural artifacts?

WADE: Part of the thing that kind of kicked it off was being in Berkeley. And of course, in 1965, you know—the anti-Vietnam and Mario Savio with the free speech. And Carol Doda would come down on some of those marches in Berkeley wearing a big T-shirt—Carol Doda, being the first big-time buxom stripper—and she wore this tight, tight T-shirt that said "Wheaties, Breakfast of Champions."

It was so different from Texas, and so different from Austin or anywhere. It was an eye-opener. And the kind of art that you would see around—whether it was San Francisco or other—was very visceral. Almost, in a funny way, it was what Austin became later.

In fact, there was a show that Dave Hickey put together in Austin called *South Texas Sweet Funk*, which was sort of based on people like Shelton and Franklin and myself.

DREYER: We should note that Dave Hickey had an art gallery in Austin called A Clean, Well-Lighted Place. And then he became a major art writer, a very important critic.

WADE: So, I came back to Texas and was looking for a teaching job. That was one way you could avoid the draft and do something good in your community. And that's how a lot of artists support themselves, anyway, if they have a degree.

So, I ended up getting my first teaching job in Waco, Texas, of all places. I'd lived there as a little kid. But I'll tell you what, you talk about *boom*! Right out of Berkeley into Waco!

DREYER: Lots of churches there.

WADE: Yeah, more than any other place per capita, I think.

DREYER: In a blurb on your book, *Daddy-O: Iguana Heads and Texas Tales*, Willie Nelson writes, "When I first saw the Giant Frogs on top of Carl's Corner Truck Stop in Carl's Corner, Texas, I'll never forget my first thought: 'What the hell is Carl on?' Now that I understand art, I realize what a genius 'Daddy-O' Wade really is."

How did you start doing the giant stuff, the great big sculptures?

WADE: In art school you learn that a lot of the early abstract painters and sculptors—whether it was Jackson Pollock or the guy Chamberlain who crushed cars—it was always big stuff. And they exhibited it in cities like New York and LA, these big places, big spaces, big everything. And so, it would have made sense if Texas had that thing going.

But I'd also like to say that having been a custom-car guy in El Paso really pushed me a long way. Number one, it's the fact that it's something bigger than you. And when you are a custom-car guy, you're having to farm out a lot of the work because you don't do custom roll-and-pleat jobs on your own. We were lucky because being on the border, we were able to send them over to Juárez and get these gorgeous deals. And to get the paint jobs.

And so you're like an art director when you're working on a custom car; you're the one who says, "Okay, I want it to look like this, I want this color to be like this." The hot rod thing has interesting parameters about it that then equate in a funny way to the art world, the formal art world.

DREYER: Right.

WADE: Now, sometimes I step out of that formal art world.

DREYER: No kidding.

WADE: I had done a number of smaller installations in museums. I put an armadillo walking towards a cactus and it had sand; it was up against the wall in the Fort Worth museum and it had special lights coming down and it looked like the sunset. It was an armadillo going off into the sunset.

That started this whole thing of big three-dimensional kind of deals. And then, with one of the first NEA grants, I was able to travel around Texas. I think my grant said something like, "Go around Texas and study the culture." And in my case, "purchase artifacts, bring them back, and put all this stuff together." And that became the Texas map at the University of St. Thomas in Houston in 1973.

DREYER: Which was a very interesting center of intellectual and artistic ferment.

WADE: That's where Earl Staley and Jack Boynton and that crowd were, and they brought me in.

So, you'd lay out this Texas map: it went from high up in the Panhandle all the way down to the sand and water areas of the coast—with all kinds of stuffed critters. I had armadillos.

MELLARD: Had javelinas in there.

WADE: Had javelinas and coyotes and the Lone Star Beer sign that was plugged in moving along and the pretty water that would flow. It came from those old paper place mats that you would eat off of in a truck stop or whatever—every state used to have them. They would have little images of what was in various parts of the state.

Then the map of the USA for the bicentennial in Dallas, 1976, was the size of a football field, which about killed me. You try to fill up this thing with every state. We put an outhouse, I think, in Arkansas, and they got upset. We were trying to support this thing by people putting advertisements. We figured the USA is all about advertisements anyway, so we get these companies to put up their gigantic billboards—RadioShack, or whatever it was. We said, "You give us $5,000, and we'll move the Arkansas outhouse to Missouri." And they did.

DREYER: So, what was next?

WADE: Well, that was '76. And then I got invited to send something to Paris, France, for La Biennale Paris.

I put together a concept of taking a Spartan Trailer Coach—it was the Cadillac of the trailers of the day, 1947 Spartan—and filling it with Texana. Had a stuffed bucking bronco—I mean, full-sized stuffed horse—upside down in this thing. Had a two-headed calf, a pair of longhorns about twelve feet long that looked real. And outside, had the horns on the front and all that.

The calf came out of the old Lone Star Brewery. I went down there and talked to a guy. I said, "Listen, I need something to send to Paris, what have you got?" He says, "I've got a critter in the back that we can't show publicly because it scares children and freaks out pregnant women."

So, he brings out a two-headed calf, and it had two tails. Now, I don't have to tell you what's underneath the tails. So, we wanted to make sure that the French would really enjoy this, because they would say, "*Impossible!*" So, we rigged up a mirror on a stick, just like in high school, so we were able to prove to the French that we were from Texas and that's what we do here.

So, we sent the entire trailer to Paris. It was called the *Texas Mobile Home Museum.*

MELLARD: What happened later to that trailer?

WADE: The trailer was loaned out to somebody, who then sold it to some gypsies. And so, somewhere in Paris is a two-headed calf with two tails, and a stuffed bucking bronco.

Actually, I went back and found the trailer years later and climbed inside. And there was a stuffed armadillo and a saddle that had been done by the Texas Kid, the old outsider artist out of Dallas, and I brought those back to the hotel. And you can imagine this person in the French hotel seeing these tourists come walking in carrying an armadillo and a saddle.

I did this book, *Daddy-O: Iguana Heads and Texas Tales*, for St. Martin's Press, which kind of documents a lot of the goofier projects with anecdotes and stories from everybody, and people like Willie commenting.

I said, "I don't want to have to go around and do these book signings where I'm sitting there waiting for people to show up, and if nobody shows up, how embarrassing is that? So I'll concoct some kind of dog and pony show."

I said, "Let me combine an iguana with the trailer, and it will become the Iguana-Mobile"—and we'll take that around and do appearances not only at bookstores but at nightclubs, beer joints, schools. You know, wear a different hat each place we go, and do the book signings. And we had a great time. I still have the crazy Iguana-Mobile.

DREYER: I've seen pictures. It had a fiberglass iguana head. Very cool.

WADE: Meanwhile, I had done this giant iguana, known as "Iggy," in Upstate New York, and I tried to figure out a place where to put that crazy sculpture.

You know, doing the iguana sort of came out of the Jim Franklin Austin scene. I wanted to do something in Upstate New York at this place called Artpark, and I didn't want to do an armadillo, because that was Franklin's and Micael Priest's, and all those Austin guys. But I thought, "Well, some kind of goofy critter"—because that's what a lot of Texas stuff is all about—"would be an iguana."

And, you know, it's like a small house. I mean, forty feet; there's a lot of houses that probably aren't forty feet. We had to have access so we could unbolt it and bolt it, and so we figured the best place to have a door would be right between its legs in the rear—size of a manhole cover. And so that became our little door back there.

Anyway, it was galvanized pipe all bolted together, covered with heavy wire mesh and window-screen wire, and sprayed with urethane foam. You could have lived in it because, like the boots, it was insulated.

DREYER: And you did have a homeless guy living in the world's largest cowboy boots?

WADE: In the boots, later, we had a homeless guy, and that was a great thing.

Anyway, [the iguana] was forty feet long. It was a big thing. I thought I'd make it in sections so it could go somewhere else after the fact.

Somebody suggested the Lone Star Café in New York. I made a cold call and Mort Cooperman, the co-owner, answered the phone and he said, "Daddy-O, I'll never ever answer my own phone again." I talk him into buying this thing, and so they gave me a bunch of money. I don't know if it was a whole *bunch* of money, but they gave me some money and a tab—and we put this thing on the roof.

DREYER: Always get the tab. We should also mention the Lone Star Café was an outpost for Texas culture in New York.

WADE: The Texas embassy. Everybody from Texas that'd go to New York, everybody would have to go straight to the Lone Star Café.

DREYER: Kinky Friedman and a lot of other people played there.

WADE: I had known Kinky from college days and then had seen him around LA, and of course, there was nothing more exciting than to hear Kinky run out on the stage in New York and say, "Welcome to Kinky Friedman and the Texas Jewboys." I'm going, "Oh, my gosh!" So here we are with Henny Youngman and those kind of guys, or Mort Sahl, or whatever. And he'd let them have it. You could just feel that irreverence.

But what we used to do in New York—and Kinky would help us with this, Doug Sahm, everybody—we'd take people up on the roof to see it. Mort [Cooperman] would say, "Wade, take these guys on the roof and show them the Iguana."

So we would take all these celebrities up to the roof; Belushi went, and Tom Cruise, we took him up there. We'd make them stand on this table and they'd pose next to the iguana, but they didn't realize their heads were right by the opening in the rear.

DREYER: And it was right up there in the sky.

WADE: It was right on the corner of Thirteenth and Fifth Avenue, and it upset the Fifth Avenue Association. And that was the first time that I had ever been involved in some kind of controversy or lawsuit.

It wasn't against me, personally, but the Fifth Avenue Association thought of themselves as this real posh kind of deal—and *Forbes* was down the street, and the high-class art school, Parsons, I think, was right across the street. You can't have an iguana on a nice building down on Fifth Avenue.

Mort [Cooperman] had been an advertising genius for the company, and he was milking this thing like you wouldn't believe—and so it stayed in the courts for years and years.

"You can't have an iguana on a nice building down on Fifth Avenue."

And we won. The judge eventually told the prosecutor, "What are you going to do, call the Statue of Liberty a 'sign'?" Case dismissed. And we won with the frogs: the frogs got in trouble, case dismissed. Houston had the giant sax, case dismissed. So, we had a lot of fun with all that.

DREYER: So, they claimed the iguana on the Lone Star was a sign!

WADE: Yeah.

DREYER: So, to leave New York, tell us about some of the other things. One is the boots; the boots are what—Guinness world record?

WADE: The boots came next. Somebody had been eating lunch across the street from the iguana in New York and said to me, "Come down to DC. I've got an empty lot—we're nonprofit down here—so build something on the corner." I kept thinking, "What can I build on this corner that would be in scale with the corner?" And the term "Texas chic" was really around a lot during that period of time.

MELLARD: Late '70s, yeah, when Texas's economy was blowing and going because of oil, and the rest of the economy, the Rust Belt was kind of sagging. And so there was this sense of looking to Texas swagger, to gain from the Texas oil wealthy.

WADE: Travolta, I think, came out the year later with *Urban Cowboy*.

So, I always had in the back of my mind all those characters who had left Texas, you know: Sam Rayburn, LBJ, a lot of people had gone to DC in the political realm, and they were always making the scene in their cowboy boots. And I said, "Ha, Texas chic: something that's tall and something that's long." So, it became this object that was perfect for this corner: a pair of cowboy boots.

DREYER: And how big were those?

WADE: They were forty feet tall. So, the iguana was forty feet wide, and the boots were forty feet tall and thirty feet long. They were perfect for that corner. And they do have a huge Texas contingency in DC. All these Texans would come out of the woodwork in Washington—and people would drive by as we were building, and they would yell, "Tony Lama!"

MELLARD: And I love that they're ostrich, too. It's a nice touch.

WADE: Yeah, I wanted to make them visually as exciting as you can make them. So I said, "Put the little bumps on them, these little ostrich-skin bumps." People like that.

MELLARD: And it worked.

WADE: Joe King Carrasco is allowing us to use his song "Hasta Mañana Iguana" on the documentary film that we've been working on for a few years called *Flight of the Iguana*. The iguana has such a crazy long history to it, and it eventually ended up on the roof of the Fort Worth Zoo.

It was delivered by helicopter from where it got restored. A giant helicopter, a Vietnam helicopter, and it was the first helicopter that went to Katrina. Anyway, a huge thing, and it picked up the iguana and flew around the zoo, up in the sky—and all the people were there drinking and having a good time—and then lowered it down to the roof.

That's the beginning of this documentary, which then goes on to document a lot of the other projects.

DREYER: Then the sax was in Houston. The seventy-foot-tall, blue *Smokesax*.

WADE: The sax was at Billy Blues. And it is now owned by the Orange Show in Houston, which you know has been around for a number of years.

DREYER: It's an interesting intersection, too, with folk and visionary art. Now, you're not a folk artist.

WADE: I'm not a folk artist.

DREYER: But there's an intersection and interaction there, and Houston has got an incredible folk art scene.

WADE: A lot of contemporary artists have been influenced by folk art—and thank goodness, because if they just went along in the old art school trip, it would be pretty boring.

DREYER: Jason, as a cultural historian, why don't you give us a little context.

MELLARD: There's something I want to say about Daddy-O's work. I don't think it's said quite enough, and I know this from traveling around with him some. It's kind of a highfalutin way to frame some of what he does—and he will probably laugh off a lot of things that I say about him—but I think he also carries me around so I can say these highfalutin things.

DREYER: So he can laugh them off.

MELLARD: Yeah. But, you know, as much as it is about these monumental works of sculpture, those are just the product of a long process, and I think the way that Daddy-O goes about making those things, the relationships that he creates in the community, are as much a part of the work as that final thing.

And not just about, you know, fighting the city over the iguana in New York City. The memory that I always cling to is this one: There was a show that Daddy-O did in Seguin, where he was creating an old honky-tonk at Texas Lutheran University. And there was a honky-tonk that he loved in Lockhart run by a woman named Lilly Serna, who had spent all of her life running this little bar in this just beautiful space. And one of the qualities of it was that all the walls were covered with aluminum foil. But not just flat, like wallpaper—it was crinkled in just this kind of way that it would reflect the neon signs and little Christmas lights she'd put up.

I remember one afternoon, sitting in that bar. We had some beers and then Daddy-O and Lilly Serna went over to the pool table and they stood there at that pool table and they crinkled up foil and they crinkled up foil and then, you know, he learned.

And that interaction with everyday people and their creativity is what leads to a lot of these monumental works. Lilly's no longer with us, but I think that's so important to know; it's kind of behind the show. Pull back the curtains and there's a whole community of people connected to this man.

DREYER: And when you're dealing with culture—when you're creating, in some ways, cultural artifacts—obviously the process and the people and the sharing, it's all part of the whole thing.

WADE: Well, *it* directs *you*; you just flow with it. I mean, what could be more fun? Jason helped on that little project. He put together a four-hour loop of some of the most fabulous early Texas music that you could ever hear in your life—and we had it kind of rigged to the loudspeaker system there at the university.

There was a jukebox and it had the chicken wire around the jukebox—which represented back in the days when these bands would go across Texas and they might not be so great and the fans would throw beer bottles at them. And that's when they started having chicken wire cages around the stage so that the band members wouldn't get hurt by beer bottles.

MELLARD: You saw it in *Blues Brothers*.

WADE: And, by the way, speaking of Kinky Friedman: Kinky ran for governor, I think, in '06, and he and Cleve Hattersley [Austin musician who was also Kinky's manager] had me do a little teardrop, baby teardrop trailer. And I had Kinky's hat enlarged in urethane foam and a three-foot cigar coming out of the front. The hat was an exact replica; he actually took his hat off for just long enough to have it scanned. They blew that thing up and made this gigantic hat and bolted it down to the trailer, which was painted fuchsia—and that thing ran around the state of Texas. I'm told they raised at least a million bucks selling T-shirts and that kind of stuff—just by having this goofy trailer.

And so, of course, we know Kinky lost—he wasn't happy, and he didn't have much time to be thinking about whatever happened to the trailer. And every time I'd see some of his people, they'd say, "We don't know what happened to the trailer." How can you lose a trailer with a gigantic cowboy hat on top?

And the guys at Texas Hatters in Lockhart—who, you know, used to be here in Austin—the Gammages. They knew I was looking for the trailer and the hat, and they said, "Bob, you won't believe it. We've got the hat in our backyard in Lockhart."

The hat has now reemerged, and this is typical of the stuff that's in my documentary, where these projects started in one place, like the Bonnie and Clyde Mobile, which is now in Marfa. The iguana moves at least ten or fifteen times. They're like your kids; they take on a life of their own. So, the next time you're in Lockhart, go to Texas Hatters. Kinky Friedman's hat is right in the front.

DREYER: Okay, gentlemen. What haven't we covered?

WADE: I can remember one time I did a show here in Austin at the old Laguna Gloria when it was still the only museum. It was in 1975, I think, and they asked me to do something down in this sort of nice formal area where there had been a Charles Umlauf piece. So I did a crazy sculpture and it had live chickens. Carlene Brady of the *Austin Sun* wrote this fabulous article, and the headline of the article was "High-Class White Trash."

In a way, I'll take it, because it has to do with being able to straddle more than one side of the fence. You can move back and forth, where a lot of people are kind of stuck in one cultural milieu or another, and they can't make that transition.

MELLARD: I like that. When you do it, it's not like it's satire; I feel like it's a loving embrace.

WADE: Exactly. And then I give it Texas-size form.

IMPRESARIOS

Eddie Wilson (*left*), founder of the Armadillo World Headquarters and owner of Threadgill's restaurants, photographed with Thorne Dreyer at KOOP radio, July 17, 2014. Photo by Roger Baker.

EDDIE WILSON

Making the armadillos dance.

Eddie Wilson reflects on a nervous Bruce Springsteen at the Armadillo, Van Morrison's shrimp enchiladas, and little girls in tutus.

Restaurateur and promoter Eddie Wilson was cofounder and proprietor of Austin's world-famous music venue the Armadillo World Headquarters (1970-1980) and managed the pioneering Austin psychedelic/country/blues group Shiva's Headband. He started the Raw Deal restaurant in 1976 and in 1981 bought Threadgill's—a gas station and beer joint where Janis Joplin got her start—from country singer Kenneth Threadgill. He later opened a second Threadgill's, Threadgill's World Headquarters, in South Austin next to the site of the old Armadillo World Headquarters.

Wilson launched the Armadillo in an old National Guard armory after another pioneering Austin concert hall, the Vulcan Gas Company, closed shop. The Armadillo provided a showcase for blues, psychedelia, and the emerging progressive country movement—and lots of other genres—and became one of the most influential performance venues in the country. The hall helped birth and nurture Austin's famed music scene and put it—and the lowly armadillo itself—on the national map.

Eddie Wilson is an old pal and Armadillo World Headquarters an old haunt. *The Armadillo is long gone now, and both Threadgill's have since closed—Threadgill's South in 2018 and the original Threadgill's in 2020, a victim of the coronavirus pandemic.*

Rag Radio engineer Tracey Schulz joins us on the show.

JULY 11, 2014, AND MARCH 24, 2017

THORNE DREYER: Austin legend Eddie Wilson is our guest today on *Rag Radio*. Welcome.

EDDIE WILSON: Thank you very much. I enjoy being legendary.

DREYER: I should also mention that Eddie is a survivor—a lung cancer survivor. So, how are you doing? How are you feeling these days?

WILSON: Got my health, got all my health. I'm just looking for a place I could buy a little fitness off the shelf and then I'd be set. I learned how to really enjoy being lazy for the first time in my life and I'm having a hard time kicking that part.

DREYER: Eddie Wilson was the impresario of Austin's Armadillo World Headquarters, one of the nation's most celebrated concert halls, in the 1970s.

I want to start with Bruce Springsteen—when he came to the Armadillo—because it's a wonderful story and also because it's a good taking-off point to talk about the role that the Armadillo played.

In 1973 the South reportedly had not been all that kind to Bruce Springsteen. Nobody knew what to think of him, this young kid from New Jersey. He had a bad time in Atlanta. They didn't understand him in Nashville. Liberty Hall in Houston may have been the only other place in the South where he was truly appreciated.

He came to Austin and he was nervous. According to Kenneth Threadgill, Springsteen was walking back and forth, side to side. He said, "That young fellow pacing back and forth, he's as nervous as a coon trying to pass a peach pit."

WILSON: You had to be there.

DREYER: The show ended up being just a remarkable event, and the person I'm going to use to talk about it—and this is from the *Austin*

Chronicle—is Micael Priest. Priest was one of the original Armadillo poster artists—a wonderful, weird, crazy guy.

Priest said, "All the cowboys in the room were standing up on their chairs. And I've otherwise only seen this in movies, but they threw their hats. They started throwing their hats. The boys onstage were so excited that they didn't know what to do. But everybody was screaming for them, so they played 'Blinded by the Light.' By the time they finished 'Blinded by the Light,' the bartenders were standing on the bars. Everybody was dancing, it was uncanny, they blew the lid off the place."

The *Austin Chronicle* wrote, "Both shows are remembered here today as the stuff of legend only the likes of Bruce Springsteen could create, concerts people still talk about forty years later."

Tell me about that night.

WILSON: Bruce was booked for Friday and Saturday. The tickets were selling fairly well, but not all that great—and I got Bruce's management to let me add him to Thursday night without really paying him hardly anything, in order to let me charge a dollar. And so, we got on KOKE radio—and I asked Alvin Crow if he would mind opening for somebody else.

Alvin told [his future drummer] Tiny McFarland, "I can't let you start drumming tonight. I can't break you in because we're opening for some real hot dog out of New York named Silversteen. And I want to put on the best show I can." So, he was pushing his band real hard. We had a large crowd for a dollar. I know Billy and Regan Gammon [Bill Gammon was one of Eddie's closest friends] were there with Regan's best friend Laura, who later ruled the White House [as First Lady Laura Bush].

Bruce was really nervous. Alvin had everybody jumping—I mean, they were really jumping—and Mr. Threadgill, who had sung a song or two earlier in Alvin's set, was standing on the side stage with me and Tiny McFarland, and that's when he looked over and saw this guy pacing back and forth. He didn't have any idea who he was; he just knew nervousness when he saw it.

But Bruce and Clarence [sax man Clarence Clemons] and the crew just came out and blew everybody away. I don't remember the hats, but it was a fabulous night. And then the Friday and Saturday, on the basis of that thunderous Thursday, sold really well.

DREYER: Probably, the fear that they had—they didn't know from cowboys—was about making the transition from the western swing of Alvin Crow. A tough act to follow, in any case. They had never played a crowd that could deal with those two things—and that tells us a whole lot about what the Austin music scene was and how it evolved.

WILSON: That was the key element and what caused the Armadillo to cause so much talk.

Actually, it was two things. It was the audience and the food. The food that traveling bands got from the Armadillo kitchen was not something that any of them had ever experienced before. And as a result, they talked and talked and talked.

"The food that traveling bands got from the Armadillo kitchen was not something that any of them had ever experienced before."

That's why shortly after that show we had Van Morrison, and Van played three sold-out nights, and on the last night he was so relaxed that he announced that he would talk. And the first thing he wanted to know was why he didn't get the shrimp enchiladas that Jerry Garcia had told him about.

The kitchen manager was there, and she promised that next time he played he would get the shrimp enchiladas. Sunday morning, they left to go play Dallas and I got a call that night; the manager asked me if I would please let Van play on Monday night. Made very little sense. How could we possibly promote a show that late?

Van Morrison had gotten on the one friendly radio station in town that would just let me say, "Guess what, we're going to do it again tonight." And I think we sold 1,100 tickets out of the 1,500 possible—on a Monday night—and Van got his shrimp enchiladas and was a fan of the 'Dillo.

DREYER: Food was an interesting phenomenon there.

WILSON: The first year I was in the process of losing fifty pounds by using LSD instead of beer. But there was no way in the world to make an economically viable place out of this thing without selling beer. So we got a beer license, and I knew that you couldn't possibly survive without giving people something to eat when they were drinking and getting dehydrated at the same time.

DREYER: Right.

WILSON: And so we started fumbling along through several different generations of kitchen operation, but it was always pretty unique. We had one of the first vegetarian menus in a place that large and yet, if you look through those menus, you'll see at the bottom of a lot of the vegetarian dishes, "Ed's sausage, twenty-five cents."

DREYER: Okay, so tell me how it actually started, all this. You went outside of the Cactus Club one night, and you looked over and you saw this old National Guard armory.

WILSON: I didn't know what it was; I saw some broken windows at the top of a big cinder block wall. I had walked out behind the Cactus Club because its bathroom wasn't working. And thirty years later, after telling this story hundreds of times, I found out that John Reed was on one side of me and Jimmie Dale Gilmore was on the other side. [At that time, the legendary Austin musicians were playing with a band called the Hub City Movers.] They had to go back in and play.

I went around the other side of that building to check out this broken-window scene that I had discovered and managed to pick a lock and raise a garage door and pull my car in it and turn on the lights—and came close to having a heart attack because it was just what I was looking for.

It looked like Noah's ark turned upside down. You could have put two of every kind of animal in the world in the damn thing—and in effect, we did. And I was the guy they handed the shovel to and I had to take the elephant poop out.

DREYER: Okay, why did this space look so good to you?

WILSON: It was like an empty auditorium, empty gymnasium—but in *extra, extra* large. I was raised by a union plumber and I went into both the men's and the women's room and realized that one thousand people could drink five thousand gallons of beer and not have to leave the building. It was the most plumbing I'd ever seen in an empty building.

DREYER: And we should note that at its apex, the Armadillo World Headquarters consumed—or its customers consumed—more Lone Star Beer than any place in the state, besides the Astrodome.

So, it's an old National Guard armory.

WILSON: It was a sixteen-thousand-square-foot armory that had high ceilings with no visual impairments.

DREYER: What Ann Richards called "a barny old place."

WILSON: I was supposed to be managing Shiva's Headband, and there was not a place for anybody to make a living playing in a band at that point—unless you were a cover band and playing the dance halls. And Shiva's was not doing that.

DREYER: So, you were managing Shiva's Headband.

WILSON: That's a joke.

DREYER: Yeah, to the extent that one could manage Shiva's Headband. Shiva's was extremely important to the Austin scene.

WILSON: Shiva's Spencer Perskin was the reason that I quit my job with the US Brewers Association—although I was about to quit anyway, but I certainly wasn't about to quit in order to get involved in rock and roll.

DREYER: A hippie rock and roll band.

WILSON: And so, I found the landlord within twenty-four hours, and M. K. Hage made me a deal. Well, the landlord had a young teenage son that he was very worried about. And he liked something about my presentation and so he gave me a very good deal. I rented that huge building for $500 a month. And part of the deal was that I try to help take care of his son and give him something to do.

DREYER: This was a time when many of us were living in Austin and paying thirty dollars to forty dollars rent a month.

WILSON: Rent houses all over, at that point, were a hundred dollars and five people would live there.

DREYER: Right.

WILSON: For the first five years, I was most often at least a year behind on the rent, but M. K. Hage didn't really need it. And so we stumbled along. We had a wonderful bakery before we had anything else going on, and the whole object was to try to figure out what we can do in this gigantic space that will make it worthwhile.

The main difference between all the other music venues and what we were doing is that we were there at seven thirty in the morning—five thirty in the morning baking bread—from early in the morning, all day long. The reason we opened the beer garden was because it was so hot inside the building, we had to go outside. There was nothing to do outside.

"Oh, well, let's go ahead and get a beer license. What the hell," I said. This is a community of German beer gardens and it just seemed like the thing to do. My job previous to that had been with the US Brewers Association in public relations—about which I knew absolutely nothing—but it was obvious that we needed beer to fight the heat, and I'm here to tell you that it still works.

And I ended up with a passion for local history, and it was years after the Armadillo that I found this brochure for the Armadillo address. It was called the Sports Center, and in August of 1955, Elvis, Scotty, and Bill played the Sports Center. Elvis was referred to as a "folk music fireball" and in a little four-paragraph piece about him, he's referred to as "the big blond guy."

All right, Elvis Presley was a blond, we're here to tell you. And Sammy Allred got his autograph the night of that show and asked Elvis, "What color is your hair?" And Elvis said, "Purple." He had started dyeing it and it was that black, drippy-looking, you know, dye. And it was from then on he was such a black-headed guy, and nobody ever, ever thinks I'm telling the truth when I tell them that Elvis was a blond.

DREYER: Oh, boy. Well, blond Elvis has left the building, so he can't tell us.

What did we learn from all this about the role that Armadillo played in that early evolution of the Austin music scene? We talked about national acts a lot, but wasn't its heart in the local groups?

WILSON: Well, that's a nice way to try to remember it, but the fact of the matter is that local didn't sell. It took the national acts to really get the audiences up. The main thing that most people forget is in 1973, the drinking age was lowered to eighteen. That's the single most important thing having to do with it finally taking off in '73. And the voting age and the drinking age: there for a while we were considered grown-ups at eighteen. Even though a lot of us by then were pushing thirty.

Eighteen-year-olds being able to drink meant that there were sixteen-year-olds out there getting away with it, and that meant that there were forty-year-old dirty old men getting off the sofas all over town and getting out and starting to root around.

Soap Creek Saloon probably was the epitome of that quintessential Austin late-night thing at that time. You know, Doug Sahm moved to Austin and immediately found a place not a hundred yards behind Soap Creek Saloon. [Sahm was a San Antonio-born musician who was a defining force in the evolution of Texas music.] It was the place that really did it, in a lot of ways, more than the Armadillo—because it was out of the city limits and it was kind of like a heavenly sort of place to break the law.

We had ballet one Sunday a month at the Armadillo—Austin Ballet Theatre. Stanley Hall got crossways with the city [falling out with Austin Civic Ballet, which he directed from 1968 to 1972]—that had allowed him to exist. He was a little bit left of the average dance studio, and he came to me and asked if they could perform. He was a little hesitant; there was a reticence about his request that was really blown away when I jumped up and down and clapped and said, "Yes, yes, yes." Because I knew it fit perfectly into what we needed to do.

We had the Guatemalan Ballet Folklórico. We had lots and lots of things, but nothing was ever really any more obvious than twenty rows of parents and grannies sitting looking at those little girls in tutus and having twenty rows behind them of hippie bikers eating nachos and drinking beer.

DREYER: Okay, you had, like, Laura Bush; you had Farrah Fawcett.

> "We had lots and lots of things, but nothing was ever really any more obvious than twenty rows of parents and grannies sitting looking at those little girls in tutus and having twenty rows behind them of hippie bikers eating nachos and drinking beer."

WILSON: The Clintons.

DREYER: The Clintons, Norman Mailer, Ken Kesey.

WILSON: We had several different bookings of my psychedelic hero.

DREYER: Hunter Thompson?

WILSON: No. Hunter Thompson came through *after* the Armadillo and got a Threadgill's bartender shirt to wear onstage with Jerry Jeff Walker at the Opry House while he was raising money for his legal troubles.

TRACEY SCHULZ: Was that Timothy Leary you were trying to think of?

WILSON: Leary, for god's sake. And Baba Ram Dass, who had started off, you know, as Leary's cohort at Harvard.

DREYER: So, we're talking about something more than just a rock and roll emporium.

WILSON: A cultural arts laboratory.

DREYER: Cultural arts laboratory. The Armadillo World Headquarters was a cultural arts laboratory.

WILSON: The largest petri dish in the world.

DREYER: And there were a lot of chemicals.

WILSON: It was just part of our duty. We had to make sure that everything was okay, so we had to take it ourselves.

DREYER: And did they say that—because so many cops came there—they were afraid to bust it because they were afraid they would bust some of their own?

WILSON: We had a horrible tragedy after the Pointer Sisters show; we had one of our people get shot. [Artist Ken Featherston was killed by a disgruntled customer.] And because of Burton Wilson's photo, because of Dub Rose, our security chief, and Henry Gonzalez—we solved the murder. And Jim Franklin. Jim Franklin was instrumental in solving that murder. And I have been told any police department puts you on a different shelf when you solve a homicide.

WILSON: Two people more responsible for what happened at Austin in the '60s than anybody will ever give them credit for—and then for what happened in San Francisco, too—were Don Hyde and Travis Rivers.

Travis Rivers went from here to San Francisco and was cofounder of the *Oracle*, which was one of the most beautiful underground newspapers anybody ever saw. And then, you know, Travis was largely responsible for the Summer of Love. Travis, I had known since junior high, and Don Hyde, who tried to sell me some of the broken-down pieces of the Vulcan.

DREYER: The Vulcan Gas Company, which was the predecessor to the Armadillo. Hyde was one of the founders, and Houston White.

WILSON: Hyde will never get the credit from the other guys, but he was the one that really started it. And Don had gone to San Francisco as a teenage dropout, you know, a runaway, and come back with a clear vision of rock and roll emporiums.

And certainly, Thorne, you're one of the great examples of how we all benefitted from the genius of Gilbert Shelton and Jim Franklin. Because the reason that I picked up *The Rag* was not because of the sterling writing about our causes, but it was to find out what the Freak Brothers were doing. It was the most entertaining thing that I'd ever seen in print.

DREYER: Gilbert Shelton created *The Fabulous Furry Freak Brothers* to liven up *The Rag*. And it worked, obviously, because it got you.

WILSON: Well, it certainly worked, and it still works. *The Fabulous*

Furry Freak Brothers were the image of our young adulthood that we still go back to. I've got my grandson, you know, just chomping at the bit to get into my stash of comic books.

DREYER: But Gilbert was so universal in his appeal that it took off everywhere, all over the world. *The Freak Brothers* has been translated into I don't know how many languages, and he's now doing it in France.

And the interface, the interconnectedness, between our alternative-culture media and the music scene and the music emporiums, was substantial.

WILSON: We were kinda like a big ol' band.

DREYER: We were just a band. We made beautiful music together. Okay, so then you bought the Raw Deal.

WILSON: Well, I just split off, I left the Armadillo, you know, with my tail between my legs. I got my butt kicked. [The Armadillo fell into bankruptcy in 1977.] And I found this little bitty place with $120 a month rent on Sabine Street, backed up on Waller Creek right across from the police station.

DREYER: Perfect location.

WILSON: And the motto was, "You found the Raw Deal, the Raw Deal didn't come looking for you." I had the simplest menu in the whole world. I had a steak, a pork chop, and hash brown potatoes. I refused to have beans.

The Raw Deal was how I got over my performance anxiety. I went and I kind of nestled down. Kenneth Threadgill walked in and I was telling him I wanted to do a bigger format. I had a menu that I was working on that was kind of a tribute to my mother, and Kenneth said, "Why don't you take my place and turn my place into that."

I thought I could remodel Threadgill's. It turned out there were only three boards that would even hold a nail, it was so rotten. And so I ended up having to completely rebuild it. But by the time I was done, it was a restaurant that I'm still proud of.

DREYER: We should mention that Kenneth Threadgill, and his club, Threadgill's, was where a lot of this mix of country and the early folk scene—where a lot of that started. He was an old-style country singer, but he was open to all of this new stuff.

WILSON: Janis Joplin and some of the girls told him that the N-word was not cool, and he immediately turned a hard left and became a wide-open, diverse culture endorser. And Mance Lipscomb broke the color barrier, taken there by [musicologist and musician] Tary Owens and some of the people that had already adopted Mance. The photographer Burton Wilson had already gone to Navasota and taken pictures of Mance. I've got a picture on my wall of Mance's kitchen in 1967.

DREYER: For those who don't know, Mance Lipscomb was a very significant blues musician out of Navasota who, I guess, was actually "discovered"—and first recorded—by Mack McCormick and Chris Strachwitz in 1960.

WILSON: Mance was the nicest guy in the whole world, and the only person that could make Mance say anything that was not completely a hundred percent happy positive was Lightnin' Hopkins—who was a nasty sort, kind of mean. The only thing I ever heard Mance say that was the slightest bit down on anybody, he said, "I taught this song to Lightnin', but he only plays every other note."

DREYER: I used to hang out at Liberty Hall in Houston and was there one afternoon. Lightnin' Hopkins was supposed to perform that night and they never could depend on his showing up. So I got the assignment from owner Mike Condray of going and finding Lightnin' and bringing him in.

And he was sitting on a porch in the Fourth Ward, drinking, with no indication that he was getting ready to go anywhere. So I loaded him in my car and took him to Liberty Hall.

WILSON: I love Mike Condray. I had a lot of fun in Houston. Houston is soulful. Never had any fun in Dallas. Dallas is scary. Molly Ivins used to say that Houston is like Los Angeles with the climate of Calcutta. But, she said, to define Dallas you have to completely redefine the whole meaning of evil.

DREYER: Molly Ivins grew up in Houston, in River Oaks.

SCHULZ: Glen Alyn wrote Mance Lipscomb's biography, talking about a bunch of his time here.

WILSON: And he wrote it in the vernacular right straight off the tape recorder. To read it you have to really work at finally being able to talk it. By the time you end up reading it, you sound like Mance.

DREYER: And Mance became an Austin hippie; he sort of merged into the community. I remember going to an outdoor party in East Austin, and there was Mance out there just sitting and playing and everybody was drinking tequila all night long.

WILSON: Mance never went to bed until everybody else was down. He would play until the sun came up and keep going if there was anybody still awake.

DREYER: So, you bought Threadgill's—this was Mr. Threadgill's original bar—and rebuilt it as a restaurant.

WILSON: When I opened, I didn't even have Kenneth playing there because I was desperately hoping to get my act together. Finally, when I thought that we could add a little wrinkle to the new operation, I asked Kenneth if he and Bill Neely would start playing on Wednesday nights. And he said, "Eddie, you know you're gonna have to pay us thirty-five dollars because that's scale."

And I said, "Kenneth, I'm going to pay you a hundred dollars each." He said, "No, you can't do that Eddie, you'll go broke." And I said, "If I can't make it, I'll ask you to back up, but that's how I want to do to start off because I don't want you passing the tambourine—because you're going to make me look like a cheapskate. And all the people are going to say, 'Wilson, come on, what are you making this old man play for tips for?'"

DREYER: The old man who had set much of this stuff in motion.

WILSON: And so he said, "Okay, we'll see if you can do it." And son of a gun, it didn't stop him: he immediately started passing that tambourine anyway. And he always said, "This is my favorite instrument in the band, it pays for itself every night."

DREYER: Then you decided to start Threadgill's South. What year was that?

WILSON: Well, in the '90s; it all runs together. They had built that cafeteria next door to the Armadillo in '72, and it was scary. I thought that was going to be our demise at the Armadillo, but we got along great. I think Jimmie Vaughan was the first musician I ever knew that was a vegetarian, and he ate at the cafeteria every day.

One day I was driving up to the original Threadgill's—and was afraid the light-rail up there was going to wipe us out during the construction period. I was just scared to death of it, and then all of a sudden there was that same cafeteria with a "For Lease" sign on it. And in no time at all I had it remodeled enough for us to open Threadgill's South.

DREYER: Okay, so you opened Threadgill's South with Threadgill's home cooking. I mean, great Southern cooking—you know, meat, vegetables, seconds on the vegetables, please.

WILSON: Have the largest vegetable selection of any restaurant in America.

DREYER: Threadgill's South also has an outside performance stage and does some really fine booking.

WILSON: We had Shiva's Headband just a few weeks ago and it was just fabulous.

Left to right: Thorne Dreyer, Margaret Moser, and screen actor Sonny Carl Davis. Moser was interviewed on January 24, 2014. *Rag Radio* photo.

MARGARET MOSER

Patron saint of Austin music.

Margaret Moser reflects on producing the Austin Music Awards, her years as a groupie and a rock journalist, and her critical place in the evolution of Austin music history.

    Author, music producer, and award-winning rock journalist—and my friend—Margaret Moser was known as the "Grande Dame" of the Austin music scene and the "patron saint of Austin music." She made epic contributions to the cultural development of the city. Moser, who started writing for the Austin Sun *in 1976 and later was a music critic and senior editor at the* Austin Chronicle, *directed the* Chronicle's *annual Austin Music Awards during South by Southwest from 1983 until her death in 2017 and served on the Austin Music Commission.*

    She performed with Dino Lee and the White Trash Revue and with the Jam and Jelly Girls, was a commentator for National Public Radio, worked as an assistant to Liz Carpenter, worked in Austin's Comedy Workshop, and cofounded the South Texas Popular Culture Center in San Antonio. In 1971, as a teenager, Moser became a noted groupie, leading a troop tagged the "Texas Blondes," and she was known later in life for mentoring and producing teenage musicians.

    At the time of this interview, Moser was undergoing chemotherapy for stage IV metastatic colon cancer, first diagnosed in February 2013. She died three and a half years later, on August 25, 2017.

Rag Radio *engineer Tracey Schulz joined us in this interview.*

JANUARY 24, 2014

THORNE DREYER: Margaret Moser. You know we all love you, and I'm sorry that you aren't here in the studio with us. How are you doing, Margaret?

MARGARET MOSER: You know, I'm really doing pretty well—or "doing pretty good for the shape I'm in," as I like to say, quoting the Arc Angels.

DREYER: You've been open about your situation. You first wrote about it, I guess, in a column in the *Chronicle* in what, last May?

MOSER: That was when I finally got around to really writing about it. You know, it took me quite by surprise. It kind of came in stages, literally, because at first they had said that I was stage III cancer, and then they spent some tests on me and very kindly waited until after the Music Awards to tell me in fact it was stage IV.

So, that's been the thing that I've had to deal with most this year in terms of everything else that I do. Unfortunately, it means that I've had to put some of the many things that I love to be involved with on the back burner. But I'm still very focused on those things that I keep very close to me—the teen bands, the Music Awards, my work with the *Chronicle*. I also work down in San Antonio some at the South Texas Popular Culture Center—so that's got a lot of my interest these days, too. So, anything I can do to stop thinking about things.

DREYER: You've done such important work in this city in terms of bringing recognition to the music community, of really turning things around in the way that the community at large recognizes its musicians. Everybody loves you and everybody supports you.

MOSER: That's so nice of you.

DREYER: You've got a massive fan club out here.

MOSER: I think that speaks really well for Austin, because Austin in general is one of the premier music communities and scenes around the world, not just the United States. And one of the things that I believe makes us that way is Austin's real commitment to supporting itself. Somebody gets sick, somebody gets hurt, things go bad for somebody, you hit a deer with your car, you know, people will be there for you.

DREYER: There's a bio of you on the site of the Department of Communication Studies, Moody College of Communication, UT-Austin. And it says some really sweet things and it also has some information about your early groupie years and the "Texas Blondes," which we might talk about later.

MOSER: Sure. What I always say is that my experience doing that incredibly informed my opinions and knowledge of music as well as set me up with a lot of connections and people that I have maintained friendships with over the years, you know—long past the wild days.

DREYER: Well, I wanted to read something else from that bio: "Since arriving in Austin in 1973, her body of work as a rock, blues, country, and folk scribe, most notably for the *Austin Chronicle*, has left an unparalleled literary legacy. Author, performer, producer and 'Grande Dame' of the Austin music scene, Moser's grandest achievement was to provoke a response from a music industry that was at one time too occupied with its own survival. Her work both encouraged musicians to live a more intense and passionate life and drove city fathers to become more cognizant of their creative capital."

Let's talk first about what's happening with the Austin Music Awards. The Music Awards actually started out before South by Southwest, right?

MOSER: Yes. We were five years old before South by Southwest ever came along, which meant we had done six polls and five shows.

DREYER: So it started with a poll, a music poll in the *Austin Chronicle*, before there was ever an actual event.

MOSER: Yes. And that was run by Jeff Whittington, who had been one of the people working over at the *Daily Texan* at the time that punk broke, whose opinion I really cared about. I loved the way he wrote—and there was a guy who was really passionate about music.

I had always been passionate about music, but I had never been around anybody else who was so passionate about music. We were good friends and he really encouraged me to do this—and he was the one who brought me in to the *Chronicle*. So I felt very good taking over the poll from him in the early '90s.

DREYER: Tell us how that works, how the poll works—and then we'll talk about how that evolved into the actual event. I go to the Austin Music Awards every year and it's spectacular. And it's always a big surprise and everybody's waiting to see what big stars are going to show up. It's always a lot of fun.

I doubt there's anybody listening to the show, wherever they might be, that doesn't know about Austin's music scene and the importance of it, nationally, and the heritage here. But it's gone on for a long time and it's evolved an awful lot over the years.

MOSER: Yes, and it is exactly what you said. It's the heritage part of it and the legacy part of it that interests me so much these days. The poll now is thirty-three years old; this is the thirty-third one we've done. So, to take that poll and look at all of the bands and musicians and people who have been honored in it over the years really gives you this broad-based notion of Austin music that isn't just relegated to punk or rock or country, or anything.

"So, to take that poll and look at all of the bands and musicians and people who have been honored in it over the years really gives you this broad-based notion of Austin music that isn't just relegated to punk or rock or country, or anything."

One of the things that I've always been really proud of our voters for is that they seem very well informed. And so, I can usually look at the winners of any given year and go, "Yeah, that's representative of the year." May not necessarily have been the best I was listening to, but then, you know, that's what your voters are for out there.

DREYER: Let's go down through that parade of history. Tell us some of the people who have been honored in the Austin Music Awards.

MOSER: When I started with the *Chronicle*, I was young and we were all around the same age—in our mid- to late twenties—and we were very much into the Fabulous Thunderbirds, the punk rock scene that was happening out there, and so early on, that's a lot of what you saw: the Fabulous Thunderbirds, Stevie Ray Vaughn, Eric Johnson, people like that being voted in there.

But if you looked, you would see all kinds of other people in there, too. Over the years we've been able to acknowledge people like Townes Van Zandt, Willie Nelson, Lucinda Williams, the people who are not just Austin oriented but have risen above and beyond and made Texas music something that everybody listens to around the world.

DREYER: Asleep at the Wheel.

MOSER: Asleep at the Wheel. There's another one. And there's really a handful of people like that—like Joe Ely and Ray Benson and the late Doug Sahm—who I could always go to and just sort of tap on the shoulder and go, "Hey, would you put together a set for us or something?" And to me that speaks very well for their ability to perform.

I just went to the *Chronicle* site and I pulled up the very first poll that we did. And let me just read out the top ten on the very first poll. This is very interesting. Fabulous Thunderbirds were Band of the Year. The Big Boys were the second band that was in Band of the Year. Joe Ely Band, Rank and File, the Devils—must have been the Rockin Devils—Extreme Heat, Van Wilks Band, Standing Waves, and Pressure. And then Ernie Sky and the K-Tels.

That's a really interesting group of people to have been in there. And it takes you directly from the top—say, the Fabulous Thunderbirds, who were just about to start breaking nationally, and then the Big Boys, who really changed the face of hard-core punk for everybody. And then you've got Ernie Sky and the K-Tels, and the reason that Ernie Sky is really significant here is that Ernie was born and raised in Austin. He grew up here, he was part of the '60s crowd before the Vulcan, performing around town. He recorded on Sonobeat Records, which is very crucial to the formation of Austin music.

And then again you have Van Wilks, who had come from Brownwood, Texas, a little podunk town in West Texas. He'd come down here, performed around San Antonio, and had really gotten popular on his own. [You] had Extreme Heat, who were really funking it up back then. Rank and File changed the game for a lot of people. They moved here to be from Austin, and that was one of the first bands to do that. So, I just love looking at just this first poll here, 1982 to 1983.

DREYER: And then we think about all the stuff that's gone on since then. Of course, there's the Hall of Fame, that has a pretty remarkable roster, and I guess every year you add somebody to the Hall of Fame.

MOSER: We add a handful of people. I started realizing a while back that there were too many people doing too much good stuff, and that one wasn't enough. One's too many and a hundred's not enough, or something like that.

DREYER: Who are some of the people that have been added to the Hall of Fame in the last few years?

MOSER: Our Hall of Fame folks have included people from Blind Lemon Jefferson to . . . And You Will Know Us by the Trail of Dead. And right there, that's an incredible arc of people. We've also included people like Albert Collins. Clifford Antone got in there; he was only marginally a musician, but you could hardly deny his effect on the music scene. [Antone founded the influential Austin blues club Antone's and mentored a number of important blues musicians.]

One of the best ever was a couple of years ago when Greezy Wheels went into the Hall of Fame. When I was talking to [band leader] Cleve Hattersley about coming to the show, I said, "I would like for you to invite everybody who was in Greezy Wheels who you can feasibly get here." And so there were about thirty people onstage, and I love seeing that kind of thing. They are just great folks.

We have one of the great rockabilly stars from the old times, Ray Campi, who's in there. We also have, of course, Roky Erickson, our architect of psychedelia, Stephen Bruton, Steven Fromholz.

DREYER: Who just died. This last week.

MOSER: Yeah. The year that Steven Fromholz went in, his daughter got to walk him across the stage; Dorothy walked him across. So, I really love this particular category. This one means an incredible amount to me, you know.

DREYER: One of the things that's so wonderful about the Austin Music Awards is that it happens during South by Southwest; it has since the first few awards. When did it actually start being a show, an event, and not just a poll?

MOSER: From the first show. The first time we did it in 1983, we did it at Club Foot. We were not only surrounded by our peer musicians that we had been hanging around with—when I say "we," I'm talking about the folks at the *Chronicle* who put it together—but all of a sudden we'd reached into these other genres of music that coexisted but didn't necessarily cross over with each other.

In much the same way, the early Austin music scene—I'm talking about the '50s—had three distinct operating factions. There was the Threadgill's folky one, the Victory Grill East Side [a historic music venue that nurtured many legendary African American musicians], and then the kind of Tejano community that was going up. And those three coexisted, but there wasn't a lot of crossover in them. So, one of the things that the Hall of Fame has done is present all of those people, from all those genres, in one platform.

DREYER: The other thing that happens at the Austin Music Awards, there's always surprise guests—and often we sort of know they are going to be surprise guests.

TRACEY SCHULZ: Well, there is this particular thing that happened where Alejandro Escovedo was onstage with Joe Ely, and then he brings out a friend of his, and he introduces this extra guitar player that he brought.

DREYER: Margaret, this was one of the worst-kept secrets of all time—that Bruce Springsteen was going to come out—and what a jam that was.

MOSER: Oh, I can remember. There was such electricity in the air for that whole show, and, you know, he didn't sound check or anything. But when I was at sound check and I heard Garland Jeffreys step up and do "Beast of Burden," I knew it was going to happen. Still, it wasn't until the moment that he set foot in the building that I was really sure that it was going down.

And I just should have quit after that show. I just say, "That's it, you know, I've got Bruce Springsteen, we're out of here." But of course, I didn't get Bruce Springsteen, Alejandro brought Bruce Springsteen. And this is part of the magic of the Music Awards. These musicians enjoy playing the show, they enjoy getting the recognition, and they want to pass it on. And so, you know, that was something that just worked out unbelievably well, much like the year that Pete Townshend showed up and performed with Ian McLagan.

DREYER: And there was a pretty good jam last year, too.

MOSER: Yes. Gary Clark comes in and plays his one and only set at South by Southwest, unannounced, with us. And I mean, not only was that really unannounced, it was really unplanned. The moment they realized that Gary was probably going to go up onstage with Bill Carter and the Blame, they didn't have a guitar. So, Steve Chaney and Wayne Nagel are running around with the Trishas and got one of the Trishas to loan them a guitar—and that's what Gary's playing up onstage, for all you guitar freaks.

DREYER: I think it's wonderful, too, because all the different kinds of awards that are given and the different kind of performances during the show—it's just such an incredible range. And it shows what a wide range of music is happening and coming out of Austin at this time in history.

MOSER: I absolutely agree. It is one of the things that I really try to go for when we put together the show; I sit down with Louis Black and Raoul [Hernandez] from the *Chronicle* and several other people and we discuss all of the various possibilities—and almost every one of those slots fulfills two or three things. And that's really what I look for: not somebody who just represents great Americana songwriting, but also maybe has some country roots or maybe some old punk rock roots, or something like that.

So, you know, I think that has worked out very well for us in terms of being able to really show people who come to Austin what Austin music is all about. I would say that probably more than half of the people who are in an awards show audience are local people. But many, many of them come from South by Southwest to see who's hot around Austin; particularly, they're looking for the best new band.

We're at the Convention Center again this year, not at the Music Hall. I really like that because we are absolutely on-site when we do it. So, whatever is happening at South by Southwest—and in the beehive there in the Convention Center—we will get a little part of that by being right there with them when we kick off that Wednesday night.

This year they have all kinds of interesting folks coming from my favorite period, which was like the '80s. I know Gary P. Nunn is going to be there and Blondie is going to be there, and this is the stuff I really like.

South by Southwest does a remarkable job of bringing in international music from everywhere—as well as keeping its fingers on what was once very hip and popular and where they came from.

SCHULZ: We have the interactive portion, we have the music, we have the film, but the thing that kind of seems to have stirred a lot of talk is about Jimmy Kimmel: he's coming in and filming his show here for the week of South By.

MOSER: He's going to be over at the Long Center, but here's what people don't realize about Jimmy Kimmel's band: it's being led by Cleto Escobedo III. Cleto Escobedo's father, Cleto Escobedo II—or Cleto Escobedo Jr.—was from San Antonio and he was an original member of the West Side Horns. He was one of the ones that put together the West Side Horns—or what became the West Side Horns—in the late '50s and early '60s.

He was part of that movement of a lot of Tejano and Chicano soul musicians who had migrated out to the West Coast and then to Las Vegas, where they got lots of work—and the work wasn't necessarily as musicians. I believe that Cleto Escobedo II worked as a waiter for a good long time before his son got this gig with Jimmy Kimmel. And his son said, "Hey, I want to bring my dad on the show." And so, you hear those twin saxophones, which is one of the hallmarks of San Antonio music, every night on the Jimmy Kimmel show.

DREYER: Do you agree that the work that Doug Sahm did—in an intersection of musical genres and forms—has become symbolic of what Austin does, musically?

MOSER: I would absolutely agree with you and I would absolutely say that Doug Sahm, to me, is the quintessential Texas musician for that reason. Because San Antonio stands there at the crossroads of I-35 and 10. You can go east to west from there, you can go north to Duluth, Minnesota, or you can go down to Laredo from there. And that crossroads right there is pretty much imprinted on the sound of San Antonio—which is equal parts white, Black, and brown, when you put it all in the mix there.

And Doug understood that better than anybody else. You could see that particularly in his early days in the late '50s, when he was recording for Harlem Records. And he was doing this sort of post-Elvis thing, but his heart was very much in the rhythm and blues as well as the Tejano sounds that were happening.

I wouldn't say that that was Tejano proper that he was taking it from. It was still pretty much the traditional Mexican music that was being played in San Antonio that he was deriving all of these little bits from— in much the way that Manny Guerra, who was then one of the big guys behind one of the record labels down there.

Guerra said, "Hey, we need our young bands to be hipper. Let's put away the accordions and give them Farfisas, or Vox organs." And so that's where you get that sound in the '60s coming from that. "Wooly Bully" and "96 Tears." "She's About a Mover." That's where all that came from.

DREYER: I saw the Texas Tornados with Doug's son, Shawn, leading them, at Gruene Hall in New Braunfels. What a trip; they're still spectacular.

MOSER: He is his dad, you know.

DREYER: He's just a shorter version. He's got the same energy and the same sort of physical presence.

MOSER: Talks just like him. A mile a minute. And he's also got that, you know, understanding of San Antonio music that I go back to.

You know, the San Antonio and Houston music scenes were very closely related, much more so than San Antonio and Dallas, for example. But a part of it was because back in the '50s, when Don Robey started his little empire there during the Chitlin' Circuit days, his guys were running the San Antonio Chitlin' Circuit clubs. [Performance venues on the Chitlin' Circuit during the segregation era featured African American performers and catered primarily to Black audiences.] So, Don Albert, who had the Keyhole Club there, was the main guy, and he brought in all kinds of people via Don Robey. So there's a very close connection.

DREYER: When we talk about lore, Doug Sahm got some national attention thanks to [Houston music producer] Huey P. Meaux, who created the Sir Douglas Quintet and decided to pass them off as a British band. Which is just a wonderful story. I mean, there's a lot of amazing stories around Huey P. Meaux, for that matter. You know, wonderful and tragic and sad.

MOSER: And they even photographed the Sir Douglas Quintet in shadows so that you wouldn't see that you had four Mexican guys there and that they weren't maybe from England.

DREYER: They weren't from Liverpool.

MOSER: Right. And then of course, Trini Lopez outs them on *Shindig!*, so the jig was up at that point.

DREYER: This book that you reviewed, Vicki Welch Ayo's book, *Boys from Houston*—which is a self-published book that I also wrote something for—talking about the Houston scene at that time, is pretty amazing. Houston in, I guess, the '50s and '60s had an unacknowledged, very significant music scene.

MOSER: Very significant. You know, you had everything from Billy Gibbons's father, Fred Gibbons, who had the orchestra back then, to Don Robey, who was the magnate of the Chitlin' Circuit. And really, he kind of turned the town on its ear because he not only booked all these bands, but he had the record label, he had Duke-Peacock Records, and also Back Beat Records. And then he opened the Bronze [Peacock] ballroom there so that he could showcase a lot of these people—and they reached out and had his guys going to San Antonio and stuff.

That influenced a lot of the young rock and rollers that were coming up, all of the fine rhythm and blues history that Houston has. And I think that's why when you hear a lot of those Houston bands from the mid-'60s, you hear so much of that blues influence in there.

DREYER: And then you had Kenny Rogers with his band.

MOSER: First Edition.

DREYER: You had the Moving Sidewalks, you had Bubble Puppy, of course, who weren't actually originally from Houston. The [13th Floor] Elevators were down there for a long time.

MOSER: And then you had bands like Fever Tree, who were very popular at the time, you know, and who are considered kind of cult bands now. And the Clique; I think they were from Beaumont, but I remember listening to their version of "Splash 1" on KILT in Houston.

DREYER: Part of why Houston's music scene was so strong was the fact that there was such an incredible radio scene. And Vicki, in her book, she does talk a lot about that radio scene. It was pretty phenomenal.

MOSER: Vicki's book, I think, is really fascinating. If you're looking for heavy scene analysis and stuff like that, you won't find it in there. But what you've got there is the witnesses talking about what they saw, and to me that's the real value of that book.

DREYER: It's got your basic first-person accounts. The great interviews. I highly recommend it to people who are interested in the evolution of Texas music.

MOSER: Me too.

DREYER: And another thing about Houston is the whole influence—as you said—of R&B, of blues. You had people like Lightnin' Hopkins and Mance Lipscomb—who wasn't from Houston but who I used to go see at Liberty Hall, which was a wonderful rock venue.

MOSER: Great venue.

DREYER: We had Chris Strachwitz on this show—Arhoolie Records—who was one of those people who was a music detective. There's a documentary about him, *This Ain't No Mouse Music*. And of course, he came chasing after Lightnin' Hopkins and Mance Lipscomb and was responsible for a lot of indigenous music actually seeing the light of day, in terms of the larger public.

MOSER: Yes.

DREYER: When you look back on it, what are some other turning points in the music scene in Austin? I know that you were involved when there was a big, rich punk movement that had a lot of different tendencies in it—as well as infighting, that whole story.

MOSER: Well, that's very true. All those scenes were very friendly with each other back then; toward the end of his life you might see Clifford Antone hanging out at the Broken Spoke with James White. But I guarantee you that twenty years before, that did not happen. And not only was the punk scene pretty insular at that time, but they were really kind of at war with the fraternity community, too. So there was a lot of politics for the local punks to build their scene on.

Which was good, because one of the basic roots of punk was politics anyway, or at least as it came out of England. Certainly, we didn't have the kind of unemployment and, you know, government with [Margaret] Thatcher that they did—but there were plenty of other things to rebel against with punk.

DREYER: One of the things that always happens at the Austin Music Awards is that you never know who's going to walk out onstage and jam with somebody else. How much do you know what's going to happen, and how much of that just is because one of the musicians talks somebody else into coming and showing up?

MOSER: It's about fifty-fifty. I mean, some of it I actually orchestrate by saying, "Would you consider having such and such with you as a guest?" But just as often they will either come to us at the last minute and go, "Oh, by the way, we're going to have Bruce Springsteen come." Or they just show up with them. Or in the case with Gary Clark last year, he just happened to be on-site and we just sort of said, "If you want to sit in with Bill Carter . . ." And that's what happened with that.

DREYER: And that just went on and on; they went for a long time.

MOSER: He was smoking.

DREYER: Oh was he. That was incredible.

Okay, and I quote, "Aside from her next role as columnist for the newly arrived *Austin Chronicle*, where she helped spark the rising punk movement centered around Raul's nightclub, [Margaret Moser] found other avenues to champion musicians, her most infamous contribution being ringleader of a troop of groupies known as the 'Texas Blondes.'"

Tell us about the groupie days.

MOSER: It's funny, because it kind of came in two eras for me. The first was around 1971, in San Antonio, when I was a young teenager and San Antonio at that time was still pretty much the center of touring bands coming through this part of Texas. And so you weren't getting Jimi Hendrix in Austin, you were getting him down in San Antonio. You weren't getting Janis Joplin playing with her band in Austin, you were getting them down in San Antonio.

So it was a wide-open scene, literally, for me to get in. I'd been reading in *Rolling Stone* about all these girls like Pamela Des Barres who were having a good time with their group, the GTOs. And I really knew that I wanted to be in music, but I didn't know how. I knew I wasn't a singer; I knew I wasn't a musician, you know. And that was never what I wanted to be.

I would instead read and just voraciously devour all this information about rock and roll, largely through *Rolling Stone* and magazines like *Creem*—and all of a sudden at some point I realized, "Hey, I could maybe meet some of these people." So I started showing up backstage at these shows, like at the Municipal Auditorium in San Antonio, with Rod Stewart and the Faces, or Jethro Tull, and I mean—that was it.

It was all wide open back then. There weren't phalanxes of security guards to get through or anything like that. Really, you know, everybody was there for the party. So that kind of continued for me. I wasn't doing much of that in the late '70s, but then when punk rock came around again, it was more of a way to really hang out with the bands. People always assume that there's just tons of sex going on, and there was, but it wasn't necessarily for me.

It was really just sort of my inroad to the scene—and so that's how I ended up being buddies with Iggy Pop, you know, twenty-five years later, and stuff like that. So, it was a very fun time for me, and I managed to get out of it before things got really icky with bad diseases and stuff like that—because there were very definitely downsides to that sort of thing. But all in all, I really considered it having been a very positive experience for me, because I was the one who was in charge of it.

DREYER: Okay. We started *The Rag* in 1966, and then the *Austin Sun* was started by Jeff Nightbyrd and Michael Eakin, I guess.

MOSER: Yes.

DREYER: In what year?

MOSER: '75.

DREYER: '75. And you sort of wandered in? That was where you got your start in journalism, right? But it wasn't a direct path to being a music writer.

MOSER: No. I read the *Sun* from front to back, and I would always read the classifieds. So, in the classifieds one day was an ad asking for somebody who wanted to come clean the offices and answer the phone. And I went, "Oh, that's for me." I just had a feeling that some way or another this was going to be my way in—that maybe I could tell people about what it was that I was so excited about. I think that that was more the impetus for me to do this than anything else.

[Managing Editor] Dave Moriarty hired me there and I started working, cleaning up their offices and stuff. But the first thing I realized was their music files were in terrible shape, and so I said, "Do you want me to organize these?" And they said "yes." And then I realized that nobody was really taking care of the club listings that came in, and I said, "Well, do you want me to call the clubs and get the listings?" Boom! That was it. All of a sudden, I knew who all the people were, you know, who were having live music in Austin and was in touch with who was booking them, or who was handling them for the club.

And that, to me, was really my ticket to ride because suddenly I could not only walk into the club but I could ask for the person I'd talked to on the phone. They were always very happy to see us, you know. We were giving them kind of free press with the listings and everything—and that was really how I got my feet, my foot in the door.

DREYER: When I mentioned *The Rag* and then the *Austin Chronicle*, of course, afterwards—well, the *Austin Sun* was sort of a segue. *The Rag* was an underground newspaper and the *Austin Chronicle*, I guess, was what was called an alternative newspaper. It's not all that alternative, I don't know, anymore.

MOSER: No. Alternative to the daily.

DREYER: There was a lot of overlap among, in these transitions, among these three papers—a lot of people that were involved or played some kind of role in the evolution of the Austin scene. The *Austin Sun* was there at a really critical time, wasn't it?

MOSER: Very much so. And I really could not get enough of any of the publications around town. I remember that right around the time the *Sun* started, not only was *The Rag* still around, but there was that nice little publication *Free and Easy*. And I'd really gotten the feel for all this stuff back in San Antonio in the late '60s when Pleas McNeel had printed the *Eagle Bone Whistle* down there—which I have copies of now and have been going through.

But what I really liked about it back then—and this was coming out of the hippie era—there was very much a sense that we were in this together. And there was so much political undertone in *Eagle Bone Whistle* and in *The Rag* and in the *Sun* that would be carried over to the *Chronicle* in a very different way. But back then there was almost that kind of "them versus us," you know, "feds and heads" kind of thing, that was reflected in those earlier newspapers. And I really thrived on it and I believed it. I believed that we were—that these kinds of papers were—the right voice for the young generation.

DREYER: There's been some other cities that were involved in really important evolution of music, but I wonder where else there was such a tie-in between the politics and the music.

MOSER: Possibly only San Francisco. But I wasn't part of that scene, so I'm just sort of guessing.

DREYER: Well, that was just an offshoot of Austin, wasn't it?

MOSER: Absolutely. I call it the great "Texadus"—and the "Texpatriots"—that went out there. Because there's not a medium out there that's associated with that era of San Francisco that there weren't Texans who were behind, you know, pulling the strings.

DREYER: Ranging from people like [Dave] Moriarty and Rip Off Press to Chet Helms and the Avalon Ballroom, you know, and Janis.

MOSER: Bob Simmons on the air.

DREYER: Okay, when we look at that transition, what do you see happening now? I mean, everybody always says, "Well, Austin was wonderful back then." And it doesn't matter at what point in time you are: it was always greater "back then." But we have to acknowledge that there's incredible changes going on and, you know, the good old days was always whatever happened ten years before.

MOSER: Sure. [*Laughs.*]

DREYER: It's becoming so expensive; it's almost becoming unlivable for people who are entry-level musicians. Well, I mean, all musicians just about have to work and have to have a second job. But what do you see happening now with the Austin music scene?

MOSER: I'll tell you the trend that I like most about it is that the clubs are no longer relegated to just the downtown area. As a matter of fact, I think some of the more soulful clubs are nowhere near downtown. And to me that's one of the best indicators of the health of the scene.

And I imagine that South by Southwest has had a great deal to do with that—if only because it brought the larger sense of industry to a town that had a kind of Peter Pan notion of what the industry was about. We've always had record labels here. And I absolutely think that it was the booking policies of the Vulcan [Vulcan Gas Company, Austin's first psychedelic rock hall], and then the Armadillo, that created what we think of now as the amazing Austin "Live Music Capital of the World."

DREYER: In all of this discussion, Shiva's Headband and the Conqueroo and Powell St. John and people like that don't get mentioned a whole lot.

MOSER: They don't—and you know, funny you should say that. I'm going to pimp a little book here right now that's just come out. It's called *Sonobeat Records*—I mentioned Sonobeat Records earlier—and it's by Ricky Stein, whose father was Rick Stein, the singer-songwriter here in town through the '60s and '70s and '80s. And the subtitle of the book is "Pioneering the Austin Sound in the 1960s." I've just finished reading and I'm actually doing a piece on it right now.

Sonobeat Records was around from 1967 to 1976, and in that short period of time it put out twenty-three singles and two albums, which included stuff by Rusty Wier's early rock band, Lavender Hill Express, and also Ernie Gammage's early rock band, the Sweetarts, to a more sort of straight-line trio called the Lee Arlano Trio. To the recording at the Vulcan of Johnny Winter known as *The Progressive Blues Experiment*.

And so, Ricky has focused on this particular period of Austin in the mid-'60s, when radio station KAZZ was recording a lot of live shows in the clubs and being kind of the start of that. And I would say he's probably right: although Sonobeat starts the same year as the Vulcan, in a sense it comes from previous years—sort of innocent post-Beatle years—and the initial British rock years before psychedelia and blues rock kind of take over rock and roll.

Sonobeat Records is the puzzle piece that's missing from what everybody knows about Austin music in the '60s.

DREYER: Very interesting. Tracey has something he wants to ask.

SCHULZ: I'm really excited about a lot of things you've been doing lately with the under-eighteen bands—I guess the "youngblood" crowd, as they're being tagged. And that's a showcase that you're bringing to the Austin Music Awards, that you're highlighting this year.

MOSER: Zeke Barbaro—the son of publisher Nick Barbaro from the *Chronicle*—when he was a teenager came up with the term "U-18," and so I grabbed that term and I used it to apply it to all the young teen bands. But it's been a few years since we did that, and I've been informed that "U-18" is now a passé term—and they do prefer to be called the "youngbloods," or at least this particular little crowd does.

This crowd I'm talking about sort of centers around William Harries Graham, who is the son of Jon Dee Graham, and he is assembling just this monster lineup of young musicians whose parents grew up in the scene, too. And so they're absorbing all of that, and—at the ages of, you know, twelve and thirteen and fourteen—they're thinking like we were in our midtwenties to late twenties. And yet they're just sort of getting their feet on the ground as far as getting real experience that goes with this music.

And because sentiment is always such a big part of the Music Awards, I always like to try to bring that stuff together. So I've put together a set this year called "The Youngbloods Choir"—that's what William has named it—and William will be having Marlon Sexton; Sara Hickman's girls, Lili and Iolana; Finley Sexton, Will Sexton's daughter; and then they will be bringing the parents out at the end. So, to me, that's really going to tie it together very well.

SCHULZ: It's kind of a nice little bridge between the old Austin—and celebrating what's come before—and giving attention to what's emerging.

MOSER: Very much. And remember that back in the '60s, when all this started, it was teenagers who were playing rock and roll.

MUSIC MAKERS

Virtuoso guitarist Bill Kirchen (*left*) performs on *Rag Radio* in 2018. At right are Thorne Dreyer and Tracey Schulz (*center*). Photo by Roger Baker.

BILL KIRCHEN

The elegant and the funky.

Commander Cody guitar virtuoso Bill Kirchen reveals his love affair with his Fender Telecaster, his experiences with Iggy Pop, and how he became the "King of Dieselbilly."

The Grammy-nominated Kirchen, who was named a "Titan of the Telecaster" by Guitar Player *magazine, was the guitarist with the original Commander Cody and His Lost Planet Airmen from 1967 to the mid-1970s, and his trademark licks drove the band's classic "Hot Rod Lincoln," into the top ten. Kirchen's work in the early 1970s with Commander Cody "helped set the stage for Waylon Jennings, Willie Nelson, and other outlaw country bands." He is also a pioneer of the Americana radio format.*

Bill's career has spanned over forty years and includes guitar work with Nick Lowe, Emmylou Harris, Doug Sahm, Elvis Costello, and many more. His work celebrates an American musical tradition "where rock and roll and country music draw upon their origins in blues and bluegrass, western and honky-tonk." Kirchen, who tours worldwide, grew up in Ann Arbor, Michigan, and is now based in the Austin area.

FEBRUARY 17, 2012

THORNE DREYER: The first question I want to ask you, Bill, has to do with a love affair: a man and his guitar. The *Washington Post*'s Mike Joyce said, "The folks who make Fender Telecasters ought to stop what they're doing and cut Bill Kirchen a big fat check."

BILL KIRCHEN: All right. I'll go check my mailbox.

DREYER: Tell us about the famous guitar that you used for years and years and the story of how you got it.

KIRCHEN: I started out and picked up a guitar after I learned the banjo back in the big "folk scare" of the '60s. That's what drew me into the whole thing. And I started on an acoustic guitar and fingerpicking. I wanted to be Mississippi John Hurt and went to the Newport Folk Festivals, but somewhere along the line the electric guitar loomed, and the first one I actually owned I bought when I hooked up with the Commander Cody bunch and we started that band. I bought a guitar off one of the guys in the band. But I ended up trading it.

I was working as a motorcycle messenger in San Francisco. The Cody band had temporarily broken up. I traded guitars with a guy sitting next to me. He had a Telecaster and I had just figured out that all my favorite guitar players at that time—Buck Owens's guitar player, Don Rich; James Burton with Elvis and Ricky Nelson, or at that time just with Ricky, probably; and Roy Nichols with Merle Haggard—they all played Telecasters. So I wanted one.

I traded with this guy as we waited for the next load of blueprints to drive around San Francisco on our motorcycles. And that Tele stuck with me and I played it pretty much straight for forty years, to the point where I wore it down to a nub. I still play a Telecaster, I'm kind of identified with that. It was one of the original styles of guitar that dates back to—well, it's about as old as I am. It started about the same year I was born, in '48 to '49.

It's just a slab and a stick and a couple of pickups, you know—one, two pickups, two knobs, one switch—it couldn't be any simpler. Anyway, that's the story of me and the Telecaster. I wrote a love song to the Telecaster while I was here in Austin a couple of years ago, called

"The Hammer of the Honky-Tonk Gods." I wrote it on the way to go see the great Redd Volkaert at a club here in town.

What I wanted to do at the beginning, I wanted to play the acoustic blues and acoustic music. I got seduced by the electric, though, and I play more electric than acoustic now. But I thought, just to be a gentleman, I would show up with my acoustic guitar today.

DREYER: That's very polite of you.

KIRCHEN: Thank you very much. It's a much politer instrument than the electric guitar.

DREYER: I understand that you went to high school with Iggy Pop and Bob Seger in Ann Arbor, Michigan.

KIRCHEN: I didn't know Seger at all, but I knew Jim Osterberg, who became Iggy Pop before my very eyes. He was an interesting guy. He was a drummer in a band called the Iguanas, hence "Iggy." And then he was the drummer in the great local blues band the Prime Movers that had a big influence on me. I learned some music that stuck with me until this very day by listening to those guys.

But Jim was the drummer in that band and he used to sing the blues song, "I'm a man, that's spelled M-A-N." At some point he started singing—this would have been about '66—"I'm a tricycle, spelled T-R-I . . ." We knew something was afoot at that point.

DREYER: He just gained a couple of extra wheels is all.

KIRCHEN: It was the first Stooges show ever, on Halloween, and they were the Psychedelic Stooges then. And I have to admit, I wasn't impressed. I got there late and by the time I got there, Jim and Ron and Scott Asheton had covered themselves in silver or gold spray paint, I think, and Jim had—or Iggy, as he was then known—had a mic and he was sticking it in and out of a vacuum cleaner. And I remember watching and going, "What a waste."

But we started doing gigs with the Stooges back then, and right away he was just such a fantastic performer. It was like, "Okay, I get it." Plus, he had great songs back then, like "No Fun"—all the great songs.

DREYER: Austin and Ann Arbor—it seems like there were some similarities between the two places.

KIRCHEN: We knew about each other, Ann Arbor and Austin. They were liberal college towns, little oases.

DREYER: What was it like in Ann Arbor then?

KIRCHEN: It was a great place to grow up. Back then I remember Bill Monroe came to the area and I saw him. Bob Dylan played at my high school solo, then I saw a band with Bloomfield and Gravenites, and then later that year I went to the Newport Folk Festival for the second time, in 1965, and saw some of those people, mainly Bloomfield backing up Bob Dylan when he went electric. I remember seeing Ralph and Carter Stanley—the Stanley Brothers—and Carter was still alive.

But, yeah, it was just a great musical town, and I hung out with the guys in the college. Matter of fact, there were some people there who had been involved in the rediscovery of Mississippi John Hurt and some of the bluesmen of the day, and it was a great place to grow up.

DREYER: When did you first see the MC5 in Detroit?

KIRCHEN: I went and saw them early on. There was a ballroom in Detroit—probably like your Vulcan Gas here, later the Armadillo—where all the big bands came through, the Grande Ballroom. And a guy who got me my very first gig with my first band, John Sinclair, lived first in Detroit and then in Ann Arbor and was a big mover and shaker in the music scene.

DREYER: John Sinclair has been our guest on *Rag Radio*. I guess he managed the MC5 for a long time.

KIRCHEN: He did.

DREYER: Founded the White Panther Party.

KIRCHEN: That's right.

DREYER: The Lost Planet Airmen started in 1967, and the name was inspired by 1950 film serials featuring the character Commander Cody, and from a feature version of an earlier serial, *King of the Rocket Men*. How did that band get pulled together?

KIRCHEN: It was an art school kind of a wacky, admittedly stoned, local Ann Arbor thing. Initially it had a floating cast, and the guy who we had made be Commander Cody—we'd assigned him that role—George Frayne, had a lot of charisma; he was a Jones Beach lifeguard.

DREYER: He was perfect for the role.

KIRCHEN: Yeah, big old lantern jaw, barrel-chested, "follow me, men," Nick Fury type of guy, and he played great boogie-woogie piano, and he eventually is the guy that did the talking songs, one of which was a big hit. But the band used to have a floating membership.

We had the fabulous Green Sisters; they would do the twist dressed in green bra and panties onstage. And then we had someone else do a jumping jack with an American flag. I remember once we played some gig where it seems to me that the Commander's brother was showing films of dental extractions behind the band while we played. So, we really weren't following the playbook.

DREYER: More fun than having your tooth pulled.

KIRCHEN: The band kind of folded when John Tichy went off to get his doctorate in mechanical and aeronautical engineering.

DREYER: That's just what I was going to say: pop trivia quiz, "What founding member of Commander Cody became an important scholar?"

KIRCHEN: Yeah. John Tichy. So, he got his doctorate. George Frayne went off to teach art in Oshkosh, and I did the "go west, young man" thing and went to California. And then at some point I was able to talk the band into joining me in California in the late '60s—'69 it would have been. I remember because I celebrated my twenty-first birthday, which would have been in '69.

DREYER: Your guitar work was referred to by some as "rockabilly." Commander Cody was one of the pioneers of country rock, and that whole phenomenon. But so much of what you've done—like so much of what we've seen here in Austin—has been sort of merging of different musical styles.

KIRCHEN: I never did think of myself strictly as rockabilly, but we did play a bunch of rockabilly and I was certainly informed by that. I certainly know a few rockabilly licks, and so I can identify with that. But I've always felt like that was a little bit limiting, especially once rockabilly became, in America, kind of like a very specific dress-up gig. Which is great, but it was sort of like the way for a bunch of people to bond and perhaps spawn.

DREYER: Perhaps in that order.

KIRCHEN: They spawn then bond. But anyway, rockabilly was just sort of the name for the rock and roll that sprang up early in rock and there was still a big country influence and it was a neat thing. It was real, you know. At the same time, I listened to tons of blues guitarist Hubert Sumlin back in the day—who I was delighted to meet once I got to Austin.

DREYER: It was interesting because you had this psychedelic music phenomenon, and there was country rock, and then there was a lot of country rock that kind of went psychedelic. And in Austin, or in Texas, the whole Cosmic Cowboy, progressive country phenomenon started, and I know you've worked with Asleep at the Wheel and knew those guys. Was all of that just sort of like a blip in music history? What role did it play, do you think?

KIRCHEN: I have no idea where its historical importance is going to lie, but I know this: I know that we did turn on a whole generation of people to country music, to hard-core, blood-and-guts country and western swing that they did not have access to. Because I know I didn't have access to it. I saw Johnny Cash in Newport, but I didn't know from all that, and it wasn't really embraced by the folk scene that I'd come up in.

We did gigs with Merle Haggard and played western swing back then, and then Asleep at the Wheel came along later and did the same thing. I used to say that we sold more Merle Haggard records than Commander Cody records, and maybe that's a good thing. When I would do "Mama Tried" back in the late '60s, I was just trying to copy the Merle record. I had really nothing to bring to the table, you know.

As a matter of fact, once we had an interesting experience. We were opening for the Grateful Dead and Bob Weir, who was very young at the time—he was probably a late teenager. But he came up to me and he said, "Man, I like that song you're doing, that 'Mama Tried.'" He said, "But you guys"—and he used these words—"you guys ought to update your tonalities."

And so, "Yes, Mr. Weir, but what do you *mean* by that?" And he sang me "Mama Tried" and he kind of imitated me imitating Merle Haggard. And then he sang it how *he* would do it and it had that LA style. I like Bob, he's a good guy and everything, but we made fun of him for years for telling us to "update our tonalities."

DREYER: When you talk about folk music—and you came up out of that folk music scene—folk music and jazz were the first things that really hit me, touched me. And then when I came to Austin—and I came up here in '63 from Houston—Austin had this folk singing group that met once a week. And it would be a big circle of people in the Student Union—I guess it started at Threadgill's—and a lot of them were folks like Janis Joplin and Powell St. John and John Clay. And people would take turns, they'd sit around and play. And some of them became stars as the music scene evolved.

KIRCHEN: Right. And I think back then people were searching out. It wasn't the biggest and best and brightest time in pop music—it was kind of pre-Beatles, almost, and the sort of boy band stars from Philly had run their course—and so everybody was searching, searching, I think, for more adult content.

And that's what drove people towards folk music, because these old magical songs had been kicking around for x number of years. And then there was country music. I loved it because it had adult themes and to me a deeper emotional content to what I was getting from rock and roll radio at the time.

"I'm a big fan of mindless, slack-jawed, ham-fisted rock and roll. It's a beautiful thing. I will play that until I die."

But don't get me wrong. I'm a big fan of mindless, slack-jawed, ham-fisted rock and roll. It's a beautiful thing. I will play that until I die.

DREYER: Dieselbilly.

KIRCHEN: That's a genre I made up myself so I could play anything I wanted to, since I am the self-crowned, self-anointed "King of Dieselbilly." I think I used to say it as a joke and then when I was touring with Nick Lowe as his guitar player, he would have me do one song a night and I would do "Tombstone Every Mile" because it was the title of my first CD, a truck-driving song. And he would introduce me with this fantastic aristocratic British accent: "Ladies and gentlemen, Bill Kirchen, the King of Dieselbilly." And so, it just stuck with me, so I *am* the King of Dieselbilly.

DREYER: Nick Lowe called you "a devastating culmination of the elegant and the funky," adding, "He's really a sensational musician with enormous depths."

KIRCHEN: Wow. Thank you, Nick. Elegant and the funky? I thought he said "the elephant and the monkey," so I'm glad to know it was the elegant and the funky. That's fantastic.

No, he's good, I'm a big fan of Nick Lowe. He produced a record by my band, the Moonlighters, back in the early '80s, late '70s, and then I got to record with him and tour the world with the guy. I love playing with my own band and being my own boss, but if there's one guy I love working with, it's Nick Lowe. If he comes off as big hearted and smart and funny in records, he's even more so in all those categories in person. He's a delightful human being. So, a big fan of that guy.

DREYER: What made you decide to settle in Austin?

KIRCHEN: I love Austin. My wife and I love Austin and we'd been living in Buda, which was just a little too far away to really feel a part of the hub and the bub. When we lived here before, our daughter joined us, and she stayed here when we moved back to DC—back six, seven years ago. We have a granddaughter here and that was the final straw that pushed us over the edge. But we like Austin and had considered moving here just for the sheer love of the town.

Kick a can and three musicians, three guitar players, will rush out clutching their Grammys and their Stratocasters. I mean, every corner it's like that. I went out and sat in a bunch with the great Alvin Crow, who I knew back from his Pleasant Valley days, back when I played here with Cody. I got to sit in with them some, and John X. Reed. I did a gig with Marcia Ball at the Christmas Bazaar, who is just a treasure. The Flatlanders live here, Jimmie Dale and Butch, and I played with them a little bit out in California, but that's a fantastic group of original Texans. What a bunch of characters.

DREYER: The Armadillo, of course, was one of the great rock halls in the country.

KIRCHEN: Well, everything club. Not just rock, but back then it embraced so many things. Yeah, we came from California to play there twice a year and ended up making a live record there. I think we dug in for about a four-day run, and back then it was all recorded on two-inch tape, of course, so we had these giant carts full of reels of tape. Waylon opened for us at the Armadillo one time, back right before he blew up and became huge. We played with Greezy Wheels.

DREYER: Maria Muldaur?

KIRCHEN: Yeah, she's great. I once played New Year's Eve at San Quentin Prison with her. That was strange. It made me think I don't want to ever, ever be there on the other side of that proscenium.

DREYER: You both played at the "Last Dance at the 'Dillo" [the final night of performances at the Armadillo World Headquarters].

KIRCHEN: I used to see Maria when I was a high school kid and she was in the Kweskin Jug Band, and I was quite infatuated with her, I'll have to tell you. Who would not be?

DREYER: You guys were around the West Coast, you were in San Francisco around the time all the stuff was happening. When everybody was bringing their flowers.

KIRCHEN: I kind of missed the real Summer of Love in '67; I got there a little late for that. So, the bloom was already off the rose in Haight-Ashbury.

DREYER: I was there the summer *before* the Summer of Love, and you could see the bloom already starting to wilt.

KIRCHEN: But it was still exciting times and, you know, wonderful. I lived there from '68 to '86.

DREYER: A lot of Austin people went to San Francisco.

KIRCHEN: Yeah, the Family Dog.

DREYER: Chet Helms. The Rip Off Press—Gilbert Shelton and all of those guys—and, of course, the 13th Floor Elevators and Janis Joplin, Powell St. John and Travis Rivers, and all those people.

KIRCHEN: And all them, yeah. Doug Sahm.

DREYER: Doug Sahm. A lot of people don't know that that whole phenomenon out there was really a creation of the Austin music scene.

KIRCHEN: I was a big fan of Gilbert Shelton. I loved Gilbert Shelton.

DREYER: Gilbert Shelton started the *Fabulous Furry Freak Brothers* comic strip in *The Rag*. Said we needed a little more humor.

KIRCHEN: Oh, really, good for you.

DREYER: Gilbert lives in Paris now, or near Paris.

KIRCHEN: He was my favorite. I found a font once—I was looking through fonts back when I first moved to DC in '86—and I saw a font called "Gilbert Shelton," and I went, "Hold on, oh, doggone," and I took it and used the letters. They were like circus letters, they're kind of jaunty, tipped in different directions, and I'm sure he drew it. And that was my logo for a while, with Too Much Fun. And I never saw that font again until I was in Avignon, in France, and boom! There it was on a poster that Gilbert Shelton had done.

Shelton adhered to what I love, the story. Robert Crumb was a genius, of course, too, but I was a big fan of Carl Barks's work on Scrooge and Donald Duck. That's what I grew up on, so when I saw basically the same format except with *The Furry Freak Brothers*, I bought the whole program. I couldn't wait to get my hands on the next one.

DREYER: I think Jim Franklin did one of your covers for Commander Cody.

KIRCHEN: Yeah, he sure did.

DREYER: Jim Franklin developed the surrealistic armadillo that graced, among many things, a number of covers of *The Rag*.

KIRCHEN: Freddie King. [Franklin immortalized the blues guitarist in a mural that depicted him with an armadillo bursting from his chest.]

DREYER: Album cover and poster. And he [Franklin] was also the MC at the Armadillo for a long time.

KIRCHEN: Franklin does the introduction on the live album. He goes, "Live from deeeep in the heart of Texas, Commander Cody . . ." That's him. All dressed—I think he had a robe and a staff with some sort of a skull on it and perhaps an armadillo.

DREYER: So, what have you been up to lately? You tour a lot.

KIRCHEN: We did some interesting gigs last year. We played in Palestine, which was so cool, brought over there by the American consulate in Palestine—there's no embassy because they're not a country. But that was fantastic. We played in Jenin [in Palestine], and we played up in—slightly less interesting, but we played up in Lapland, up north of the Arctic Circle.

As you can imagine, less happens in Lapland.

DREYER: Why don't you sing a song for us?

KIRCHEN: All right. This is one of my "good to be alive" songs—I wrote this song, as a matter of fact, when I was walking my dog when I lived in Buda. And you know how dogs are, they're just happy to be alive. So, I wrote a "good to be alive" song encouraged by his enthusiasm, and I was going to cut him in on the royalties. I was going to give Rufus half the royalties—but then I realized, Thorne, he's fixed, he doesn't need the money.

DREYER: Give the dog a bone.

KIRCHEN: [*Singing*] . . . I'm gonna live each day like there's no tomorrow / Crank up the love, turn down the sorrow / Get my ducks in a row . . . / One more day . . .

But if living truly is a terminal disease / All I'm askin' for is a brief reprise / And I can rattle and roll / One more day . . .

DREYER: Very cool. Thank you, Bill. It's been fun. My best to your dog.

Jazz musician, composer, and Beat movement pioneer David Amram talks and performs on *Rag Radio*, September 28, 2012. Photo by James Retherford.

DAVID AMRAM

Ambassador of good cheer.

Composer and jazz virtuoso David Amram reflects on playing with Charles Mingus and Dizzy Gillespie, his experiences with Jack Kerouac and Woody Guthrie, and his early days as a Beat musician.

David Amram was called the "Renaissance Man of American Music" by the Boston Globe, *and the* Washington Post *called him "one of the most skilled musicians America has ever produced." In 1957, Amram joined Jack Kerouac, Philip Lamantia, and Howard Hart in a poetry and music performance at the Brata Gallery in New York, an event often credited as the "birth of the Beat Generation."*

Amram, who was eighty-one at the time of this interview, is a composer, conductor, virtuoso jazz musician, actor, and author. Amram has composed more than one hundred orchestral and chamber music works; written movie scores, including Splendor in the Grass *and* The Manchurian Candidate; *and penned two operas and three books. A pioneer on the jazz French horn, Amram is a multi-instrumentalist who has collaborated with Leonard Bernstein (Amram was the New York Philharmonic's first composer in residence in 1966), Jack Kerouac, Dizzy Gillespie, Langston Hughes, Dustin Hoffman, Willie Nelson, Bob Dylan, Allen Ginsberg, Charles Mingus, and many more.*

In September 2012, the Austin Civic Orchestra produced the Texas premiere of This Land, *David Amram's folk-inspired symphonic variations on a song by Woody Guthrie, commissioned by the Woody Guthrie Foundation. I was there for an exceptional performance—and David Amram was a delightful guest on* Rag Radio. *His tales of Kerouac and Guthrie (and our mutual friend, musician-historian Bobby Bridger) were riveting, and his positive outlook on culture and society was inspirational.*

SEPTEMBER 28, 2012

THORNE DREYER: David Amram, welcome to *Rag Radio*, welcome to Austin one more time. I know you're a regular here and you love Texas.

DAVID AMRAM: The beautiful thing about Texas, at least in my experience—as I'm still a work in progress as I approach eighty-two this November—is that when I came here in the '40s, and Austin was considerably smaller, and so was I, the country players, the jazz, the folk players, the western swing players, the symphony players, the opera singers, the folk singers, everybody seemed to appreciate everybody else's work and efforts.

As [the famous Hill Country character] Hondo Crouch of Luckenbach, population seven, said: "Everybody is somebody in Luckenbach." In Austin, everybody who loved music or participated had a place in their heart for everyone else's work and everyone else's expression.

And I don't know why that is, but it's still that way in Austin today, all these years later. And that's a beautiful thing and that's inspiring enough to come. When I came to Kerrville first in 1976 and saw every genre of music was appreciated as long as you were sincere—to me, that reflected what Texas is like.

DREYER: I understand that our dear friend, historian and musician Bobby Bridger, was responsible for your first coming to the Kerrville Folk Festival.

AMRAM: It was amazing. I met him at the Lion's Head Bar in 1975 in New York. Vine Deloria Jr., the great Native American writer, called me on the phone. I was writing a symphony for the Philadelphia Orchestra based on texts of Native people that Vine had given me—and Floyd Red

Crow Westerman and others had taught me all these songs and I was grinding away. He said, "Dave, how's the symphony coming?" I said, "Well, Vine, it's slow, but I'm cranking it out."

He said, "You put down everything and come right now; there's a guy I would die for—he's like my brother even though he's not an Indian—named Bobby Bridger from Monroe, Louisiana, now living in Texas. Get over here." So I went running down to the place and met Bobby. He came to my little apartment in the Village and he started playing me his "Twilight of the Sioux," and I realized he was a country singer-songwriter doing the same thing in that genre that I was doing for the Philadelphia Orchestra.

I said, "Wow," and he said, "You know, there's this little festival in Texas in a town called Kerrville. I think you would love it and I think they would like you." So, I came, and I've been coming back ever since; I've been there, I guess, thirty-four times. They even had a classical series of chamber music and baroque music—and, whatever it was, everybody appreciated and loved it. [The Kerrville Folk Festival, which has run yearly since 1972, lasts eighteen days and encourages emerging singer-songwriters.]

And when we went to the campfires with some of the members of the Austin and San Antonio symphonies, and sat around and played with the pickers afterwards, everybody felt at home with everybody else.

DREYER: Incidentally—and this is a perfect lead-in to our mail—we got a number of messages for you, and here's the first one: "Thorne, can't wait to listen to this one online. David and I have been pals since 1975. Please tell him I said 'hello' and would have been there for the concert if possible. Cheers! Bobby Bridger."

AMRAM: Oh, my word.

DREYER: Here's another one: "Thorne, wish I could be there. Please give David Amram my very best. He's an exceptional human and a joy to hang out with. Hugs, Crow Johnson Evans." And: "David Amram is a treasure, great you're interviewing him. Jonah Raskin."

AMRAM: Wow. Well, I thank all three of you for your kindness. I'll try to live up to those accolades. All three of you are still doing what you love to do, and that's the best thing young people can see in us older people. Crow Johnson has been a great songwriter for so long, Raskin's terrific, and Bobby Bridger is my main man.

All of those people who are now past their teenage years, when a teenager or a young person sees them—and hopefully myself—they can see that we love what we're doing. We're grateful to be able to do it, we're thankful that anyone will show up and listen. They can realize that maybe they can go beyond their career counselor's advice—that if they're twenty-four years old and they don't own a skyscraper and therefore they're a failure and a disgrace to society.

"Work harder than is expected, realize that if you give more than you receive, you're not an imbecile or a business failure, you're simply doing what the highest level of a human being can do, which is to make a contribution."

Give it a few more years, not just as a musician or artist, but if someone wants to be a rancher, a doctor, a lawyer, an astronaut, professional athlete, whatever you want to do, that you should do it with love. Work harder than is expected, realize that if you give more than you receive, you're not an imbecile or a business failure, you're simply doing what the highest level of a human being can do, which is to make a contribution.

I'm living proof of that because I have so much fun doing what I'm doing, including being here at a radio station that's cooperatively run. That's the reason why Marconi invented the radio: to dispense valuable, interesting information to other people. In Feasterville, Pennsylvania, where I was brought up, when we worked in the cornfields during the Depression, we had two tin cans with a string, and when we got tired and when our folks weren't around to see we were goofing off, we would scream into the one tin can and that was our mass communication.

Marconi and the other folks who invented the radio, I think, did it as a way of sharing information of lasting value. And that's what stations like this do, and that's a beautiful thing.

DREYER: I want to talk a little bit about Woody Guthrie, about the piece that you composed that's being performed here in Austin and in other places around the country. I want to talk to you about how you put that together, how you got into Woody Guthrie's head a little bit.

This is from an interview that you did. You said, "Ahmed Bashir and I had walked over to this little place in the Lower East Side, and there was Woody Guthrie, a very small, wiry man sitting at a kitchen table, and the amazing thing was he was wearing cowboy boots and I'd never seen anyone in New York City wearing cowboy boots."

Tell us about Woody Guthrie; tell us about your first impressions.

AMRAM: That was 1956, and Ahmed Bashir, who introduced me, was a good friend of Charlie Parker and Sonny Rollins—and I was playing with Charles Mingus in 1955 when I met Ahmed. He was staying at my place for a while and he said, "Man," he said, "you want to go tomorrow and meet Woody?" And I said, "To meet Woody Herman?" And he said, "No, no, Woody Guthrie." I said, "Sure," because I knew Cisco Houston and I knew Pete Seeger and I knew Ramblin' Jack Elliott, but I had never met Woody, and heard so much about him from them and from his beautiful songs.

So, we went over and he spent the whole day talking about politics, about traveling around the world as a merchant seaman, about Bach and Beethoven and Shakespeare and country folks and Cajuns; he was like an encyclopedia. And just such a wonderful, vital guy. Fortunately, he was having a good healthy day.

Many, many years later I knew Arlo, Woody's son, and Nora, the daughter, Arlo's sister, when they were little kids. I would see them when I was with Jack Elliott, when Nora would come from her dance classes—and run into them and their mom, Marjorie, over the years.

Many years later, about forty years later—just as I bumped into Bobby Bridger in the Lion's Head and that became a whole part of my life—Nora called up and said, "You know, we're doing a whole bunch of things about Woody. Our favorite piece as children was listening to Aaron Copland's *Appalachian Spring* because my mom, Marjorie"— that's Woody's wife at the time—"was the lead dancer in *Appalachian*

Spring, and that's where she and Woody met and fell in love and got married."

So they said, "We'd like to have a piece honoring Woody for a symphony, but not an elevator schlock-o pop ghostwritten piece with eleven people with synthesizers turning his songs upside down, but actually a piece of music." And they said, "Well, maybe you could model it on the *Theme and Variations on 'Red River Valley'*"—which I wrote after meeting Hondo Crouch and which gets played all over the world now.

And I said, "Well, boy, that would be great." So I thought, well, maybe I could take "Pastures of Plenty" or the "Deportees"—which have such gorgeous melodies, like something from Tchaikovsky or Brahms's *Variations on a Theme by Haydn*. That's the kind of melody that Brahms would have used. So I said "okay."

I called up Nora and she said, "No, no." She said, "I love those, too, but we have to use 'This Land Is Your Land.'" And I said, "Uh oh," because I had played that with Woody's son Arlo probably a hundred times; I imagine, with Pete Seeger, maybe three hundred times; every Farm Aid I played with Willie Nelson, we'd do that one, just about. And it's so great without any orchestra, without anything. I figured, boy, an orchestra would just wreck it.

So I thought, "What the heck am I going to do?" And I was sitting there tearing up paper and throwing things away and Nora called up again and said, "How are you coming?" I said, "Well, I'm trying to figure out what to do." She said, "Read Joe Klein's biography of Woody—there are a lot of things in there that most people don't know. And secondly, remember that most of his three-thousand-plus lyrics that he wrote for songs, he didn't just jot them down in an afternoon. He spent years writing a verse here and there when he traveled around the country."

I said, "Wow, that's my MapQuest."

So, the piece starts off with a big fanfare, and there's a section, first variation, based on the kind of music that's used in an Oklahoma stomp dance. I wrote my own melody, but based on that beautiful genre.

The second movement is Woody being in church, because Pete Seeger told me that that melody for "This Land Is Your Land" is actually an old church melody Woody probably heard in church.

Then the third variation is when he moved to Pampa, Texas, and I had what's called the "Pampa Texas Barn Dance." Actually it doesn't sound exactly like a real barn dance, because you don't need an orchestra for that, but I made up one of my own.

The next variation is when he was working in the fields with the Mexican workers, called "Dreaming of Mexico." The variation after that I called "Dust Bowl Dirge"—which was when he was in the Dust Bowl and actually almost died during one of those Dust Bowl experiences.

And the final series is when he moved to New York, and the neighborhood scenes. First, there is a distant West Indian band that you hear, then a klezmer wedding, then a Turkish-Greek-Armenian Middle Eastern bazaar, then a Salvation Army hymn, then a big jazz band welcoming home the troops in a block party, an Afro-Cuban band, and then finally the finale.

And in every one of those variations you suddenly hear, snuck in there, that "This Land Is Your Land" melody playing in counterpoint with everything else. Now, this is nothing original. Palestrina, Bach, Beethoven, Mozart, all did that, too, where you would take variations of a theme and where you would have the theme subtly come in and fit into everything else you were doing.

So, it was almost like building a boat inside of a bottle. I was sitting there cranking it out with the tweezers—only, I didn't use tweezers, I used music paper. I still write it down by hand. I don't wear a white powdered wig, but I still write it down the old-fashioned way.

And we just did it with the Colorado Symphony in Denver, and it's going to come out as a recording. We didn't have to outsource it to a former Iron Curtain country where the guys get ten dollars a day. We actually had a regular through-the-union arrangement, the great players of the Colorado Symphony.

And the other one we did was *Theme and Variations on "Red River Valley,"* which I wrote for the Kerrville Festival, dedicated in memory of Hondo Crouch. So, the two generically American oriented pieces played by American musicians.

DREYER: As you were describing this, I couldn't help but think of a theater piece. Of staged theater—it sounds like it would adapt wonderfully to a piece of theater.

AMRAM: Well, I'd love to see that, or as a ballet.

The nice thing is when the piece gets played, people can hear it and they get something from it. And that, of course, is the special blessing; because of my being an octogenarian, my idea in music school was if you're going to write a significant piece of music, it's supposed to empty out the house, cause a riot, and make everybody go home with a headache, looking angry, and saying I want to go back and hear some doo-wop music.

The reason for that is that when *The Rite of Spring* was premiered in the beginning of the twentieth century, it was so hard that the musicians got lost after about twelve measures—and messed the whole thing up. The dancers got lost because the orchestra was goofing up, and it was a disaster and the whole audience started booing and caused a riot. And because of having the telegraphic communications that were just beginning, that became a worldwide story of the riot, which got more publicity than the people that liked the piece.

So, the idea from that time on was, if you're really going to be a significant artist, you have to do something that offends everybody. Kind of the insult-comic syndrome. And, obviously, you could do something new that people don't understand. People said Kerouac was a speed writer. Jackson Pollock didn't know how to paint. Charlie Parker and Dizzy Gillespie were just playing a lot of wrong notes out of tune. History has proven them wrong.

So, people don't have to necessarily dig it the first time, but there has to be something there. At least the musicians or some other people know that there's something happening. And I was so delighted and so thrilled that the Austin Civic Orchestra could play it.

DREYER: This is from the *Cleveland Plain Dealer*: "[David Amram] grew up in farm country and had a storytelling uncle who was a seaman. At age twelve his family moved to Washington, DC, to what was then called a checkerboard neighborhood, Black and white, and heard, day and night, jazz, blues, and rhythm and blues. He played piano, percussion, and French horn and had a French-horn-playing girlfriend in Palo Alto."

You had all of these influences. Tell me about that process. Tell me about when music started doing this stuff to you—and all the different kinds and forms of music and how that got synthesized for you.

AMRAM: Well, it still happens every day. Every time I see, hear, or look at something that touches my heart, I just figure, "Boy, I'd like to know a little more about that." And when I was a little boy on our farm, we used to have the radiator upstairs—and I would hear all these different crazy sounds. Then when I heard Big Sid Catlett and Gene Krupa and the jazz drummers playing, I said, "Boy, that's like the radiator." I had the understanding that rhythm has all different forms and different styles.

And when we lived down south in Florida, I used to hear all the music in Pass-a-Grille, Florida, where I was so long ago. I heard all that beautiful southern music because my dad's side was originally from Savannah, Georgia. And my uncle, who came from Las Vegas, New Mexico, taught me about American Indian music. And my other uncle, David—who was a merchant seaman—traveled around the world.

> **"So, even though I was living on a little farm during the Depression, I had a sense that there was something out there, and the music was a gateway to traveling to those places and to look and listen."**

So, even though I was living on a little farm during the Depression, I had a sense that there was something out there, and the music was a gateway to traveling to those places and to look and listen. And it's something that I've tried to do ever since, to learn how to pay attention.

DREYER: Can you show us, with some of your implements of destruction here?

[David Amram describes and performs on a number of instruments from around the world.]

AMRAM: So, when you can learn to hear and play and get close to those instruments, you're not only able to appreciate the cultures that they come from, but you're also able to go back and listen to Mozart and Beethoven or Patsy Cline or Merle Haggard or Willie, or whatever the genre of music is, and hear that music that we were brought up with—with a fresh ear.

And Mozart sounds a whole lot hipper than it ever did before because you can relate it to the musical intent and the genre and the special place that it comes from, rather than saying, "I think he hit a wrong note in bar 243."

You can listen to music spiritually and emotionally, not only judgmentally. I'm a fierce, nasty critic of my own work, but I never let anybody know about that. Everything else, I try to approach with an open heart and an open mind and listen for the soulful human, cultural qualities.

And I think being with people who know more than you do and who come from different places than you do and have a different approach is not only good for your mental health, it makes you a much better appreciator and more creative.

DREYER: You said, "It's nice to see that at the end of the century with the embrace of multiculturalism, we find that Columbus was right. The world isn't flat."

AMRAM: Amen.

DREYER: Tell us about some of the experiences you've had in other places, discovering other kinds of music and other kinds of instruments.

AMRAM: I spent time with so many musicians. I was the State Department's cut-rate ambassador of good cheer: they figured for fifty dollars a day they had nothing to lose, so if I went out from my assigned tasks and hung out with people and disappeared, they didn't lose a big investment. As a result of that—I'm not being sarcastic—to me it was more of an honor than the two years I was happy to spend when I was drafted from 1952 to 1954, because I felt I was better equipped to represent my country as a musician than I was in my soldiering days. Although I did my best to manage to get through that, thank heavens, which a lot of people didn't, so I'm very grateful.

But when I went for the US State Department as their economy-line ambassador of good cheer, I received a trillion-dollar education in return. So I was grateful for that and also to share the beautiful music from here—Cajun, blues, zydeco, jazz, country, Charles Ives, George Gershwin, Aaron Copland, Duke Ellington, Monk, Dizzy, Bird, all those people I've been blessed by the Great Creator to stumble into and who took me under their wing—and share what I learned from them.

And in exchange, learn a fraction of what they could show me, with the idea that I would bring that back home and share that with other people. And that's what most musicians did; when Duke Ellington went to Sri Lanka, he made such an impression that when I was there, they had a Ceylonese Duke Ellington Orchestra.

And I've got a picture at home with all the men and women in that orchestra, all dressed up in their traditional garb but playing the heck out of Duke Ellington's music. And then the second half, they played all traditional Ceylonese and what they now call Sri Lankan music. And to them, both were beautiful.

Now, when Duke came back, he would always bring an instrument from a different country in one tune and include that in his work. When I played with Dizzy—I met him when I was twenty years old, back in 1951—he told me years later he wrote "Night in Tunisia" before he ever got to the Middle East because he was so fascinated with that music. And he studied enough to know the basis of some of that wonderful genre of music that they played in Tunisia. And of course, when he finally made his Middle Eastern tour, he said, "Man, I was in heaven."

When I came with Dizzy, Stan Getz, and Earl Hines to Havana, Cuba, and we were playing Afro-Cuban music and I had to learn that if the clave goes this way [*demonstrates*], the counterrhythm had to be [*demonstrates*]—and that there were certain things that fit into certain things and it wasn't just everybody bashing out and having a good time. That there were hundreds, thousands of varieties of Latin music and that Latin music was more than Carmen Miranda wearing that great hat with the bananas and the pears and the apples and grapes on top.

DREYER: As wonderful as that was.

AMRAM: And she could sing. She was a terrific performer. And Xavier Cugat was a very colorful personality. But there was a whole lot more than what we thought of as Latin music, which was lumping everything together in one big package, not paying attention to what was inside that package. And in Cuba there were so many different styles that were different than anything else in the world. And in Brazil they have more music than you could even dream of hearing.

When I was in Nicaragua, I found there was so much music that some of the Nicaraguan musicologists and hang-out-ologists—the musicologists and professors down there—can all play, sing, dance, and treasure their own indigenous music. As much as they like our jazz and as much as they like Mozart, they also include the music of their culture, which is beautiful.

So, every place I went I saw musicians who had a broad scope. They knew everything about us, and I realized we knew nothing about them. It's better to know next to nothing than nothing, so the little teeny bit that I learned in each place, I tried to bring back. Some of those I use in my—I guess, you could say—classical pieces. Sometimes I don't use anything of that sort. But anything that I do helps to enrich me.

When I was the first composer in residence with the New York Philharmonic, I mentioned my influences were Palestrina, Bach, Beethoven, Mozart, Brahms, and Hector Berlioz, my main man, and also Charlie Parker, Bix Beiderbecke, Sonny Rollins, Roland Kirk, Dizzy, Bill Evans, King Oliver. People thought, "Well, isn't that nice?"

But the management of the New York Philharmonic said, "How can you equate barroom entertainers with the treasures of European music?" And I said, "It's very simple; the commonality is they both have purity of intent and exquisite choice of notes." I thought that would do it. And he looked at me and said, "Man, what kind of psychotic, career-death-wish moron has Leonard Bernstein chosen?" This was 1966 to '67.

DREYER: This is from the *St. Petersburg Times*, by Paul Bergin: "In October 1957, Jack Kerouac, Philip Lamantia, Howard Hart, and David Amram staged the first public poetry music performance at the Brata Art Gallery in New York. It was the first group statement by artists who would quickly—and speciously—become known as the Beats, and it is the moment most chroniclers of the period regard as the birth of the Beat Generation."

I would like to mention that in our announcement for this show, we included a photo Jim Retherford sent us of Gregory Corso, Jack Kerouac, the artist Larry Rivers, David Amram, and Allen Ginsberg. Wonderful, wonderful photo, sitting in a coffee shop—I don't know where that coffee shop was—but this all brings us to the fact that Jack

Kerouac is being honored with three movies and more. Tell us about that era and what you brought with you from all of that.

AMRAM: I had met Allen Ginsberg and Gregory Corso in 1955, when I was playing at the Café Bohemia with Charles Mingus. I was a twenty-four-year-old hayseed studying classical composition, and Mingus, by a miracle, chose me to be in his band. So, they all came down, and apparently Jack came down then, too, but I had never met him, and Cecil Taylor also was there. That's where we all met and I met Thelonious Monk, Sonny Rollins, all these great, great people during that time when I was at Manhattan School of Music on the GI Bill, studying French horn and composition and orchestration, music theory.

In 1956, I was at a "bring your own bottle" party, and the painters always got the biggest space at the lowest rent so that they could have their own one-man or one-woman shows by having a party and inviting people to come up and see their stuff. So, the mantra of that time—before the Maharishi came over and started merchandising "mantra"—was, "Where's the party?"

DREYER: That was the mantra here, too.

AMRAM: Which I think is pretty good; certainly develops the spirit and keeps the economic woes at a distance because they were "bring your own bottle" parties. BYOB. And people would bring something to drink or some potato chips or a new dance step or a poem they'd created, or their own charming selves, and show up and recite from Shakespeare or do just about anything.

And the painters would always have their paintings about eight or nine feet off the ground so that when the party really got cooking, they wouldn't have cigarette burns put on them or drinks spilled on them, and we'd just have a good ol' time.

And I was at one of these and a young man came up with a red-and-black-checkered shirt looking like a Canadian lumberjack and said, "Play for me." So I said "okay." I had my penny whistles and my French horn with me, and as soon as I began to play, it was like when I was playing with Mingus and Sonny Rollins, when I played with Dizzy and these great people, and a lot of other people no one ever heard of who were fantastic; the minute you started playing you just got that feeling that you were tuned into them and they were tuned into you. We just got taken to a different place.

And then he went running off and went dancing with some very nice woman and I was running around, and I kept bumping into him. Finally, he told me his name was Jack Kerouac, he was from Lowell, Massachusetts, small mill town; and I was from Feasterville, Pennsylvania, before we moved down south again. And he spoke French at home before he spoke English. My mom had translated French, so I loved the language as well. He had been a football player; I'd been a gym teacher when I was going to college as part of my extracurricular activities.

He loved Mozart and Shakespeare and jazz equally, and I did, too. And he was a wonderful, friendly, warm person. He would always find the most insecure person in the room and purposely hang out with them. He was very musical; he was a good scat singer. He could do that because he could hear it, he felt it, he respected it. He was one of the first writers I ever met who really understood jazz, because he could sing it and he would bash it out on the piano.

He was very musical and very respectful and a great listener. So, any time he was some place where you played, all the musicians knew that among the throngs of the somewhat stoned-out people, there was one person that was actually listening to what was happening, which made us play better.

So, all that being said, he finally had *On the Road* come out and in one night became a world-famous figure—and being very shy, and wanting to be considered to be a writer, he never could quite deal with that.

And as far as any kind of a "Beat movement," I never even knew there was such a thing until I began to read about it later on. That's why I wrote my book *Offbeat: Collaborating with Kerouac*, just as one person's viewpoint of what it was actually like, and what it was like after Jack passed away, and what it's like today.

Next month I'm going to London, England, another suburb of Austin—I guess it's west of Pflugerville—and they're showing the scroll that Jack wrote his tenth version of *On the Road*, the great big famous one with the twelve-foot sheets, all attached to a scroll. And I'm going to play a concert there of music from the era.

And I'm also going to include, as I do when I go to schools and do a "Cairo to Kerouac" program—they show the film *Pull My Daisy* that we made and then I have young people come up and not only read Kerouac but read their own poems, and get young musicians to come up—because what Jack believed in, and what I believe in, and which most people do, is that our gig is hopefully to inspire others to be creative and tell their story.

Everyone's born with a story, with a song, with a history, with a family, with a place that's unique. And, hopefully, what we can do is to make that person—or those people—feel, first of all, they visited the places we've been, and secondly, they can then tell us their story.

And that was what Beat was about. Jack said it was "beatific," not the negative stereotype of the stoned-out like, "Man, I hate everything." There was certainly a place for that and there are fans of the Marquis de Sade and the morbid and in a free society you can believe anything you want, but Jack Kerouac was much more than that.

He was the engine that pulled and continues to pull the train, and like Woody Guthrie and Will Rogers and so many other people, makes us see ourselves and treasure the place that we live. Treasure the blessings of our own country and all the people who live here and realize that we live in a global culture and we can all somehow join hands in some way, and that starts out by digging yourself and your own story.

DREYER: Okay. I understand that your acting career has been reborn; tell us about the Norman Mailer movie.

AMRAM: Well, in 1959, when I did the score and the title song for *Pull My Daisy*, with lyrics by Neal Cassady, Allen Ginsberg, and Jack, I was supposed to play Mezz McGillicuddy, the deranged French horn player. I said, "Well, what am I supposed to do, Jack?" He said, "Just be you." I said, "Wham, instant Stanislavski, make an actor without even having to go to school."

So, forty—no, fifty-two—years later, I got a call back for a film made by Matthew Barney, a fabulous painter, filmmaker, where they were going to have a wake for Norman Mailer, with real people like Larry Holmes, the ex-heavyweight-champion boxer; Dick Cavett [the talk show host]; and myself, who knew Norman, and restage a party where we would just kind of improvise our lines. And they also had Paul Giamatti and some great actors.

So, there I was in a movie playing me, more or less—a decrepit me with these fantastic actors. I was really embarrassed to be with these super pros, and they were all—Giamatti and all these great actors—were so cool and so nice and they were having such a good time being with people who respected them, that I actually said to Larry Holmes at one point, I said, "Man," I said, "This is so much fun. I think I'm going to get out of the music scene and be in the movies."

He said, "Man, it wouldn't be this much fun anyplace else, because everybody'd be in their trailer and wouldn't talk to any of us because they think they're better than we are." So, I realized Larry Holmes also had a very good appraisal of that way of egomaniacal, selfish, nasty, prima donna thinking.

I always tell kids that being a disrespectful, selfish, abusive creep is an overcrowded field in a nongrowth industry, so you've got to go the other way. And the beautiful thing about Texas that warms my heart every time I come here, and I just feel so good, is that that's definitely the Texas way. As long as you have some respect and appreciation and mind your manners, you can be anything and everybody will appreciate that.

DREYER: Got to mind your manners, though. What's going on now that you think is important culturally, especially in music?

AMRAM: Well, I believe that we are now no longer terminally incarcerated in what I call the Penitentiary of Bad Taste. With independent stations like this, with the internet, where you can go on YouTube and study some of the greatest things that ever happened—all of which are in the cut-out bins but which are not cut out on YouTube—you can find out that we can have a choice and realize that there are other things out there besides what we're told is all we deserve.

And that the beauties of the cultures of the world can now be accessible to people. And that's such a miraculous thing that I've become a vegetarian again, and I'm drinking a lot of green tea so I can live to be about 140, just to see all the great stuff that is being done every place I travel. Not only in the USA, but all over the world.

And if I could say one final thing. First, thank you for the station, thank you for what you all are doing to upgrade everybody's culture. And next month at Symphony Space in New York, I'm getting the second Pete and Toshie Seeger Power of Song Award, and they're going to show the world premiere of the film about me, *David Amram: The*

First 80 Years. And then all these wonderful people—Henry Butler and Paquita la del Barrio, Pete Seeger, and so many others, Tom Paxton and Peter Yarrow and some young classical players—are all going to play my music.

Poet and musician Ed Sanders. Photo by Miriam Sanders.

ED SANDERS

The only beatnik who can yodel.

Counterculture icon, acclaimed man of letters, and founder of the Fugs, Ed Sanders claims to be the only beatnik who can yodel.

Ed Sanders is a poet, singer, author, publisher, environmentalist, and political activist. He wrote the best-selling book The Family, *about the Charles Manson murders. Sanders has received a Guggenheim Fellowship, a National Endowment for the Arts fellowship, and an American Book Award. And he invents musical instruments, including the talking tie, featuring a keyboard down the front of a clip-on necktie.*

Ben Ratliff of the New York Times *says that Ed Sanders was "present at the counterculture's creation." He was a founder of the yippies, and, along with Tuli Kupferberg, he started the legendary satirical folk rock band the Fugs. He helped start the underground newspaper the* East Village Other. *He founded the Peace Eye Bookstore, in the Lower East Side of New York, where folks like William S. Burroughs and Allen Ginsberg hung out.*

Sanders wrote his first book, Poem from Jail, *on toilet paper after he was busted for attempting to swim out in the New London, Connecticut, harbor to board a nuclear submarine in protest. He was active in what was called the "Mimeograph Revolution," and now he says he's determined "to go out in a blaze of leaflets."*

SEPTEMBER 18, 2015

THORNE DREYER: Ed Sanders, how are you doing?

ED SANDERS: I'm doing fine. Nice day here in Woodstock, about eighty degrees or so.

DREYER: Well, we've got eight degrees on you. It's eighty-eight here.

There's so much to talk about. You are one of the most prolific human beings I know. You've made a serious mark and you're a very important American man of letters.

Ed, you sort of straddled the beatnik and hippie—we never called ourselves hippies, I never called myself a hippie—but that whole era, that whole movement. And a lot of people are looking back on it, historians are acknowledging it for its importance.

The underground press—which we were both involved in from the beginning—a lot of the papers are experiencing their fiftieth anniversary about now. *The Rag*'s fiftieth anniversary is next year. The *Los Angeles Free Press* was about two years ago. I guess the *East Village Other* is next year?

SANDERS: '66.

DREYER: '66. Okay, that's the same as *The Rag*. What a long strange trip it's been. How do you feel about what was happening then when you look back on it now?

SANDERS: We thought that things were going to change greatly in America. We thought there would be cradle-to-grave medical care and that there would be rent control for all and that guaranteed income would happen for everybody and then goof time—free, you know, everybody with a month's free vacation for all workers. Those were the type of things we thought that would happen in our lifetime. We were wrong.

But the underground press grew up because there were all of these web presses, these presses in many major cities that printed newspapers on big rolls of paper. And they were always looking to book new publications, so the underground presses just pasted up and burned their plates and were printed, just fitted themselves in. The *East Village Other* and the *Los Angeles Free Press* and others, *Great Speckled Bird*,

I don't know, many presses used these commercial printing operations because it only took an hour to print a whole two thousand copies of, say, the *East Village Other*—so there was just this availability.

And young people who took advantage of the opportunity and the low cost, you know, we sandwiched our publications into these giant presses in between church bulletins and auto repair catalogs and just whatever the commercial company would have, we would fit in and publish our things. It was then of course that the FBI got interested in stopping it, and then sort of toward the end of the '60s, they made a deliberate attempt to crush the underground press movement and it was pretty successful.

DREYER: I think this was in an NPR interview, you called the 1960s "a very fervent, fermenting era."

SANDERS: Yes.

DREYER: I remember it as being a time when just everything was larger than life and time almost stopped, stayed still. We actually thought we could change the world in real and basic ways. Part of the difference between what we did and what the Old Left had done was we thought that it also involved how you lived your life and the way you related to other people—and your inner life. I mean, obviously drugs came into play.

SANDERS: We thought people would wear primary colors for the next five hundred years and Merlin curved-toed shoes and Afghan vests that Jimi Hendrix wore and fancy shirts from London with wide collars, and we thought all that primary-color spectrum would take the day.

But there was a time in—I think it was around February of 1967—that, you know, in the South the crackers called us "walkers," civil rights walkers, "dirty beatniks." And then miraculously, in like the spring of '67, "dirty beatniks" was gone, and it was "dirty hippies." And people started letting their hair grow long. Then at the end of the '60s, the Beat attire came back. Basic black and turtlenecks and sandals never goes out of style for the avant-garde.

DREYER: It's a phenomenal thing, when we look at it now—how it *didn't* happen, you know.

SANDERS: Right.

DREYER: I mean, there was a lot that was done, there were a lot of changes that occurred. And we did some things out there in the real world, we actually helped stop the Vietnam War.

SANDERS: Right.

DREYER: What we didn't do is build anything that was really lasting.

SANDERS: We lost the battle of the textbooks. My generation, the generation that I associated with—the Beat Generation and the Black Mountain generation [from the 1930s through the 1950s, the experimental Black Mountain College produced a group of influential postmodern poets]—you know, they basically have lost their battle of being inserted into the textbooks as a prominent phenomenon. There's still a lot of books out, and publications, but the basic American textbook battle was lost.

And it's the same way they're trying to rewrite the origins of the Vietnam War now, you know. The American military has made a deliberate decision to rewrite the history of this ghastly, evil war that our nation conducted and make it into a justified march.

DREYER: One thing, too, in terms of history books is how we view the Civil War.

SANDERS: Right.

DREYER: The Confederate flag as an image is being attacked. But, you know, was the Civil War about states' rights, was it about a culture, maintaining a culture, or was it about slavery and racism? I mean, everything has complexity to it, obviously has some texture, but those things, I mean, we rewrite history.

How important is the way history is told by the historians? In Texas we have, obviously, problems with textbooks and those who approve them: the right wing, the Tea Party, especially, has been very active in trying to micromanage the way we teach history.

SANDERS: Well, it's like in the Ukraine now, they say World War II was a fight against the Soviet Union rather than the fight against Nazis. They try to twist the larger political narrative. Like somebody, you know, says, "Gee, I didn't know Paul McCartney was in a band before Wings." So history gets mishmashed, and sometimes deliberately.

DREYER: Our friend James McEnteer, who writes for *The Rag Blog* and who lives in Quito, Ecuador, went to Buenos Aires recently and said that it's all Beatlemania. He said the Beatles are everywhere right now in Buenos Aires. It's just a cultural explosion of Beatles and Beatledom.

SANDERS: It's like no one can play Bach for 150 years after he died—and then they learned how to play his music. So, music comes and goes, you know. I've been listening to a lot of Charlie Parker records, and wow, you know, I was a Mingus guy when I was a kid and I didn't really realize the great genius of Charlie Parker. So, we dip in and dip out of history and bring forth the best, you know.

DREYER: The beginning of the Beats was kind of a convergence of poetry and jazz, don't you think?

SANDERS: Right. Well, Kenneth Rexroth played jazz poetry and then Allen Ginsberg brought music to his readings for thirty years and Jack Kerouac was on *The Steve Allen Show*, reading poetry to Steve Allen. Steve Allen ran through it and said, "Okay, now that was a good rehearsal," and Kerouac said, "What do you mean rehearsal?" He walked out and that was the final take.

DREYER: Allen Ginsberg was a major influence on you—and a close friend, was he not?

SANDERS: Yes, we were close. He called me just hours before he died.

DREYER: But he also was an influence on your work, on your writing, on your poetry.

SANDERS: Yes. I always tell audiences that I would have wound up driving an Eskimo Pie truck in Kansas City if it wasn't for reading "Howl" when I was a senior in high school. You know, I memorized it and read it, screamed it. I lived in a rural area and there were cows in the field and I would screech "Howl" to those cows. I would drive around the county courthouse screaming "Howl" while my buddies would be drinking their beer.

So, then I came to New York City and, you know, that first line of "Howl"—"I saw the best minds of my generation"—I took that as marching orders for reaching out. So, I got to know Allen by just writing him a letter when he was in India. And I wrote Samuel Beckett and I wrote Burroughs, I wrote all the poets, I wrote Charles Olson, I became friends with Kerouac and Corso.

By reaching out and realizing that when I was young and still striving and had all this energy and didn't need to sleep—and, you know, sleep was something we just didn't do—and so I reached out and got to know all these people.

DREYER: I did an interview recently with the folks at City Lights Books, which has just observed an anniversary—sixty years, I think. But City Lights was incredibly important; it's continued throughout the years to be important, not only as a bookstore but a community center.

SANDERS: [Lawrence] Ferlinghetti turned it over, turned ownership over to the staff, you know—it's actually worker owned for the most part, I understand—a worker-owned enterprise. Ferlinghetti, who is now ninety-four, ninety-five, still gets around. [Ferlinghetti passed away in 2021 in San Francisco at the age of 101, six years after this interview.]

DREYER: I had a friend who saw him recently at the bookstore.

SANDERS: He still walks a lot, you know, he's a good exerciser. I admire him, and he had a great sense of what to publish and what not to publish. I'm eternally grateful for him publishing my first book, *Poem from Jail*, and Ferlinghetti also published my manifesto, *Investigative Poetry*, and so I'm eternally grateful to Ferlinghetti. And, you know, I see him around the circuit. He tours a lot.

DREYER: I want to talk about this in context with what you did with Peace Eye Bookstore, which is also very important in different ways and in a different kind of community, but we'll get to that in a minute, and we need to take a break.

[*A segment from conservative intellectual William Buckley's interview with Ed Sanders is played.*]

WILLIAM BUCKLEY: Mr. Ed Sanders is a musician, a poet, and a polemicist. He is one of the Fugs, a widely patronized combo. He has published four books of poetry and has vigorously preached pacifism for a number of years. I would just like to begin by asking Mr. Sanders whether we have serious terminological problems. For instance, are you a hippie, Mr. Sanders, and if not, wherein not?

ED SANDERS: Well, I'm not exactly a hippie. I mean, I have certain sentiments for that quote, "hippie movement," unquote. I would say that I'm different from the hippies in that I would have a more radical political solution to the problems of this part of the century. And I have my roots more strongly in, say, the classical tradition and in poetry and literature, rather than in dope and street sex.

[*Segment ends.*]

DREYER: Okay, that was when William Buckley had you and Jack Kerouac and—who was the third?

SANDERS: Lewis Yablonsky.

DREYER: Buckley is such a trip. What was that like, doing that show?

SANDERS: It was quite surreal. Jack Kerouac was very drunk and he kept smoking these little cigarillos and slugging down from a bottle of liquor. I told him that I respected him too much, I wasn't going to fight with him. We met in the elevator and he says, "You look like Ginsberg and you talk like Ginsberg and you write like Ginsberg." And I said to him, "Well, you know, I have a lot of respect for you, you impacted my life, I'm not going to fight with you."

And you know, he was—in the show—he was in the same checkered jacket that they buried him in about a year later after he drank himself to death. He was supporting Buckley for mayor of New York City, I think. And was pretty much a Nixon supporter. That was the split in the beatniks in 1960: Allen Ginsberg voted for John Kennedy and Jack Kerouac voted for Richard Nixon.

DREYER: The politics weren't really inherent in the Beat philosophy, were they?

SANDERS: No. Ginsberg was pretty political—he did hundreds, maybe as much as a thousand benefits for different causes during the last thirty or some years of his life.

Kerouac was desperately unhappy—but, you know, a very neat guy. He would call me up and read poetry to me and, you know, he would go by my bookstore on his way to visit Allen Ginsberg, who lived down the street from me, on Tenth Street.

And I never thought this guy would be so organized, but he left behind a magnificently well adorned set of files and manuscripts and letters. He kept everything, he was a pack rat, and he kept them at his mother's place. He kept an incredibly complicated personal archive. I wouldn't have thought it possible. But now it's there in the Berg Collection at the New York Public Library for anybody to read.

DREYER: How does it compare to what you have in your garage?

SANDERS: I have five hundred banker's boxes in three or four barns and it's all computerized. My goal is to be able to get anything from the past within a minute, so I can pretty well do that. I have, you know, all my files on the Manson case, on the Robert Kennedy assassination, on Sharon Tate, on the yippies, on all kinds of cases I've dug into. I have them all organized so I can get access to them.

So, I think I have a larger archive than Kerouac, but maybe not as big as Allen Ginsberg, who kept everything, including the tennis shoes he wore when he was in Czechoslovakia in '68—so he really kept everything.

DREYER: A friend of mine who I worked with on *Space City!* in Houston back in the late '60s, early '70s, went to New York and he ended up hanging out with Ginsberg for a while. And then, much later, he was doing some research, going through the Ginsberg archives. He came across some memo or document that mentioned him, Sherwood Bishop. Ginsberg says, "Sherwood Bishop was kind of an odd bird." And Sherwood said, "How wonderful, Allen Ginsberg calling *me* an odd bird."

SANDERS: So, well there's two—there's the landfill solution to an archive or there's a library solution. I mean, I often think of sending all my five hundred boxes to the landfill; it may be better for the world. But I've got it and I'll probably send it somewhere. Some college or institution will obtain it down the road, when I no longer need it.

DREYER: We were listening to "Kill for Peace" at the beginning of the show. The Fugs were an incredible phenomenon. "We are not the Mormon Tabernacle Choir," you said.

SANDERS: Right.

DREYER: You said, "We were the Fugs, we were not the Beach Boys. We were the Fugs. And we had our own pizzazz and energy and élan, especially early on; those old records just scream and steam with fun and joy and raising our fists to the sky to demand a new type of American reality."

I loved the Fugs, saw you guys live, and I'm amazed that there are people who don't even know about you. I mean, we have problems with history in this country, no kidding. And a lot of people don't know the role, the incredible role that the Fugs played, without really trying to play a role, I think.

SANDERS: It's easy to get lost in the moil and toil of time. Things are so complicated, and everything changes over. Try to listen to—try to watch your old Hi8 videotapes or listen to your old reel-to-reel tape recordings. I mean, things get turned over. It's like a big plow, a technology plow that plows everything under and then something new comes along. So, I don't mind. Plow me under, baby, I don't care.

You know, the Fugs—we did it as a joke. I mean, I thought I could have a quiet old age here in Woodstock, and nobody would know anything about my past. But people drive here to take pictures with me. I thought I could be free of the Fugs, but the Fugs are wrapped into my life all the way to Valhalla.

"I thought I could be free of the Fugs, but the Fugs are wrapped into my life all the way to Valhalla."

Which is fine, I don't care. You know, we made some mistakes. Some of our songs were not exactly politically correct in the ultimate sphere of things, but I just say, "Hey, we were a bunch of testosterone-crazed young men mainly from the Midwest and West and we have to be forgiven."

DREYER: We forgive you. And you just brought a lot of life and a lot of fun to a lot of people.

SANDERS: Well, Tuli Kupferberg was—I used to say Tuli was anarcho-Hasidic and I was Midwest rock and roll, and we formed our unison—and Ken Weaver, our drummer, was from El Paso, Texas. So, he brought a frontier, brilliant comedy line to the group. We melded together pretty well, I think. They say we're all walking the sword edge between coma and convulsion.

So, the Fugs danced along the sword edge of the '60s, coma and craziness on one side and chaos and convulsions on the other. And we did okay, you know; we survived, and we left behind art. A lot of people were great and brilliant, but they forgot to turn on the tape recorder. But we always made sure the tape recorder was turned on.

> **"And we did okay, you know; we survived, and we left behind art. A lot of people were great and brilliant, but they forgot to turn on the tape recorder. But we always made sure the tape recorder was turned on."**

DREYER: The tape recordings are important and the books are important. I mean, obviously books will be here forever, but people don't seem to read them very much now.

SANDERS: Well, there's still a lot of collectors. And vinyl records are coming back, so I don't know. Who knows? You do the best you can and then it's a shave and a haircut, two bits. That's the polite way of talking about one's funeral, so shave and a haircut, two bits.

You know, you go as long as you can, you try to do some good. I always tell people I'm going out in a blaze of leaflets. You can't forget to serve on committees, to protect the water and the environment, to do the boring thing of sitting in a town meeting and complaining. "Think globally and act locally" is an extremely difficult thing to do.

DREYER: What are you doing right now in terms of community involvement?

SANDERS: I'm on a water committee; we have an ancient, like 11,000 BC aquifer in downtown Woodstock that's where a glacier receded and left behind a hundred feet of sand and gravel which contains ten-thousand-year-old pure water. I'm on a committee that's going to write the rules to protect this aquifer. One thing, protect it from Poland Spring, from water companies who might want to come in and sell millions of gallons of this water in plastic jars.

I chaired the committee that wrote Woodstock's zoning laws quite a while ago, but it's held up and we protected—we put the wetlands on the maps and we made a bunch of environmental rules to keep Woodstock Woodstock. So, it's held up so far.

So, I don't know. It teaches you to reach out to your political enemies and realize they're always the same as you, really—humans, you know, with the same problems. And so, I reached to my political opponents, developers. Once you protect a piece of land and then the developers start adding up that you've cost them a hundred million dollars, say—then you have to reach out to them and show them the goodness of what you've done.

DREYER: Protecting aquifers is also a major preoccupation here in Austin.

SANDERS: Even right-wingers are realizing that once water's gone—once, say, fracking ruins an aquifer—that it's gone for hundreds of years. So, better to protect it now, to set up rules and regulations for property use and environmental use, and you'll have that water—not only your children but your great-great-great-great-grandchildren will have clean water.

DREYER: Hopefully, people will stop just seeing locally and will see globally.

SANDERS: Right.

DREYER: Or think globally.

The Peace Eye Bookstore. Lower East Side. Man, what a place it was. I lived there for a little while in the mid-'60s, and I know you said you lived there until there were a couple of murders outside your house and you finally moved.

SANDERS: Right.

DREYER: And now it's all, I guess, gentrified—it's just an extension of Greenwich Village.

SANDERS: Well, when I first moved to the Lower East Side in the early '60s, the World War II rent controls were still in place. A whole generation of activists in the '30s and '40s worked hard for the blessing of rent control to be placed all over New York City.

So, when I moved to the Lower East Side in 1962 or so, I could rent an apartment for twenty dollars a month, thirty dollars a month, forty dollars a month. The same apartments now get sold for a half-million dollars. It seems to me that a culture—a proper creative avant-garde culture—needs affordable housing almost before it needs cheap food.

The Lower East Side was this marvelous place and it was very diverse. There were Czechs, there were Polish people, there were Polish delis and diners there, there were Ukrainians, there were Blacks, there were Puerto Ricans, so it was a very diverse culture.

So, it was like paradise, and I was looking to form a bookstore in late '64 and early '65 and I found this old kosher meat market that had closed up and it had the words "Strictly Kosher" on the window and then the Yiddish for "Strictly Kosher." And so, I just left "Strictly Kosher" on the front window and added "Peace Eye Bookstore."

And living next to my new bookstore was the great Tuli Kupferberg— and one thing led to another. We founded the Fugs mainly to have a good time, and, too, I thought maybe I could earn a living through a combination of avant-garde bookstore and forming a singing group.

I wanted to call it the Yodeling Socialists, but Tuli had the great idea of calling it the Fugs, after the euphemism in Norman Mailer's novel *The Naked and the Dead*, and that caught on and it was just unrisqué enough that we could run it on ads and the radio stations would mention the word "Fugs." But it was right on the edge. Some people would not take ads from the Fugs, but most would.

So, then we started out, you know, we rehearsed in my bookstore and we started attracting people to the rehearsal and we began playing in art galleries. And Diane di Prima—a great poet who ran the American Theatre for Poets on Fourth Street—had a theater and we started playing there. And then we graduated to other theaters and wound up in the West Village on Bleecker Street at the Players Theatre, where we ran nine hundred performances and honed our act.

Meanwhile, Harry Smith—the folklorist, magician, filmmaker, artist—had a connection with Folkways Records and got us a contract to do a session under the guise that we were the Fugs Jug Band. And so, we went in and we got this gig to record as a jug band—and I erased the words "Jug Band" from the contract that they offered us. And that provided the material for our first two albums, you know.

Tuli and I founded the band and we slowly morphed it and warped it. None of us, as I said, went to Juilliard School, but we'd all gone through the Freedom Rides. Everybody had a guitar in their apartment in those days, so a lot of people sang together all the time. We were exposed to these great three-chord civil rights songs—"Ain't Gonna Study War No More" and "We Shall Overcome" and "Down by the Riverside."

And there was, at the same time, the "happening" movement, where you could rent a storefront and get a couple of people to take off their clothes and have somebody else dance in a bathtub full of overripe grapes and have a smoke maker, and you could charge admission for this phenomenon known as the "happening." So, we came out of the happening and the folk movement and we, you know, perfected our act.

We discovered electric guitar and we got Ludwig Drums to give us a free drum set, and so we honed our act and we attracted the attention, ultimately, of Reprise Records. And so Reprise played our demo tape for Frank Sinatra, who was the founder of Reprise, and Frank Sinatra said, "I guess you know what you're doing," and okayed the Fugs being on Reprise. We didn't know that for years later. Otherwise, on every one of our Reprise albums we would have put, you know, "Approved by Old Blue Eyes." We would have taken advantage.

DREYER: That's an endorsement.

SANDERS: Yeah, Blue Eyes endorsed it. So, anyway—one thing led to another. We finally did some concerts, we started touring, went to Europe a few times, and we went all over the United States. Sometimes we'd play a hall and we could never come back to play again because they took a listen to our lyrics. So, we could never rent Carnegie Hall—that was our big loss. In 1969 we did Rice Institute in Houston. We did a gig at Rice—and what was that, there was a club that Jim Franklin did the posters for in Austin?

DREYER: You're talking about Armadillo World Headquarters.

SANDERS: Yes. The Armadillo. We played the Armadillo, we played Rice, and then we did our final record and that was *Avenue A*, and we did a live album from the Fillmore East, and I decided that I just wanted to be a beatnik poet and I gave up the Fugs.

DREYER: Okay, beatnik poet, do a poem for us.

SANDERS: Okay.

"To the revolutionaries not yet born / I and all my comrades will falter, fail, fall / with the task unfin'd / but I call out to all the Workers of the Rose / to you, oh Revs of the Morrow / Take it onward! / Declare it! Name it! Work it! / a Permanent / cradle-to-grave society of the Sharing Rose / with freedom to speak, dream, act / & create / a place where there is no poverty / no class structure / and everyone has equal access to / the best medical care / where there is genuine protection of the environment / an organic food supply / & lots of personal freedom / That's it, oh Revs of the Morrow / Work in extra dimensions / Think a hundred years ahead / Enjoy your revolution / Show enough mercy so / that Mercy shows the way / & never give up 'til / war-hungry capital is gone / and the fields of sharing prevail."

DREYER: That's wonderful, I love that.

Our friend Ken Martin, who is an investigative reporter who publishes the *Austin Bulldog*, contacted us: he said, "Sounds like a great guest, I'm anxious to hear more about investigative poetry." So, there you go.

SANDERS: "Investigative poetry" means that poets should assume the role of describing historical events. Again, in ancient times, the poetry—the news of the civilization was carried by poetry, by the plays of Aristophanes, by Homer's *Iliad* and *Odyssey*—they used to recite Herodotus at the Olympics. They would have "Herodotus the Historian" contests.

So, that is to use the ancient role of poetry in describing historical events, bring it to modern times.

So, I wrote this manifesto in 1976, that City Lights Books published, to my gratitude. And since then I've written the poetry and life of Allen Ginsberg in poetry form. I wrote a biography of Anton Chekhov in poetry form. *America: A History in Verse, 1900 through 1970* has been published in three volumes. I've written *1968: A History in Verse*, all written in poetry form. And now I'm working on the final years of the life of Robert Kennedy, in poetry form; it's called an investigative poem. And *The Final Years of Robert Kennedy* is now about three hundred pages long; I've been working on it for thirty years and I'm trying to finish it up with final investigative work.

When the *New Yorker* does a profile of somebody, why couldn't it be in poetry form? Why do you have to give some writer a lot of money to write a prose history of something when you could assign a poet?

DREYER: When you could get a poet to do it cheap. No, I'm kidding.

SANDERS: You could get a poet to do it for a fee similar to what a regular prose writer would. It's just a way for poets to earn money. Because most people would rather go to a dentist than listen to a poem. So, the idea is to make poetry more accessible and more familiar to people. So, I don't know—investigative poetry.

DREYER: But on the prose side, *The Family*, about Charles Manson and the murders, was an absolutely riveting book. And you're releasing a biography of Sharon Tate [a promising actress who was murdered by the Manson Family in 1969]. How did you get interested in that?

SANDERS: All through the '60s, I had trained myself never to look a cop in the eye and to try to hide your joint as you walk past them. But when I wrote about the Manson Family—the first edition was published in 1971—I had to become friends with cops and investigators. And I learned that many of them are liberals and are not crushers and violent, but they are decent human beings and worthy of being.

So, I became friends with a lot of these cops and I learned some things from police sources after my book came out, about Sharon Tate. And possibly that Manson took the contract to kill her because of something she had learned about Sirhan Sirhan. So, I investigated that, and I put some of that material in my biography of Sharon Tate that's coming out in December from Da Capo Press.

DREYER: You do a television show?

SANDERS: I do a Saturday evening half-hour show about local Woodstock politics, and I also run a lot of music from the Fugs and from my own songs. But I also cover the nitty-gritty of sewer politics or the need for solar in Woodstock or the protection of the water in Woodstock, you know. So, yeah, I do that. I've been doing it for many years because "think globally and act locally" means you've got to get down in the trenches. And argue it out with all kinds of political persuasion.

DREYER: All right. You were involved with Jerry [Rubin] and Abbie [Hoffman] and Paul Krassner and Stew Albert and Judy Gumbo in starting the yippies.

SANDERS: Yeah.

DREYER: Which was, you know, a different kind of political organization. It was really political theater. Sometimes personality run, but it did some amazing things.

SANDERS: Right.

DREYER: And then you were involved in a lot of public political things like, for instance, where you swam out into the harbor [in New London, Connecticut]. Tell us about that.

SANDERS: They were launching these submarines with missile silos and each silo—I think twelve or sixteen silos—had a huge intercontinental missile with multiple warheads. Each warhead being programed to destroy a specific Russian city. So, I got together with people from a group called Polaris Action and we tried to swim out and board a Polaris submarine as it was being launched. And my goal was to get on the submarine and either vigil on top of one of these silos, nuclear silos, or, you know, maybe to try to open it up and spill salt water on it.

But we weren't allowed. They had the frogmen with ropes attached to them, and the frogmen wore flippers. So, we had no chance. They roped us in and threw us up on a barge. We then went around back in front of the submarine launching place and we sat in, and we were sent to jail. And it was in this jail in 1961, in the summer, that I wrote my first book, *Poem from Jail*, which Lawrence Ferlinghetti, to my gratitude, published a couple of years later.

DREYER: One of my greatest regrets is that you guys were not able to levitate the Pentagon.

SANDERS: Well, we did. We raised it, but we forgot to rotate it. We didn't rotate it, which, you know—that was the flaw. I mean, just raising it, that was nothing. We needed to rotate it.

DREYER: Well, I saw it go up just a little bit.

SANDERS: Yeah, well, you know, it depends on how stoned you were.

DREYER: Yeah.

SANDERS: But we forgot to twist it. That would have screwed it up really for the long term. But we just, you know, it plopped back down.

DREYER: That was quite a series of events—when we stormed through the police barricades and surrounded the Pentagon.

SANDERS: Yeah, it was a remarkable set of acts.

POLITICIANS

Senator Bernie Sanders speaks to a packed house at an Austin town meeting on March 31, 2015. Four days earlier, he joined us from Washington on *Rag Radio*. Photo by Alan Pogue.

BERNIE SANDERS

Changing politics as we know it.

In an exclusive interview, Bernie Sanders elaborated on themes that would soon highlight his first presidential campaign.

On March 27, 2015, during the height of speculation that he would soon announce his candidacy for president of the United States, Senator Bernard "Bernie" Sanders of Vermont joined us on Rag Radio *by telephone from Washington, DC. Four days later Sanders appeared at a rousing town meeting in Austin, and less than a month after that, on Thursday, April 30, Senator Sanders officially announced that he would challenge Hillary Clinton for the Democratic nomination, a run that would defy all expectations.*

Bernie Sanders would not become the Democratic Party nominee for president in 2016 (or in 2020, when he ran a second time), but he would greatly impact the political conversation, revolutionize campaign finance with his focus on small individual donations, and give Hillary Clinton a serious run for her money.

MARCH 27, 2015

THORNE DREYER: Senator Bernie Sanders, how are you?

BERNIE SANDERS: Good. I am wonderful, how are you?

DREYER: Okay. Glad to have you with us. This is an honor.

Bernie Sanders has been a leading voice in the US Senate, leading progressive voice, who is known for his outspoken advocacy for issues like income inequality and big money in politics, climate change, veterans' interests, and a whole lot more.

And we also know that Senator Sanders, Bernie, has been for some time considering—and has been frequently mentioned—as a candidate for president. And has admitted that he's looking into the possibility.

So, welcome to *Rag Radio*, Senator Bernie Sanders.

SANDERS: Well, thank you very much, it's great to be with you.

DREYER: It's going to be great to have you here in Austin, and I look forward to seeing you in person. But I have to ask you, are you going to try to catch some of that Austin music while you're here?

SANDERS: If we can, I would love to do it.

DREYER: There's a whole lot of it.

SANDERS: I know about it. You've got a great town there. I come from Burlington, Vermont, which we're very proud of, but Austin is a beautiful town.

DREYER: I should mention that you were mayor of Burlington—and had a sterling record as mayor of Burlington—and then spent sixteen years serving Vermont as its only congressman before moving into the Senate, where you've been a leading voice for those of us who believe we need some basic change, and especially towards economic populism.

Okay, I have to ask you—I would be remiss not to ask you at this point—what your current considerations are. For all I know, maybe you had your voilà moment on the way to the phone and you're going to announce right now to our audience that you're running for president.

SANDERS: [*Chuckles*] No, I'm afraid that's not going to be the case.

As I've said before, I am very proud and happy to be the senator from the state of Vermont. We have a great state and I enjoy being senator from Vermont.

On the other hand, what I recognize is that in this country today we probably have more serious problems than we have had since the Great Depression. We have a middle class which for the last forty years has been in decline, and you've got millions of people who are working longer hours for low wages, and we have a grotesque level of income and wealth inequality, just grotesque.

You know, you're talking about 99 percent of all new income today going into the pockets of the top 1 percent. You have the top one-tenth of 1 percent owning more wealth than the bottom 90 percent. You have one family, the Walton family, owning more wealth than the bottom 22 percent of the American people.

And you've got friends like the Koch brothers, who are the second-wealthiest family in the country, you know, prepared to spend more money than either the Democratic or the Republican Parties on the next election, to push forward an extreme right-wing agenda, which represents the very, very wealthiest people in this country and decimates programs for the vast majority of the people.

So, when you look—and then throw in climate change and throw in the fact that we're the only major country not to have a national health care program guaranteeing health care for all people—there is a real gap in American politics, and we need people to stand up and say, "Enough is enough." Everything cannot go to just the top 1 percent. We need to create an economy that works for the middle class and working families. We need to address the serious problems of poverty in America. We need to make college affordable for our young people. Those are the issues that people feel passionately about.

". . . there is a real gap in American politics, and we need people to stand up and say, 'Enough is enough.' Everything cannot go to just the top 1 percent."

And what I have to weigh is whether or not one could put together—in terms of fundraising and in terms of a grassroots political infrastructure—the kind of support that we need to run a serious and winning campaign. And that's kind of what we're looking at now.

DREYER: You only spent $4,000 to win the mayor position in Burlington. But we're looking at what could well be the most expensive campaign ever, in the history of this country, with the 2016 presidential election.

SANDERS: I don't think there's much debate about it. It will be the most expensive. And it's just very, very hard to run a credible campaign without raising hundreds of millions of dollars, and, you know, one of the issues that we have to be frank about is that the people who support me are not going to come to fundraisers where they're going to chip in a million dollars apiece to support the candidate of their choice.

Most of the people who support me are working-class, middle-class people, don't have a lot of money. So, can we raise the hundreds of millions of dollars you need through small campaign contributions? And that's just one of the issues we're looking at.

DREYER: And of course, you've never been one who likes to call big donors . . .

SANDERS: No.

DREYER: . . . Or work through PACs, especially super PACs.

SANDERS: No, I don't. We do receive PAC money, and I have from the unions and environmental groups, and I'm proud of that. But just to get on the phone and call up rich people: no.

What we have right now, increasingly, and I saw it last night on the floor of the Senate with the debate over the budget—this disastrous Republican budget—is that it's clear to anybody who has eyes that the Congress now works precisely on behalf of the people that make the campaign contributions. That's about it. And, you know, the rich—and now it's not only the rich, it's the super, super rich—who really control the political agenda.

When, for example, you're talking about climate change, it's not that all these Republicans are dummies and they can't read, and they don't know what the scientific community is saying. What they have to do is weigh what the scientists are saying with what the Koch brothers and what the big oil companies, the big coal companies are saying. Those are real campaign contributions.

So most of them say, "Well, I'm not a scientist, I don't know if climate change is real." Of course they know it's real. But they also know that if they speak up and say what is, in fact, true, they're not going to get the huge sums of money they need to get elected.

DREYER: So what do we do?

SANDERS: Look, the only way that I know that will move this country forward—and by moving the country forward, I mean the need to create millions of decent-paying jobs, because real unemployment is not five and a half percent, it's 11 percent if you include those people who have given up looking for work or are working part time when they want to work full time.

All right, how do you do that? How do you raise the minimum wage to a living wage? My view is that over a period of years, you would bring the minimum wage up to fifteen dollars an hour so that nobody in America lives in poverty.

How do you do that? How do you deal with pay-equity issues where women today are making seventy-eight cents on the dollar compared to men? How do you deal with the overtime issue? Not a widely known issue, but as a result of the antiquated fair-labor standards, you have people working at McDonald's who make $25,000 a year who are working sixty hours a week. They don't get overtime. And we've got to change that.

So how do you deal with inequality in America, where you have billionaires paying a lower effective tax rate than a nurse or a truck driver? How do you deal with the fact that corporations are stashing hundreds of hundreds of hundreds of billions of dollars in tax havens like the Cayman Islands and Bermuda and not paying any federal income taxes?

So, then we run up a deficit, and the Republicans say, "Oh, well, we've got to cut Social Security, Medicare, and Medicaid—and education—in order to deal with the deficit." Which is caused by the fact that we went to war and we forgot to pay for it and we give tax breaks to the rich. How do you deal with all these things?

And the answer is there's only one way to deal with it, only one way, and that is you—we need to put together a mass grassroots effort involving millions of working people, low-income people, who are prepared to get heavily involved in the political process, prepared to stand up and fight for their kids, are prepared to stand up and take on this incredibly powerful billionaire class which owns much of our economy, owns, you know, significantly, the Republican Party and part of the Democratic Party and also a lot of the media.

When you ask, am I running for president—those are the challenges that are out there. And if you'll honestly look at it, you can say, "Well, you know what, I don't know how you confront those. I don't know if you can confront those things, I don't know how you'd do it."

You've got to be honest about it. I think that's the last thing in the world you want to do is run a campaign which is ineffective. That would be the worst thing. So, those are some of the issues that I'm dealing with.

DREYER: What if you ran a campaign but you were not able to raise the kind of money needed to win, but you brought those issues out to the fore and perhaps moved—let's say the candidate is Hillary Clinton—moved her to the left? Or, if we don't want to call it the left, brought some of those issues into the mainstream dialogue?

SANDERS: The answer is, if you run, you run to win. But not everybody wins. The point is running a credible campaign. I have run strong credible campaigns in which I lost, and I was proud of those efforts. I've run campaigns which I won and was not proud of the effort. I'm familiar with politics from the state of Vermont: that I know how to do pretty well. But when you have fifty states, and you've got 320 million people, can we get millions of people involved? Are people sufficiently motivated or are they too demoralized?

The fear that I would have is, if you don't do it well, it's better not to be done, because it would disparage the views that we hold. I think this country needs to join the rest of the world through a national health care program. But if you run and I carry that banner and I do badly, then our opposition says, "See, nobody really agrees with that. Nobody thinks we need to change national priorities in America. Nobody thinks we need to have the rich and large corporations pay more in taxes.

Nobody thinks we need to make college affordable." And that's what I don't want to do.

So, what we are weighing right now—and one of the reasons I'll be excited to be in Texas, and California before that, and in Chicago after that—is just to get a sense for how people feel. Are they prepared to jump into a strong grassroots effort? That's kind of what I want to ascertain.

What do you think? Do you think there is the energy out there or not?

DREYER: I think there's a lot of energy out there, and I think that one of the problems that people have with the Democratic Party is that it doesn't seem to have a vision and there's no one that seems to be pushing a vision—and maybe the populist wing is the only place where there are real ideas.

But I absolutely think there's lots of grassroots activity. Jim Hightower was on our show a couple of weeks ago and talked about all the grassroots efforts that are happening in lots of different areas, whether it be labor or it be the Moral Mondays movement [civil disobedience protests started in 2013 by Reverend William Barber and other progressive religious figures], or the Keystone Pipeline movement [protests against the oil pipeline system that runs from Alberta, Canada, to Texas]. And he thinks that those things are coming together into a serious grassroots populist movement. I think that that energy is there—and that a lot of it is outside the electoral system.

SANDERS: By the way—Jim, he's an old and dear friend of mine, and I guess you should be very proud of your local agitator in Austin.

DREYER: Yes.

SANDERS: And I think, and I hope, that Jim is right.

I just literally an hour or two ago spoke to a group of young students—college students who are part of the National Student Association—who are fighting now for free tuition in public colleges and universities and lowering student debt, which is a huge issue in this country. And I think Jim is right in the sense that we have to bring all of these folks together into a powerful political movement.

What does make me optimistic is that on issue after issue what we find is, in fact, the American people are not as divided as the pundits

> "What does make me optimistic is that on issue after issue what we find is, in fact, the American people are not as divided as the pundits tell us that we are."

tell us that we are. People want to raise the minimum wage, they want to create jobs, they want to deal with climate change, they want to make college affordable. They are outraged by the greed of the top 1 percent and the grotesque level of income and wealth inequality.

The challenge—which is not an easy challenge—is to bring people together around that progressive agenda, get people who are demoralized about the political process. Here in this last election in November, you had 63 percent of the American people not voting; 63 percent. You had 80 percent of young people not voting. How do we, in fact, make people aware of the importance of politics and get them involved in that?

DREYER: One of the things we face, too, is not only making people think it matters but making people think that they can actually have an effect on what happens.

SANDERS: Right.

DREYER: And so, I would ask you—with *Citizens United* [the landmark Supreme Court decision about campaign finance], with all the incredible gerrymandering, and I would say the Republicans' tendency to try to consolidate power, state power, with all these different voting rights issues—how much of an obstacle is that?

SANDERS: Huge. I mean, it's huge. Before you go to war you've got to know what your opponent is, who they are, and their strengths and weaknesses. These guys are extraordinarily powerful. I mean, they're powerful in the sense of their control over the economy, where you have on Wall Street six financial institutions that have assets of over 60 percent of the GDP of the United States of America. They write two-thirds of the credit, issue two-thirds of the credit cards and half the mortgages in America. Think that's power?

You have the Koch brothers, who are worth $85 billion, who are prepared to put not only money into campaigns—they go beyond that. They are involved in the universities, they are involved in think tanks, they are involved in media. Their goal is to make a counterrevolution in America and move us back to the 1920s—enormously powerful, smart people, well organized. They have a database, a political database now, which is stronger than the Republican Party.

And what their agenda is about is literally to repeal every piece of legislation passed in the last eighty years. Social Security, Medicare, Medicaid, education, do away with the concept of minimum wage, climate change. They are funding all of the climate deniers. They're very powerful people.

Then you have—as you've indicated—the Republicans understand that their ideas are not widely supported when people know their ideas. So, what you've got to do is make it harder for poor people, people of color, all the people to vote. So, you engage in voter suppression efforts, they engage in outrageous gerrymandering. Gerrymandering is not a new idea. Republicans in the last few years are not the inventors of the concept, but they have taken it to a whole new level, which is what they do.

And then, in terms of media. I'll give an example of something. At four o'clock in the morning last night, I voted on the budget. That budget includes the ending, the repealing of the Affordable Care Act, Obamacare. It also calls for $440 billion cuts in Medicaid. If you add that together with the repeal of the Affordable Care Act, twenty-six million Americans would lose their health insurance, and with the cuts in Medicaid, eleven million Americans would lose their health insurance.

That's twenty-seven million Americans, based on the vote last night, if that were to be implemented—which it will not—twenty-seven million Americans would lose their health insurance because of the Republican budget. Do you think that might be a front-page story in every paper in America?

DREYER: No.

SANDERS: Well then, do you think it should be a front-page story?

DREYER: Yes.

SANDERS: Have you read one word about that?

DREYER: No. It's good, I'm going to be your chorus.

SANDERS: You know, so this is what we're up against. In other words, Republicans can pretty much do what they want to do. For all twelve people who were watching C-SPAN last night at three in the morning, they saw it. But the papers don't cover this stuff for a variety of reasons. Significantly, because of corporate control over the media. You look at this Trans-Pacific Partnership trade agreement: do you know how much time the major networks have devoted to that?

DREYER: No. I'm trying to come in on my cue here.

SANDERS: All right. We'll make it, we're a good team here.

DREYER: Yes, yes.

SANDERS: I'll lay it out and you say "no." That's your job, okay?

DREYER: Okay, I got it.

SANDERS: You got it?

DREYER: Yeah. I don't even need to practice.

SANDERS: But this is what you've got. You have the most important trade agreement in the history of the United States of America, which had zero discussion on the major networks on television. So, I mean, how do you break through all that stuff?

Well, you guys—and by the way, congratulations for having a cooperative radio show that talks about real issues that impact real people. We need to multiply what you do by a million times, and, you know, we have a lot of good websites out there. But these are the kinds of fights that we have to wage.

DREYER: And it's a task. When you talked about the health care law—and the ones who really seem to right now have the power to get rid of it—that would be the Supreme Court. Do you have a feel for what's going to happen there?

SANDERS: I don't. You know, it comes down to one judge or something and I can't speculate what he's going to do. But you know, what I can tell you is that this Supreme Court has been a disaster, has undermined democracy, and has been working day and night for the wealthiest and most powerful people in this country.

I think the *Citizens United* decision alone will probably go down as one of the worst decisions ever made by a Supreme Court. It essentially tells the billionaires, "Hey, you own much of the economy, now you can own the United States Government." And they are seizing that opportunity big time.

DREYER: Okay. We just have a couple of minutes left. I wish you could stay with us for a couple of hours, but maybe we'll do it again sometime. But let me leave with this: one of the things that freaks the Republicans out, especially, is the concept of redistribution of income, redistribution of wealth, and they don't seem to have a problem with it when it's from the bottom up.

SANDERS: Yeah. That is exactly right.

DREYER: Do we need to redistribute wealth in this country?

SANDERS: Do we? Of course we do. You know, your point is well taken, and people don't know it. But from 1985 to the present, there have been trillions of dollars of wealth, trillions of dollars of welfare that have been redistributed from working families to the top one-tenth of 1 percent. Let me just mention one factor, and maybe we'll end on this note.

We just discovered—it was actually in *Forbes* magazine—between 2013 and 2015, two-year period, the wealthiest fourteen people in this country, and that is Bill Gates and Warren Buffett and the Koch Brothers and a bunch of others, the wealthiest fourteen people in this country saw an increase in their wealth in a two-year period of $157 billion. An *increase* in their wealth. That is more money than the bottom 40 percent of the American people have, and that's in a two-year period.

So, do we need to redistribute wealth back to the working families of this country? Many of them have $2,000 in the bank or nothing in the bank, and many of them would go under if they had an automobile accident or a divorce or a serious illness. Of course we do.

Let me just end on this note: this country is moving pretty rapidly toward an oligarchic form of society where a small number of people have incredible wealth, incredible economic power, and incredible political power, where ordinary people have no political power, have no money, and certainly very little economic power.

That is not the kind of country I think most Americans want to live in, and that's the struggle that we face right now.

DREYER: Okay. Thank you so much.

SANDERS: Nice to chat with you.

DREYER: Senator Bernie Sanders, thank you for being with us on *Rag Radio*.

SANDERS: Bye-bye.

Progressive populist pundit Jim Hightower has been our guest on *Rag Radio* ten times. This picture was taken at the KOOP radio studios in 2016. Photo by Roger Baker.

JIM HIGHTOWER

A corporation is not a person until Texas executes one.

Jim Hightower riffs on "tinkle down" economics, the crime of privatization, and the rich history of Texas populism.

Jim Hightower is a progressive populist commentator, an orator, a political activist, and a New York Times *best-selling author. Serving as Texas agriculture commissioner from 1983 to 1991, Jim was narrowly defeated by Rick Perry in his run for a third term, giving Perry his first shot at statewide office. A Bernie Sanders surrogate during Sanders's presidential campaigns, Hightower is on the board of directors of Our Revolution.*

Hightower, a former editor of the Texas Observer, *publishes a monthly populist newsletter, the* Hightower Lowdown, *that has close to 150,000 subscribers, writes a newspaper column distributed nationally by Creators Syndicate, and does syndicated radio commentary. Hightower's books include* Swim against the Current, Thieves in High Places, *and* There's Nothing in the Middle of the Road but Yellow Stripes and Dead Armadillos.

Jim Hightower was born in Denison, Texas, and now lives in Austin. I've known him for many years, dating back to the mid-'60s, when he was editing the Observer. *He has been a frequent guest on* Rag Radio, *but this interview is taken from his very first visit. At the time, the United States was experiencing what Hightower characterized as a "populist moment." The Occupy movement—which started with Occupy Wall Street in September 2011—helped transform the country's perceptions about wealth disparity and brought the term "the 1 percent" into common parlance.*

APRIL 6, 2012

THORNE DREYER: Molly Ivins said, "If Will Rogers and Mother Jones had a baby, Jim Hightower would be that rambunctious child—mad as hell, with a sense of humor."

Jim, it's an honor to have you on *Rag Radio*.

JIM HIGHTOWER: Oh, my joy to be here. This is terrific—and right in the coop of KOOP radio.

DREYER: Right in the chicken coop here. And we should mention that we're free-range community radio.

HIGHTOWER: I appreciate the chicken wire across the windows there so we can't get beer bottles thrown at us.

DREYER: You once wrote that any small dog can raise his leg on any tall building.

HIGHTOWER: Right.

DREYER: And we might extrapolate from that: if we got a whole bunch of dogs together . . .

HIGHTOWER: There you go.

DREYER: . . . And if they understood their power, the power of their bark—that they could surround that building, and, well, I should let a sleeping metaphor lie.

Jim, you are perhaps the best-known progressive populist thinker in this country, and populism is a fascinating thing. It has a grand tradition, a grand history—and especially in Texas.

I would like for you to tell us what you mean by "populist." Populism has been applied to lots of different kinds of movements. Sarah Palin. The Tea Party was called populist, which is kind of odd since it was actually bought out by right-wing corporate think tanks. But George

Wallace and a lot of white-supremacist and conspiracist movements in the past have been labeled as populist.

I would like to know what populism means to you and if you think that true populism has a class nature to it and is inherently progressive.

HIGHTOWER: Bingo. It definitely has class and it is very, very progressive. You know, there's an old saying. You could question somebody and say, "How many legs does a dog have if you count its tail?" "Well, four, because calling a tail a leg doesn't make it one."

Well, that's the same as Sarah Palin claiming to be a populist. She can call herself one, but she's not, because populism is about taking on the entrenched power of money. And that's where populism came from in this country, right after the Civil War. That has been its history throughout: that it takes on the concentrated power of corporations and big financial institutions, Wall Street.

". . . populism is about confronting money and power in our society and realizing that too few people control too much of the money and power and they're using that control to get more for themselves at our expense."

And if you're not doing that then you're not a populist. You might have populist elements in your movement; certainly George Wallace did, for example. But again, populism is about confronting money and power in our society and realizing that too few people control too much of the money and power and they're using that control to get more for themselves at our expense. And that pretty well defines what's happening today.

I think we're in a big populist moment in America right now. Wall Street—the corporate executives—are doing extremely well while the working class gets knocked down. The latest numbers were out on unemployment and it's lower than they anticipated. Lower in part because more and more people have given up even looking for a job, there are so few out there. And it's just debilitating to keep batting your head against that wall.

More importantly—as importantly—are the underemployed, the vast majority of folks in this country who are working part time or taking lower wages or not being able to get the kind of work that they're qualified to do. That's a very, very weak economy.

So, the few are doing extremely well. But you know, they seem to think that they can separate their well-being from the good fortunes of the many. And that's not America. They get to thinking they're the top dogs and we're just a bunch of fire hydrants out here in the countryside. That's really the way that their economic policy—which I call "tinkle down"—we went from Ronald Reagan's "trickle down" to the Koch brothers' "tinkle down" economics in this country in a pretty short period of time.

DREYER: We're still here with our dog-leg-raising metaphor.

HIGHTOWER: Yes. And I think that's what the rebellion is about. That's what Occupy has been all about, the inequality, the disrespect, the knocking down of the middle class. And that's what the Wisconsin rebellion was. [The Wisconsin protests of 2011 centered on opposition to legislation prohibiting collective bargaining in the public sector.] I was at that big rally in February a year ago in Madison, Wisconsin—150,000 people. We spoke from a platform at the state capitol, and just as far as you could see were people—and it was twenty degrees, snow on the ground. Not only workers were there—there was a tractor-cade of farmers going around.

It was just a beautifully spirited moment because that right-wing nutball governor of theirs, fueled by the Koch Brothers and some of the Koch-funded front groups, decided he could just pull the props out from under the middle class and nobody would pay any attention.

DREYER: It turned out people were paying attention.

HIGHTOWER: There was a great sign that a woman held, which I saw as I was speaking. They had a bunch of homemade signs and this sign said, "You screw us, we reproduce." And that certainly is happening all across the country.

DREYER: There you go. But we reformed Wall Street, didn't we? What's the problem?

HIGHTOWER: Yeah, we did such a good job of that—but they're balking even at the little minor wrist slaps that were put on them. And, in fact, Congress passed and Obama signed a law that they call the Jobs Act. Now that's adding insult to injury because the act doesn't create a single job and in fact the word "jobs" is not actually in the act.

"Jobs" is an acronym that is basically about business. It's done in the name of small business, but it defines small as a billion dollars a year in sales. So, in the name of small business, in the name of jobs, all the benefits go to the speculators and the corporate interests in our country.

So, these kinds of frauds are wearing people down, and that's why I think we have a strong populist moment, a strong populist possibility to make fundamental change. Not just to regulate Wall Street with little puny regulations—and they've got hordes of lawyers that specialize in finding the loopholes in regulations—but restructuring Wall Street.

We have plenty of banks in this country and right here in Austin—credit unions and community banks—that can do the job of actually making loans to enterprises that create jobs and create genuine economic activity at a local level.

Why in the world would we allow Citigroup and Goldman Sachs and JPMorgan Chase and the rest of them to actually concentrate power after they had stiffed us, rather than taking that power away from them and decentralizing that money out to the countryside, where it could do some good? There's the old saying, Thorne, that "money is like manure. It only helps if you spread it around."

DREYER: The Occupy movement was certainly a response to the discrepancy in income and wealth in this country, and then spread out to other issues. And it certainly created some increase in class consciousness. How important do you think that movement was?

HIGHTOWER: Oh, it's extraordinarily important. It ignited the imagination of the American people. And no matter what their numbers were in the actual camps last fall, the public support for them was overwhelming. I said, "Yeah, these people get it. That's exactly what we're talking about."

The Wall Street bailout was the initial spark for the Tea Party movement, and it got captured by Dick Armey—a lobbyist, Koch-funded organizer, a Republican organizer in Washington, a former member of Congress out of Denton, Texas. And Armey captured the whole thing and turned it into a right-wing Republican corporate-hugging organization that just dismayed the rank and file of the Tea Party.

I'm kind of a lucky duck: I do a lot of traveling and speechifying around. And one great event, for example, is in Wisconsin every year. It's called the Fighting Bob Fest and it's for "Fighting Bob" La Follette, who was a great progressive leader, founder of the Progressive Party in the 1910s and '20s, ran for president and got about 25 percent of the vote as a third-party candidate. But that spirit of "Fighting Bob" lives in this festival.

We had a model of it here about a decade ago called the Rolling Thunder Down-Home Democracy Tour. We had it here in Austin [in 2002]; we had five or six thousand people out there and then we took that on the road some. But Wisconsin kept it up and it's a daylong festival of politics. They had speeches by all sorts of folks, some US senators but also people like Cornel West and other great speakers.

But they also have fun. They've learned how to put the party back in politics. They've got about twenty restaurants doing food all day long, and they've got more than a hundred community groups organizing people. They have an actual breakout session where the people themselves come up with an agenda to take to the legislature.

Why let the lobbyists and the politicians decide the agenda all the time? People themselves can do that—and they've won some of those fights. And they have great music and, of course, the Wisconsin beer. You've got to lubricate the movement, as you know.

"Why let the lobbyists and the politicians decide the agenda all the time? People themselves can do that—and they've won some of those fights."

You know, I was down in Sugar Land, Texas, the home of [disgraced former US congressman] Tom DeLay, last fall, and they've got a progressive coalition organized down there, particularly among Asian Americans, because there's been a huge population growth in that community there—a population that's not been paid attention to, really, by either political party. But now they're doing that.

You know, DeLay—when he got indicted here in Austin—I saw a guy on TV, one of his fellow Republicans, say, "Well, sometimes Tom's his own worst enemy." And I said, "Not while I'm alive he's not."

DREYER: There's a lot of stuff happening. One thing—and it's under the radar—is all of this counterinstitutional and cooperative worker activity all over the country. That people are not that aware of.

HIGHTOWER: I did a *Hightower Lowdown* issue on co-ops—which, of course, this radio station is one of. The air we're on at this very moment. Along with Wheatsville Co-op—and I'm a member of the Black Star, which is the first cooperatively owned, worker-managed co-op brewpub in the country. [Wheatsville and Black Star are both in Austin.]

And all of the co-ops cooperate, which is very, very important, you know. They get together, they help each other out, and through that coalition effort you gain more strength than you individually would have. So, the co-op movement is extraordinary in this country, and there's very little coverage of it.

DREYER: Carl Davidson was here and we did a whole show about the Mondragon Corporation in the Basque region of Spain, with their cooperative model, which has had some impact in this country.

HIGHTOWER: They're here working up in Ohio right now in particular. The steelworkers' union has been very active in that—and they have done some very, very strong work. So, you know, that is a role model for us, the whole co-op movement. And that gets us to populism because that was the economic model that made that movement succeed.

And it's an alternative both to just hard-core socialism, government ownership—and then an alternative to corporate management of the free-enterprise economy. This is a cooperative management, democratic management of a free-enterprise economy. And it just works beautifully and is so important and it's thriving in this country.

So, we've got plenty of models that we can go to and it gives us an alternative to be able to go to people and say, "Yeah, here's another way to organize it." It doesn't have to be the CEO, you know, getting $50 million a year and workers having their wages knocked down and their health care and other benefits taken away. "There's another way to do this."

And that, I think, is essential. A movement can't survive on outrage. It can only survive with hope. And so, you have to have victories for that hope to remain there—and then you've got to have alternatives.

DREYER: And you have to be willing to recognize victories.

HIGHTOWER: Yes.

DREYER: To accept them as victories—because everything can look so bleak in the larger picture.

HIGHTOWER: Let us celebrate. Smile every now and then.

DREYER: Jim, we talked about some of the things that are happening in the country. The Republican Party seems to be willing to shoot itself in the foot with all of the antiwomen activity. This, it would seem, has way increased the gender gap between the two parties. And these reactionary state governments coming out with all this anti-union activity: has this perhaps reinvigorated the union movement a little bit?

HIGHTOWER: Yes, it has. And in fact, Rich Trumka, the head of the national AFL-CIO, declared that he was going to make Wisconsin governor Scott Walker the "organizer of the year" for the union movement, because it's given them—not only their own sense of history back and their own spirit back, but the recognition that the public is with them. [Walker's executive actions, including anti-union legislation, became a lightning rod for organized labor and the student movement and helped inspire the demonstrations in Wisconsin.] And so, all this anti-union rhetoric that the chamber of commerce types have been pounding for years into people's heads—using Fox and all that—that is not the mainstream thought in America.

Another sign is the bevy of new and good candidates that we have running for office all across the country, for all levels of office.

The Occupy folks are mostly not in camps anymore, and I think that's a good thing. Instead of being holed up somewhere, we need them out there doing organizing, not necessarily in politics. They're going after ALEC, for example, the American Legislative Exchange Council that pushes a lot of the right-wing legislation state to state.

DREYER: Not only pushes it, writes it.

HIGHTOWER: Writes it—and, yeah, again, a Koch-funded front group. They are taking on the *Citizens United* decision. Many of them are involved in the Move to Amend movement and also the Free Speech for People, two web-based organizations that are trying to repeal, through constitutional amendments, the *Citizens United* decision. This grotesque absurdity that a corporation is a person, you know. As we say here, a corporation is not a person until Texas executes one—and then we'll know.

DREYER: Okay, *Citizens United* was just a monstrosity—but the floodgates have opened. And all this incredible amount of money; can we turn it back?

HIGHTOWER: Yes, of course.

DREYER: How do we do it?

HIGHTOWER: One way is to pass a constitutional amendment overturning it. And some people say, "Oh, well, that takes forever, you can't get that done." Well, actually you can. The last constitutional amendment was the eighteen-year-old vote, and that passed in a matter of months because we had Vietnam veterans coming home who couldn't vote. They weren't twenty-one. And so that quickly passed.

But the other thing is that it's a terrific organizing tool; and we don't have to convince people that *Citizens United* unleashing unlimited amounts of secret corporate money into our election is a bad idea. Sixty-eight percent of Republicans want a constitutional amendment to overturn that. Eighty-five percent of independents, 87 percent of Democrats. So the numbers are there.

What we've got to do is organize it, and that effort is going on. And you go back to the SANE nuclear freeze days, the protest against nuclear bombs and nuclear power. That was another issue that Washington wouldn't touch, so people went to the countryside and they got their city councils to pass resolutions and their county commissioners and state legislators to ask for a constitutional amendment—and they organized and organized and they got that done.

DREYER: Right.

HIGHTOWER: That's what's happening now. The Los Angeles City Council unanimously passed a resolution, the State of New Mexico passed a resolution saying, "Congress, send us a constitutional amendment that we can put to the people, to a vote." And if we get that to the vote, we win.

DREYER: I did two shows with Tom Hayden recently and Tom said that he thinks the way we are going to bring about progressive change in this country right now, especially electorally, is on a regional level.

HIGHTOWER: And Hayden's a very useful citizen for exactly that reason. Because he's very articulate and he's absolutely right. It's something that I've been preaching all over the country, particularly to people who are disillusioned by Obama. They say, "Well, you know, god, we tried, and he got in there and he disappointed us so I'm dropping out."

Well, what the hell good does that do? All right, maybe you don't want to be in the Obama campaign, but you've got somebody out there that you can support, or somebody local you can support. All of these elections count, and we've got to create a farm team that moves up rather than waiting on whatever next politician steps in and says, "I'm ready to be your senator or your president."

Instead, build from the grassroots—and that is what is happening. A good example is the food economy, something I've been involved in for many decades now. We've had a revolution in food in America. It did not come from any corporation, it didn't come from any government, it came from farmers saying there's got to be a better way than all these pesticides and all the cost of this stuff and making bad food and poisoning our animals and genetically manipulating our animals and that's just not natural.

And then the other group were consumers saying we don't like industrialized, conglomerated, globalized, chemicalized food. We want *real* food. And the two found each other. And it began with, you know, ex-hippies selling bad tomatoes out of broken-down VW buses in the '70s. But then came the Wheatsville Co-ops and then farmers' markets, which I'm proud to have assisted in this state. We had none, and when I came in as agriculture commissioner, we helped to establish more than a hundred of them, just by putting the tools in the hands of local people.

Now we've got a dozen farmers' markets every week right here in Austin or the Austin area. It's a huge boon and it helps farmers, it helps consumers, it helps the local economy. A guy came up to me—I guess a year ago at the Sunset Valley farmers' market—and said that he appreciated the fact that I had helped, you know, make this available. He said, "Thanks to you, I'm able to do this." And I said, "Well, how's it working out?" He kind of paused and he said, "Well, I'm still poor but I'm poor on my own terms." So, there's progress.

DREYER: But the agricultural business is still controlled by these massive corporate-conglomerate-run factory farms. One hopeful thing is the movement that Willie Nelson's involved in.

HIGHTOWER: Willie's Farm Aid is a tremendous boon linking up not just consumers but with chefs, et cetera.

DREYER: Is it putting a dent in it?

HIGHTOWER: Oh, absolutely. And the biggest movement in the whole food economy is in local, sustainable, or organic, diversified production—exactly what we ought to have in a food economy—and that has been a remarkable revolution. So successful that the companies themselves now have to say, "Well, we're local, too; I mean, we're United States of America, isn't that local?" Never mind that they bring it in from China. But, so, even they have to adopt the rhetoric of it and that's a sign of its power.

It's a tremendous movement and has helped with all the independent farmers that we have right here in the city. We have a dozen farms in Austin—Boggy Creek being the early leader of that, but many more now. And linking up with chefs and linking directly with restaurants and directly with government institutions that buy food. There's just so many ways that we can take charge of our economy and keep all that money right here doing something good for the people of our area.

DREYER: Van Jones, who was briefly in the Obama administration, wrote a very interesting analysis that we ran in *The Rag Blog*, talking about the fact that maybe Obama failed us—but that we also failed Obama because we didn't create that movement out there to give him that left flank.

HIGHTOWER: It's not just individuals out there. There tend to be groups and coalitions that are putting these things together and seeing that we're all battling the same bastards. And that unless we address that big question of who's got the money and power, then we're going to be fighting this forever.

When Obama was first elected, my message immediately was that Obama is not the answer. He is a means—and we need to buck him up when he's wrong and back him up when he's right. Unfortunately, he's been more wrong than right on big structural issues. In fact, he's mostly refused to take on the big structural issues. Which is what I think our country has got to have done: big change.

"Not only are they getting theirs, they're getting ours, they're getting our wages, our health care, our education, our air and water, our democracy."

Because this is a big time; this is another "when in the course of human events" moment that Jefferson wrote about. It's a kleptocratic moment; the thieves are just taking it all. Not only are they getting theirs, they're getting ours, they're getting our wages, our health care, our education, our air and water, our democracy. Go right down the list, they've got it. So that's not going to change by us . . .

DREYER: . . . Chipping around the edges?

HIGHTOWER: Yeah. Hoping that somebody will do something or waiting on somebody to come do something. I was with our friend Bernie Sanders not long ago—up in Vermont, campaigning with him. And a guy came up—we were in Montpelier, their state capital—he came up wearing a political button and it said, "Wearing a button is not enough." You know, we can't be a nation of button wearers.

DREYER: I think you had something you wanted to share with us—about Woody Guthrie?

HIGHTOWER: Well, really, it relates to everything you're talking about: privatization and populism and Woody. Woody comes out of that populist red-dirt Oklahoma culture that Jimmy LaFave [the late Austin singer-songwriter], for example, comes out of. I grew up in Denison, Texas, and I was just one flood away from being an Okie on the Red River there. And we consider ourselves the first line of defense against the Okies.

But we share a lot of progressive history, a lot of populist history. Populism came out of Texas, out of Lampasas. Four farmers sitting around a kitchen table over there in about 1868 and saying, "This is killing us." You know, the railroad monopolies and the bankers putting the squeeze on them; they're going broke and they had to find some other way, so they established what became the Farmers' Alliance.

Their initial effort failed, but within a couple of years the effort came back. It spread through Texas, all up through the plains states, went through the South, all the way to New York State, all the way out to California. Huge people's movement. And the great book on that is *Democratic Promise: The Populist Moment in America*, by Larry Goodwyn, who was one of the earliest of the *Texas Observer* editors.

DREYER: Terrific writer and great guy.

HIGHTOWER: Wonderful guy. And that's a super book that lays it all out. But Texas was the nub of this, and some of their best thinkers came out of here. Because this was not a spontaneous movement, it was not Sarah Palin running for president or something. Initially it had no political attachment at all.

It was an economic movement—cooperatives. They created cooperative financing mechanisms so farmers could get capital without being gouged by the banks. And then a holding mechanism for their crops, storage facilities, so that they could be in charge, and then a marketing mechanism, all of it cooperatively run. Massive economic enterprise, millions and millions of dollars at the time, in real money.

And it was also a cultural movement. Rural people were illiterate. They didn't know how to write; they hadn't read history. So, they had educational courses, they had cultural programs, they created choirs and concerts, and they had parades and fun. They made it a movement you wanted to be a part of, and you did feel a part of. So, everybody could join in.

And everybody included African Americans. Back in that day, the 1870s, there were not only African American Farmers' Alliances, as they were called, but there were actually African Americans serving on the State Alliance Committee, the governing board of the populists. Yes, there was plenty of racism—I'm not dismissing that or making light of it at all—but there was an intentional effort to try to build a real people's movement; so it's a model for us.

That movement collapsed politically because, one, they aligned with the Democrats when they shouldn't have, in the William Jennings Bryan race. [Bryan was a populist politician and presidential candidate who served as secretary of state under Democratic president Woodrow Wilson.] But the banks also came and busted their co-ops, a deliberate effort.

The original Texas Constitution outlawed banks. You were not allowed to create a bank in the state of Texas. They hated them because we were settled by debtors; there were people fleeing out of Tennessee and Alabama and Mississippi.

DREYER: Throw the money changers out. Or keep them out.

HIGHTOWER: Totally. So, yeah, we've got that spirit.

DREYER: Something you've written about recently: there's no economic system in the world that isn't a mixture of public and market systems, but the United States, of all the Western democracies, is the one that skews the furthest towards the private pole, towards the market system; the public arena in this country is already limited, and right now it's being chipped away at in very significant ways.

You've written in "The Hightower Report" about the move to abolish the post office, about moves on state parks, and you also talked about the private espionage industry, the private military industry that has become so massive and is just now getting on the radar.

HIGHTOWER: Well, it's very dangerous, Thorne. It's dangerous for our democracy, it's dangerous for our health, it's dangerous for our economy, it's dangerous in all of these aspects because it allows a few profit-seeking organizations to take charge. Privatization means giving up democratization; you give up your authority to have any say whatsoever over whatever has been privatized.

And the big push, of course, is on the post office, saying that they're just completely wasteful and inefficient, they're broke, they're bankrupt, they lost billions of dollars last year and we just can't sustain it. They can't compete with the internet and with FedEx, et cetera. Well, that's just complete—as we say out in Lubbock—bovine excrement.

DREYER: We say that here, too.

HIGHTOWER: The post office last year had a profit, an operating profit of $700 million. A profit. Yet we're told that they're broke.

So, how's that? Well, because the Congress under Bush in 2006 passed a provision that requires the US Postal Service to pay in advance now for the retirement of all of its employees for the next seventy-five years. That includes employees who have not yet been born. So, it's got to set aside money, and this has to be paid out by 2016. That's five and a half billion dollars a year that the post office has to lay out from its stamp money.

The post office doesn't take tax money; it makes its money by selling stamps and services. It does a remarkably good job of that, and it could do even more if they were to get creative, and the postmaster general is not at all creative and the postal governing board is anticreative because they want to kill the post office in the name of privatizing it for the FedExes and those outfits to take it over.

But the post office—I mean, think about it. What can you get for fifty cents? You can't get a cup of coffee, you can't buy a newspaper, you can't get anything for fifty cents—except you can get a first-class stamp and then get a nickel in change. And then they will take your letter and send it across town—across country—for forty-five cents, and if your recipient is not there, they will bring your letter back to you. That's a pretty good service.

DREYER: I loved what you wrote in "The Hightower Report." You said that the United States Postal Service "is an unmatched bargain, a civic treasure, a genuine public good that links all people and communities into one nation." And that it actually is profitable. But, "When has the Pentagon ever made a profit?" you asked. "What about the FBI, Centers for Disease Control, the FDA, the State Department, FEMA, the Park Service? These weren't designed to make profit."

HIGHTOWER: Exactly.

DREYER: These are for the public good.

HIGHTOWER: Nor was the post office, nor should it be. Yeah, this is about the common good. And again, the post office is in every community in America. They're in those gated compounds of the wealthiest people and they are in the colonias in South Texas. They deliver by pack mule, they deliver by planes, they deliver by boats in Maine. You know, they get the job done.

Yes, there are inefficiencies. Yes, there are things that need to be fixed. But that doesn't mean you throw this thing away. And by the by, it is the most popular federal agency in all of government. People feel an attachment to their post office that they don't feel, say, to the Pentagon. Because it is a community center and it's important.

DREYER: You also wrote, talking about state parks—and I think this was in your Creators Syndicate column—you said that "by axing parks, politicos are stealing the people's property."

HIGHTOWER: Exactly.

DREYER: And the whole question of the commons—the things that we hold in common that make us a people. And so much of that is being taken from us.

HIGHTOWER: Workaday people—the majority of the people of this country, particularly now—they don't fly to Aspen when they need a weekend. They don't summer in France. They go to their parks, and again, these are jewels; we've got a wonderful system here in Texas of city, county, and state parks, as well as federal parks.

And yet, we're abandoning them. Perry [Texas governor Rick Perry, in office from 2000 to 2015] and the legislature just whacked the hell out of them—so low that our state parks director was reduced to having to go to the public and say, "Please donate some money to your parks system." We're out there with a tin cup, on the side of the street, saying, "Anybody got a nickel for state parks?"

It's ridiculous. And then Perry's giving money away to any corporation with a lobbyist who'll put money in his campaign pocket. So, it's a complete abdication of long-term responsibility to the people of this state and future generations.

DREYER: And we're also privatizing schools, we're privatizing the prison system; the privatization movement is a very scary thing.

HIGHTOWER: And now, as you are indicating, it's moved with almost no public notice—much less any discussion by lawmakers—into the military and into the intelligence agencies. And they're not over there just to do administrative chores; they are doing war planning, they are targeting the enemy, they are killing the enemy. But unfortunately, also killing civilians, as we've well seen.

DREYER: And the more we privatize, the more we take away any kind of public accountability.

HIGHTOWER: That's the thing. I mean, are we going to give up the government's most sensitive activities to corporations who, by the way, have as their number one loyalty the constituency of their wealthy shareholders, which includes the CEOs? Their loyalty is not to the United States of America, it is to the bottom line, the profit of the shareholders. So it's absurd that we would let that become the guiding rule over military action and intelligence work.

DREYER: The private intelligence community, the military contracting, has become so big, and it's so secret that nobody knows *how* big it is. It is massive.

HIGHTOWER: You know, I was stunned. I started writing this in our current issue of the *Hightower Lowdown*—and beginning to look into it, and I had no idea it was this big, this extensive. They're not government employed, not public employees; they belong to corporations. This is insane. It's what one group has called a "foreign legion" that we've allowed to grow up within our own country, within our own government.

NEW LEFTIES

Tom Hayden (*right*) speaks in Austin, August 25, 2012, at a *Rag Blog*-sponsored event. Photo by Carlos Lowry.

TOM HAYDEN

You can never underestimate an empire in decline.

Tom Hayden reflects on the lasting legacy of the Port Huron Statement on its fiftieth anniversary, the crash landing from empire, and the significance of the Occupy movement.

Hayden was a driving force behind the Students for a Democratic Society (SDS), the leading organization of the '60s New Left. In 1962, he was the primary author of the Port Huron Statement, SDS's "Agenda for a Generation," which historian James Miller called "one of the pivotal documents in post-war American history."

Tom was a Freedom Rider in the Deep South; a community organizer in Newark, New Jersey; and among the most visible and articulate opponents of the war in Vietnam. He was one of the Chicago Seven charged with conspiracy following demonstrations at the 1968 Democratic National Convention in Chicago. He and Jane Fonda, to whom he was married for seventeen years, initiated the Campaign for Economic Democracy, and they worked closely with California governor Jerry Brown, promoting progressive causes. Hayden served for eighteen years in the California State Assembly and California Senate.

Hayden, whom I knew since the early days of SDS and the student movement, might have been the most eloquent and influential of the New Lefties and was always an inspiration to me. The Port Huron Statement was a call to action for an entire generation. In more recent times, he became a regular contributor to The Rag Blog *and was a guest on* Rag Radio *five times.*

Tom Hayden remained a leading voice for peace and justice until his death on October 23, 2016.

JANUARY 6, 2012

THORNE DREYER: Tom Hayden, it's been a while. Welcome to *Rag Radio*.

TOM HAYDEN: Hey, Thorne, it's great to hear your voice. I admire what you've done over all the decades; you're like one of the old trees in the forest of the '60s.

DREYER: Oh, dropping a few leaves, but hanging in there.

HAYDEN: Well, of course, it's thinning a little bit. We won't let it be clear-cut, but it's trying to get at you.

DREYER: Okay. We have a lot to talk about. Not only is it a new year, but it's the fiftieth anniversary of the Port Huron Statement. And so, I think we can look back and we can look forward.

But I wanted to start with something very important, Tom. You were, if I'm not mistaken, the batting champion of the Los Angeles Dodgers Fantasy Baseball Camp in the 1980s. Are you still playing baseball?

HAYDEN: That's kind of a shocking way to start. I think, yeah, I think it was 1988. I'm a streak hitter and I did well over a six-game period. I still am. I'm struggling, I'm seventy-two years old, but I'm part of a very harmonious and enjoyable team called the Santa Monica Monarchs. We play every Sunday. That's one of the reasons I live in California: the weather.

So, yep, I'm still healthy. I'm dying in stages, you know, parts have to be surgically removed every few years, but the vital organs are still there, and I think, like the rest of my generation, we face our natural death. People have been trying to kill us artificially and politically, but there is a natural and organic process going on, and I'm happy to have seen so much, happy to be teaching, and delighted to see the end of the Iraq War and the emergence of the Occupy protests. And I do what I can every day.

DREYER: It's amazing to me that you've continued to do such important work consistently throughout the years. You've been an inspiration to all of us.

HAYDEN: I appreciate that.

DREYER: The Port Huron Statement was an inspiration for me and for much of our generation. I came to Austin in 1963; I wasn't in on the very beginning of SDS, but I jumped on board as soon as I could.

HAYDEN: Well, you entered the picture just when the early idealism was about to be plunged into horror. The Texas-based assassination of John Kennedy in '63 was not forecast or anticipated by anybody in the 1960 to '62 crowd. And in general, I think, nobody on the left or people that study social movements had paid that much attention to the force and impact of assassinations in preventing or derailing promising progressive projects.

But there was a period that was almost golden by comparison to the rest of the '60s, and that's when the sit-ins started in Austin and cities and campuses all across the South. And the Port Huron Statement was written, inspired by those student movements in the South, and was discussed in December 1961 and finalized at the Port Huron, Michigan, convention in June of '62.

That's one of the reasons that there is some fuss and some attention to it in 2012. There are conferences at UCLA, where I teach, at UC Santa Barbara, at NYU, at MIT, at the University of Michigan, probably the University of Wisconsin, the LA Times Book Festival, and so on. So, I think it's a time for trying to contrast and compare what happened at Port Huron and participatory democracy to the new movements of today. And time for a last look at the legacy going forward.

DREYER: Ken Handel wrote an article for *The Rag Blog* about the anniversary of the Port Huron Statement. He wrote, "The fifty-nine SDS members who assembled in the small Michigan town of Port Huron in June 1962 could not accept a status quo that tolerated the possibility of nuclear annihilation, state-sanctioned racism, and a nation suffering from extensive poverty amidst affluence."

And the Port Huron Statement started out—and anybody who was involved in SDS or involved in the student movement or the movement against the war in Vietnam, knows these words—"We are people of this generation, bred in at least modest comfort, housed now in universities, looking uncomfortably to the world we inherit." And it ended, "If we appear to seek the unattainable, as it has been said, then let it be known that we do so to avoid the unimaginable."

I got an email this morning from Alan Haber, who was your colleague in the very earliest days of SDS and who was the first president of SDS.

HAYDEN: Kind of the founder president during the period when nothing was happening. He saw ahead and he kept trying to promote the idea, and then after the sit-in period in the South—'60, '61, '62—things started to take off for the organization and he got us that far. I became the president; it was a rotating office year to year. Yes, and Al is still around Ann Arbor.

DREYER: He said he was going to be listening today. He's involved with MDS—Movement for a Democratic Society—now. He wanted me to ask you about something. He said they're working on a new manifesto for today, or a "mini-festo" as he called it.

HAYDEN: I know what that means, right.

DREYER: He wanted to know what you thought about whether it's time for another manifesto or whether that's appropriate now. It seems to me that the Port Huron Statement is, in many ways, a living document. It continues to resonate and much of it is still relevant. But what is different about these times from those, and how would a manifesto now differ?

HAYDEN: Well, that's a good question. I mean, I wish Al all the best in that effort. It seems to have been attempted for about a decade. I remember, going into the Seattle confrontations [militant demonstrations in 1999 against the World Trade Organization and economic globalization], that there were some students around the country trying to write one.

But I don't know if you can replicate a document like that. Certainly we need to recognize our heritage, and one lesson is that these kind of crazy inspired visionary documents often come from the young and liberated and innocent. I mean, most of us who wrote it were twenty-one

> "Certainly we need to recognize our heritage, and one lesson is that these kind of crazy inspired visionary documents often come from the young and liberated and innocent."

years old. And it remains to be seen whether such a document materializes again.

In any event, it's a little uncanny how the words of the Port Huron Statement echo today—because it's used in classes and a lot of the students can't tell when it was written. There's some weirdness in it: we refer to people as "men," for instance. That was the entrenched sexist vocabulary of the time.

But you know, the imminent threat of the nuclear-arms race and bombs going off, the rise of anticolonial revolutions and the opposition by the United States to those revolutions, the rise of the military-industrial complex, the appearance of affluence in our economy masking 40 percent poverty rates, the continued institutionalized racism: all that makes the document seem very, very current.

In my class at UCLA, we go through it week to week and then the students, in small groups, ponder the words for today. And they're revising it in a sense by coming back to the class as a whole, to come up with the revisions that they would make, based on their experience.

One is to compare and contrast. It's very interesting: in a footnote in the Port Huron Statement, the 1 percent I referenced—I think it's 1.4 percent who own virtually everything—they were identified fifty years ago as the 1 percent of economic dominance.

We solved many, many things, but we never made much progress on changing the economy in its dynamic that seems to be compelled to create have-nots repeatedly in the midst of affluence. The underemployment, the unemployment, the chronic poverty, the understandable total anxiety of the middle class. Those are the things that are today's issues that I think are the new challenge.

The Cold War is gone but not the threat of nuclear weapons. And I think the Cold War has been replaced as a template by the global war on terrorism, which requires secrecy, excessive military spending, the shrinking of civil liberties, and all the rest. And so, for the past generation, the past ten years, the war on terrorism has come to replace the Cold War in the framework that the Port Huron Statement used.

And we haven't had, thank god, a president assassinated lately, or a candidate. But we've had stolen elections, particularly the Gore election, which robbed us from seeing whether an environmentalist could make a difference as president of the United States. So that was a terrible setback. So many of the issues that plagued us as young people then plague students today. But I think the big difference is the economic recession and the gloom.

DREYER: When you talked about the idea of whether we could write a new Port Huron Statement today—and I think your point is very well taken—that we were innocent then. We are much more jaded; there's been a great loss of innocence. When you mentioned the assassinations and the effect that they had, maybe 9/11 is the nearest thing that could be a parallel.

HAYDEN: Yep. I think that's part of the global war on terrorism.

But the interesting thing, you know—because it is the fiftieth anniversary of Port Huron—there's a tendency to dwell in the past. But participatory democracy is really alive and well. I got a memo today, for example, from somebody in Uruguay. They're having a big conference; it's not that I'm going, but I think it's quite interesting because nobody follows a lot of this global stuff. This is a conference on direct democracy in Latin America, with Uruguay as a model. Uruguay, where they have heavy emphasis on citizens' initiatives and they want to expand. So they are having a meeting.

If you think about Latin America over the past ten years, there has been a huge democratic—small *d*—revolution. I interviewed some of the Venezuelans who were involved before the election of [Hugo] Chávez, and they spoke of "participatory democracy" in their Bolivarian circle. And I asked them, "Well, where did that phrase come from?" And they said they didn't know. It just seemed an alternative to the bureaucratic dominance of a multiparty system in which all the parties were more alike than not.

You've now seen "participatory democracy" as a phrase used by somebody on Pacifica like Phyllis Bennis to describe the doings in Tahrir Square in Cairo [in 2011]. The Facebook revolutions [mass-scale protest movements in Iran, Egypt, and elsewhere that were organized through social media] are definitely an extension of the idea of direct democracy or participatory democracy. I think as long as the institutions fail to the degree they do to meet human aspirations, people will turn to taking matters into their own hands and will invent participatory movements into the future.

> "I think as long as the institutions fail to the degree they do to meet human aspirations, people will turn to taking matters into their own hands and will invent participatory movements into the future."

I think that's the lasting legacy of the SDS manifesto. The phrase actually came, I think, from the philosopher John Dewey and it was transmitted, in my times, to a professor named Arnold Kaufman at the University of Michigan. Kaufman happened to use it in a graduate seminar that a lot of the SDS people were enrolled in back in—it must have been '61 or something like that.

DREYER: "Tom Hayden changed America," writes Nicholas Lemann in *The Atlantic*. "He created," quote, "the blueprint for the Great Society programs," writes former presidential advisor Richard Goodwin. He was, quote, "the single greatest figure of the 1960s student movement," according to a *New York Times* book review.

During his time in Sacramento, when he was a state senator in California, he was described as the "conscience of the senate" by the *Sacramento Bee*'s political analyst. *The Nation* magazine recently named him one of the fifty greatest progressives of the twentieth century.

HAYDEN: You know that's all hype.

DREYER: That's all hype. Well, what was it you said? That you're part fact and part fiction?

HAYDEN: That's right. I get blamed for what I didn't do and get credit for what I didn't do.

DREYER: You have said that two of the greatest influences—both on you and on perhaps the whole student movement, the whole '60s movement—were Texas boy C. Wright Mills, the sociologist, and [Albert] Camus and his existential rebel. I did want to ask you: do you feel like Sisyphus sometimes?

HAYDEN: You know, my wife, Barbara [Williams], has written a song about Sisyphus for the trade union movement, and she invented a verse—I wish I could sing it—but basically it says, "You're rolling the boulder up the mountain and it falls back down and you roll it up and it falls back down, but in itself the process makes you stronger." So, that gave me a little more hopeful picture of what seems to be the Sisyphus dilemma, as described by Camus.

DREYER: This morning I picked up my *Austin American-Statesman* and there's a story that originated with the *LA Times*. It says, "Obama outlines plan for a leaner military. He outlines a new defense strategy that would shrink the army and marines and refocus military spending to counter dangers from China and Iran." Is this a move in the right direction? Is it a serious move?

HAYDEN: It could be far worse. The Republicans are blaming him for the loss of Iraq and they don't have a clue as to what he's supposed to do there. I think what you said about me, with all those accolades and so on, is also true of the way people focus on Obama as a symbol. I think we should think in systemic terms and not in personality terms, despite the temptations.

From that point of view, I think that the system is responding to obvious failure and frustration in Vietnam, Central America, Iraq—now Afghanistan, Pakistan—and is incorporating lessons that the costs on every level of these ground wars may be just too high to be sustainable.

And so, the shift that you see in the budget, the Pentagon's new plan, is toward, first and foremost, a new Cold War with China. A lot of bases and alliances on the Chinese border, a lot of attention to aircraft carriers on those seas, and that would be coupled with a quite frightening focus on doing something drastic towards Iran. I think the linkage is because of the oil and the Straits of Hormuz.

So, it may be a move away from ground wars of the Iraq and Afghanistan variety. It will take much more work by grassroots groups like Progressive Democrats to push Congress to cut off funding for these wars, specifically in Afghanistan. But I think that the use of force and the threat of force and the use of drones as a defensive fallback are going to be with us until somebody persuades the country that we need a different paradigm than the Cold War model applied to the newest threat.

That's what I see in this budget. So, is it good? Well, it reflects the reality that we can't afford these wars. It's not going to automatically bring them to an end, but it's a realistic budget. We certainly don't need the surplus of troops—over every other country in the world combined. But it moves us into a whole new period of conflict and threats involving the possible use of force with China. And that's going be the next generation's issue.

DREYER: How can we actually end up cutting the defense budget? There are so many people dependent upon it. We've got such an elaborate military-defense complex. And now the espionage industry has become massive. Nobody knows how big it is.

HAYDEN: Right. It's a secret budget for spies. We have no idea. Some people say it's $80 billion, some say it's $40. I don't know. And you're absolutely right, Thorne, there's no way of knowing. It's just ridiculous.

DREYER: With our whole approach, which you refer to as the long war—the huge counterinsurgency, everything that's gone on since Vietnam—it seems like we're so set in those patterns, those ideas, which have never worked. How do we break out of that?

HAYDEN: I'm afraid, you know, there's only two ways. One is persuasion, political persuasion. And there's a substantial number of people that want to break out of that, but not a majority. And the other way is a—instead of a soft landing, a crash-landing, and that's what's happening.

It's just disgraceful and sorrowful that so many Americans are dying on these battlefields in combat over objectives that they don't understand. Once a war begins, so much of it is about the reputation of the war maker, saving face, not the symbolic future threat. And so these wars, even when they become totally unnecessary and counterproductive in terms of their original purpose, they grind on.

I think that the peace movement has done a good job in a protracted struggle against these wars. The long war—which is a Pentagon doctrine, not a Tom Hayden headline—is ending. That's what the Obama budget really says. That doesn't mean there won't be drone wars against Al-Qaeda, militants, and others, but that's far different than sending one hundred thousand or two hundred thousand troops anywhere soon.

So, I think we have to argue that these policies do not make us safer, that there are ways to create jobs programs other than making weapons that we hope are never used. And that there has to be a retooling of the military industries into the manufacture of civilian products, specifically clean-energy products and solar collectors and so on.

The difference between China and the US militarily is unbelievable, if you look at what is spent on the military side. But while we're ramping up against the Chinese military threat that may be imaginary, China is ramping up to create the biggest solar and renewable energy enterprises in the world.

How could anything be more out of whack than that? But that's what's happening. And that's going to take organizing and arguing and persuading and demonstrating on an indefinite basis, because even when the opposition runs out of ideas, they don't run out of lobbyists, they don't run out of permanent institutions.

We're a voluntary force, we're the Continental Army of American rebels. We don't have any money and we come and go, but they are permanent. And they will argue for the obsolete. I feel sometimes this is what the dinosaurs were doing just before the end of their era, standing around and having cocktails with lobbyists.

DREYER: There's an incredible disconnect in this country between politics and reality. Talking about the dinosaurs, in the '60s the American empire was ascendant, we were flexing our muscles all over the place, we were hot stuff. Now, I think it would be a great understatement to say that the American empire is in decline. Do you think there is any chance that we will ever "go gentle into that good night," or, shall I say, "go *graceful* into that good night"?

HAYDEN: The soft landing. Well, I think you can never underestimate an empire in decline or an opponent that's in decline. They always can pack a punch; they always, you know, will do a Margaret Thatcher [the British prime minister from 1979 to 1990]. They are, some would say, more dangerous as they decline.

But it does seem to me that one of the things we should emphasize in our messaging is that other empires have ended and the quality of life for people has improved. It's not a simple story but it's the fact. When the British empire ended, the UK got a national health insurance program.

Despite all the troubles in Western Europe that we're seeing now, they've had a good run since empire; they've had a good twenty, thirty, fifty or more years in which their quality of life has been better than ours. They've lived longer, they've worked less hours of the year, they've had more time for vacations, the education's better, they're ahead of us in energy efficiency. It's just not true that you have to have an empire to somehow have a superior quality of life for the majority of your people.

If we learn that there's life after empire—I think that's a hard message to get across—but there's a certain American isolationism that I don't think we should ignore. People will say, "Yeah, we don't want to police the world. What are we doing in all these other countries?"

We should tap into that and talk about what I would call the "quality of life" index and have the politicians run against each other on where we stand in the rankings of the world. Why are we behind so many countries in health care, in infant mortality, and air pollution? And what are the politicians going to do about it?

I think that there's a chance—not in Texas, but in twenty or thirty states—where you could start with state initiatives, the way California has done for decades on energy efficiency, solar power, antinuke, and fuel-efficiency standards for automobiles. And linking up with other states they begin to create a powerful political and economic force for an alternative.

That's the only way I see to strengthen the power of the progressive cities and states and their partners in Congress. Much more than seeing it as a question of who's president and focusing all of our attention on national races.

DREYER: But, you say, Texas. Oh wait, I forgot. We're run by the oil business, aren't we?

HAYDEN: Not the good people of Austin.

The death penalty alone, which is disappearing as an event in most of the Western world and places like California, is just rampaging in Texas. It's to the point where if you're going to commit a serious crime, you don't want to commit it in Texas. I mean, it's just bizarre that we have no single standard on that criminal justice policy, but we don't.

DREYER: Tom, you were a critical supporter of Barack Obama, as was I. We were both involved with Progressives for Obama. There are a lot of people who are from the Left who will have nothing to do with Obama, believe that we should be looking for a third party, believe that we should be looking for an alternative in the Democratic Party, believe that he was a total fraud.

And you made the point earlier that we are not talking about personalities, we're really talking about issues. But how do you feel now, and what do you say to those people?

HAYDEN: I think you and I both felt, with Carl Davidson and many others, that we wanted to support Obama for all kinds of reasons. In my case it was my historic roots in Mississippi, Georgia, and the civil rights movement.

But at the same time, we wanted to establish the legitimacy of an independent position on the issues. In particular, I was opposed to his Afghanistan position during his campaign. I was very concerned that he would retreat on WTO and NAFTA reform, and so on. So I felt, at the time at least, that it was comfortable to be all out for Obama and at the same time to be all out on the issues. It doesn't seem complicated to me to have both views. And I'm still more or less in the same place.

Do I think that he has performed less well than I would have hoped? Yes, absolutely. But it's an experiment, it's a learning enterprise. He positioned himself as a centrist, and he's always going to be a disappointment as a centrist because he needs to have a Left against him in order to counterbalance the Right.

Sometimes these are imaginary categories but it's almost mathematical: he can't be in the middle. He can't be a centrist and at the same time left of center, period. So for us, one of the choices is you can bang on him to do the impossible—that is, to move him away from the center—or you can create a climate of opinion and a voter dynamic that moves the definition of the center so he has to catch up.

So, I'd concentrate more on the movement-building emphasis and the organizing around issues and trying to find empowerment and coalitions around issues, with a close eye on whether they're working to bring the White House and members of Congress in our direction, and view this as what might have been the '60s without the Kennedy death.

I can understand the frustration. I do think there's a lot of delusion also, where I hear people saying the Iraq War is not over. I don't know what they mean. I guess they mean because we have an embassy and two hundred marines and sixteen thousand contractors—what, we're going to, like, retake Iraq? I don't know what it means.

You can't shift the goals. If the goal was to get the American troops home, and that was the basis for the mass protest, that's been accomplished. If the goal was to end imperialism, I don't remember that as being the goal. I remember that as being a point of view in the movement, a point of view in the protests from the states, but I don't think you end imperialism in one capital or one country. It goes on and you want to inflict a price so that they don't send the troops again, and I think that's what we're about.

We should appreciate our impact, but if we're so frustrated and angered by what we had to go through to get to this point, I feel badly for people. Because, you know, you don't get utopia, you don't get all of your objectives, but you are entitled to take some credit and have some satisfaction for having made some difference in people's lives and certain public policy.

DREYER: We've never been very good at winning, or at seeing small victories along the way.

HAYDEN: Well, no wonder. When was the last time we won?

DREYER: Roger Baker, my colleague, wants to know, will the Democratic Party split over issues raised by the Occupy movement?

HAYDEN: Well, I don't think the Democratic Party will split in the way the Republican Party seems to be splitting or the way the Democrats did in the '60s and the McGovern campaign. But there is a big difference in the Democratic Party between the funding class, the people that give the money, some of whom are very liberal, very good people. But we've become on the left dependent on very, very rich people to fund some of our programs.

But in general, the funding class is closer to Wall Street than to Main Street, and on the other hand, the activist groups like Progressive Democrats, larger groups like SEIU [Service Employees International Union], and the unions, the women's groups, the civil rights groups, the environmental groups, they all are somewhat dependent and somewhat independent.

But that's the force that makes all the difference in Democratic success. So, they will keep the pressure on Obama, and they will, I think, have to focus much more on *Citizens United* and taking down the infernal power of finance capital and corporations over the campaign contributions.

On Occupy, I don't know, because one of its great strengths is the anarchistic, bottom-up, mobile, spontaneous quality. So it's there as a phenomenon, and as long as we have our economic misery and Wall Street is out there as a big fat plutocratic target, I think Occupy will keep coming back in different forms.

But one of the reasons Occupy doesn't want to make demands—and I'm not a big advocate that they must make demands, or anything like that—but it's partly the anarchist view that reform of the state is impossible, that reform itself is not going to happen and it's not worth it, and that, you know, it all has to go down.

DREYER: And that we have to build counterstructures?

HAYDEN: Counterstructures, but that leaves a wide space, because that's not the view of most of the Occupiers. They are, I think, more pragmatic than that. But I think that they will keep making their presence known, and they should be supported.

And on the other hand, those of us who believe that reform is important should be asking why the hell—instead of sitting around wondering which way the wind is blowing, to coin a phrase—why don't the

Democrats and the governors and the people in the large organizations finally implement some tangible reforms that make a difference for the working class on Wall Street issues and corporate issues?

DREYER: Okay, Tom. Is there a way that we can actually change our political system, change what's happening in this country, without a change in the composition of the Supreme Court and without undoing *Citizens United*?

HAYDEN: Of course. We can end the war in Afghanistan without waiting for the Supreme Court. [President Joe Biden announced a complete troop withdrawal from Afghanistan in 2021, nearly twenty years after the initial US invasion.] And that's my specialization. But in general, in terms of the system, no. I was very surprised and kind of interested that President Obama took the Supreme Court on right in the middle of the State of the Union address a couple of years ago. But where are we now?

I think what's happening now is there is a rising movement at the grassroots level—at the city and state levels as well—to fight back against the definition of corporations as people, and to fight against the *Buckley v. Valeo* 1973 decision that said money is an instrumentality of power.

And our Democratic Party—and most candidates in either party—are crippled in wanting to only have some reform because everybody depends somewhat on these contributions. And, as they say, they don't want to "unilaterally disarm." Which means we have an arms race—that's what they're actually saying—and I don't remember the last time arms races were healthy for children.

So, no, I think you have to keep going at it—and it may be a long fight, it may require a new generation of law school graduates working their way into the courts, but right now the shattering of that nexus between money and elections is, to me—well, there's nothing more important.

DREYER: The Occupy movement—are there parallels with what we did in the '60s? Is it a hopeful phenomenon?

HAYDEN: Sure. If you read the manifesto of Occupy Wall Street, I believe the very first principle in their statement of principles is a transparent participatory democracy. So, they are obviously, you know, carrying on the participatory democracy tradition. Whether they're conscious of it—or what level of consciousness—I don't know.

And they—these movements always come like the wind. They come out of nowhere, they come by surprise, and it's not over. They just have to—they obviously have to change locations. But I think it's very hopeful and it's become a universal consensus that they've changed the dialogue to income inequality and poverty.

The only problem I have with that is that I'm glad to see the national conversation changing. I'm glad to see the media coverage. But where's the money? Follow the money; nothing yet has happened.

Sixties activists Bernardine Dohrn (*left*) and Bill Ayers (*right*) speak at an event in Austin, June 21, 2017, sponsored by the New Journalism Project. Photo by Carlos Lowry.

BERNARDINE DOHRN AND BILL AYERS

Fire from below.

Sixties activists Bernardine Dohrn and Bill Ayers tell us about Obama's "palling around with terrorists"—meaning themselves—and address the political issues of our times.

Dohrn and Ayers were preeminent if controversial figures in the '60s and '70s New Left. Both were leaders in the Students for a Democratic Society (SDS) and then led the organization's radical offshoot, the Weather Underground. Dohrn was on the FBI's Ten Most Wanted Fugitives list.

Bernardine Dohrn, activist, academic, and advocate for children's rights, women's rights, and peace, was a clinical associate professor at Northwestern University School of Law, now retired, and a founding director of the Children and Family Justice Center at the Bluhm Legal Clinic at Northwestern.

Bill Ayers was a distinguished professor of education and a senior university scholar at the University of Illinois at Chicago and was founder of the Small Schools Workshop. Ayers is a leading education theorist and activist and has written books on educational theory. He authored Public Enemy: Confessions of an American Dissident, *a sequel to his critically acclaimed memoir,* Fugitive Days.

Bernardine Dohrn and Bill Ayers have been married since 1982. The two of them (and Tom Hayden) came to Austin to headline Rag Blog-*sponsored events.*

JANUARY 17, 2014

THORNE DREYER: You folks were certainly controversial figures in the late '60s and '70s as leaders of the Weather Underground. But you're not just legends from the past; you've been doing important work all the way through the decades.

You both live in Hyde Park in Chicago, which was Obama's neighborhood before he became president. And Bill, you call Bernardine your, and I quote, "partner, comrade, friend, coparent and grandparent, inspiration, coauthor, lover, and soul mate for close to half a century."

BERNARDINE DOHRN: Woo-woo! Thorne, it is such a pleasure to be here in Austin and to be here with you on this show, in life.

DREYER: Thank you, Bernardine. Thank you both for joining us.

Bill. Tell us about the controversy that arose during Obama's first run for president in 2008. There was a potluck seminar with students at your home in Chicago. Set the stage for us, please.

BILL AYERS: Bernardine and I were both professors for the last several decades and often had our seminars at our home because it was a nicer way to do things. And one night in April 2008, I had my graduate students over to the house and we were discussing their theses, their dissertations, their research, and we were eating. And when the seminar ended, somebody who described herself as a "political junky" flipped on the TV to see the very end of the Hillary Clinton–Barack Obama debate, the one that was on ABC.

I paid little attention until George Stephanopoulos started bearing down on Barack Obama about his friends and his patriotism, and he talked about [Chicago pastor] Jeremiah Wright. I looked over and then Stephanopoulos said, "Now, in regard to the question of your associates, what about this fellow William Ayers? Your campaign says you're, quote, 'friendly.' Could you describe that relationship to the voters and explain why that won't be a problem?"

I was stunned, but my students were absolutely thunderstruck—

several fell on the floor and couldn't believe it. And Obama responded, "Well, this is a guy around the neighborhood who's an English professor or something and he's never endorsed me, and why I would be held responsible for despicable acts he committed forty years ago—there's no connection, George."

And my students were just absolutely astonished, and one of them turned to me and said, "My gosh, that guy has the same name as yours." And another student helpfully explained that that's because we were the same guy.

We saw this thing percolating in the fever swamps of the right wing, but this is when it became kind of a national story and I was suddenly this cartoon character, the former domestic unapologetic terrorist thrust into the campaign because of a relationship that we had with Barack Obama and Michelle Obama in Hyde Park.

DOHRN: In the neighborhood.

AYERS: A guy around the neighborhood.

DOHRN: And I think one of the things that people don't remember—because Sarah Palin, six months later, upped the ante so much—is that it started with Hillary Clinton and that's just an interesting footnote.

AYERS: Yeah, it was her narrative. People couldn't figure out how to run against this charismatic young senator from Illinois, and so the narrative that Hillary developed was, "We don't know much about him. He's certainly very charming and intelligent, but let's look at his friends." And it was Jeremiah Wright, the so-called fiery Black nationalist preacher; it was Rashid Khalidi, the Palestinian scholar; Father [Michael] Pfleger, a radical priest from the South Side; and me.

So, they started to demonize these characters and we always felt—Bernardine and I felt—that the most unfair characterization was of Jeremiah Wright, a real fixture of not just the South Side but of Chicago and the nation. A decent, lovely, important thinker and activist around supporting South Africa early on, around African support, around neighborhood rejuvenation, and a lot of other things.

But the demonization of those characters was only part of the problem. The deeper problem was guilt by association—an old and disgusting tradition in American politics—and that was Hillary's plan. It failed for her, but McCain-Palin picked it up. Palin introduced that deathless phrase, "palling around with terrorists," which, you know, is kind of still on the agenda.

So that's how it started, Thorne.

DREYER: What does it tell us that it failed?

DOHRN: I think that's an important point because you've seen—since we've been in Austin—people all the time coming up to Bill and asking to take a picture with him. And then they say—they always say—"Now I can't run for president." And Bill always says, "To the contrary, actually, you can win the presidency now that you know me."

So, it's a funny kind of dichotomy. People think both that it's still scary and that the smear association is effective. And you have to kind of point out, "Hey, actually he's won two terms in a row, you know—he's the president."

AYERS: I like to think it didn't work because guilt by association seemed so desperate in the case of both Hillary and McCain-Palin. It seemed like a desperate move, not like a thoughtful move. I also think it's a generational shift. I mean, people look at the New Left and they're like, "Whatever," you know. "That's a long, long time ago."

DOHRN: "It was my uncle, that was my . . ."

AYERS: "Yeah, my grandfather was . . ."

DOHRN: "That was my great aunt, that was my mother."

AYERS: And I think there's another thing, too, which is that the more that demonization tried to get a foothold, the more it caused especially young people to look in a different direction. So, when they were hammering Obama for being a socialist, actually, the polls pointed out that toward the end of the election—among voters under twenty-five—socialists had a favorable rating of over 50 percent, whereas Republicans had a favorable rating of under 40 percent.

So, what they meant to do to tar him turned out actually to be something that kind of enhanced socialism. I can picture some kid in Wyoming, you know, googling the word "socialist" and saying, "Oh, my gosh, 'from each according to his ability, to each according to his need.' Sounds pretty biblical."

DOHRN: But you remember that—hard to remember now, these six years later—that Obama was running on an anti-Iraq War platform, which really suited the country, the mood of the country, and particularly young people. And it was both that demographic shift and really a shift in the recognition of racial transformation.

DREYER: Right.

DOHRN: I don't want to say that racism is anywhere near over. Obviously, I don't think it is even a little. But I do think that the fact that someone like him could run for the presidency does, and did, frighten the right wing and certain dug-in Americans who think white supremacy is the standard. So, you know, you want to note it was a turning point on those matters. That is very important.

DREYER: I don't think there's any question about that. They also overplayed their hand a whole lot. And those young people who googled "socialism"—probably, after a little while, they said, "Wait. This guy's no socialist."

AYERS: Right. Right.

DREYER: And that leads to my next question. You have said—and it was my impression, too—that Obama never really put himself forward as any kind of progressive. He was always, to me, a triangulator. He even presented himself as a moderate.

AYERS: We knew him as a politician in Illinois; we knew him as a person in Hyde Park, a guy around the neighborhood. And the way he advertised himself in 2008 struck us as absolutely true. He said, "I am a moderate, middle-of-the-road, pragmatic politician." He might have added . . .

DOHRN: . . . "Ambitious."

AYERS: He might have added "ambitious," and Bernardine likes to kid me because we used to talk about how ambitious he was before he was even really an elected official. A nice guy and an intelligent guy, but very ambitious. And I used to say, "He's so ambitious, I think he wants to be mayor of Chicago." And that will tell you the limits of my imagination.

But he said who he was, and the right wing looked at him and said, "No, he's a secret socialist, a secret terrorist who pals around with terrorists, and a secret Muslim." And the Left looked at him and said, "I think he is winking in my direction." But he wasn't winking, he was telling the truth about his record.

DOHRN: We saw him get elected to the Illinois Senate, and he was a state senator for seven years, and so you can look at his record there and it's a predictor for what's going to happen next. He was friends with everyone, he crossed borders, he tried to put together coalitions to make incremental changes—and meanwhile the issue roiling in Illinois during that period of time was wrongful convictions and the death penalty.

And so here this tremendous turmoil was going on, where the majority of people on death row in Illinois were found to be innocent—not just wrongfully convicted, but actually innocent. And being taken off of death row. And in that, you know, he played no significant role. So that's just telling. But it is who we—everybody in Hyde Park—certainly got used to. Smart, intelligent, thinking about the big issues, but that was the stance.

DREYER: How significant was his election in terms of the fact that he was the first African American elected? And how significant is it in terms of what progressives have learned and should learn from the process?

DOHRN: I think that the fact that he did divert his career to go work on the South Side of Chicago as a community organizer—and he *used* that, but he also *did* it. He sat at kitchen tables of people who were working poor and unemployed poor for several years and he knows what that means. I do think that he held himself out during the campaign in ways that were surprising and startling, and nobody had ever done it before.

For example, when he and Hillary were down to the wire and going head to head, somebody said to him, to Barack, "Well, what would Martin Luther King think?" And he said, "He wouldn't have an opinion about either of us; he'd be out in the streets organizing a movement for change." Now, that came right out of the community-organizing part of his history, not out of the ambitious-political-candidate part of his history.

So, I think that resonated. And of course, by the time the economy bottomed out right at the end of the election, the last two months of the election, it really resonated. And all kinds of people who couldn't have imagined themselves, you know, being for him, found in him hope.

AYERS: I would echo, and maybe add one thing. I think the echo is to what Bernardine said, that Obama's election was a blow to white supremacy, but it was nowhere near a fatal blow, or final blow. So, I think we can recognize that there was something important about a nation with the history we have, having a majority vote for an African American. It was, I think, a big thing. But it wasn't the end of the battle. So, we now have voting rights eviscerated, we have mass incarceration, and a lot of other iterations of white supremacy, and we have a lot of work to do, obviously.

But the other thing I would add is that it's worth noting that all the great moves forward in the last hundred years came from fire from below, movements on the ground. And so, we tend—and I think the Left actually gets caught up in this in a dangerous way—we tend to look at the sites of power like the White House, the medieval auction house we call the Congress, the Pentagon, Wall Street, and we look at them kind of as if those are the only sites of power.

But in reality, there's power in the neighborhood, the community,

---

> "... it's worth noting that all the great moves forward in the last hundred years came from fire from below, movements on the ground. ... there's power in the neighborhood, the community, the street, the school, the workplace, the shop, and that's the power we have absolute access to."

the street, the school, the workplace, the shop, and that's the power we have absolute access to. So, why would we wring our hands wondering what Obama's going to do, when it's predictable? While what we ought to be doing is spending our energy building a movement for peace, a movement for single payer, a movement to raise the minimum wage to fifteen dollars an hour, and also create a maximum wage.

DREYER: If nothing else, we're creating a left flank that brings pressure

AYERS: But, really, we ought to look at history and note that huge changes, huge transformations, like abolition—Lincoln was never part of an abolitionist party—and the civil rights movement—Johnson was never part of the Black freedom movement. But these things happened because of fire from below. Our job is to create fire from below.

DREYER: Bill, we started out by talking about your students and this potluck dinner work session and this incredible phenomenon of George Stephanopoulos asking Obama about your history and, as you put it, sort of turning you suddenly into this cartoon. How did the students then respond? Did they want to know about what had really gone on with the movement and what you guys had been involved in, and how did you explain that to them?

AYERS: I think my students had this sudden out-of-body experience— that they had known me very well two minutes before and now they didn't know me at all.

DREYER: Did they, in theory, know about your background?

AYERS: Not really.

DOHRN: Sometimes—usually by the end of a semester—everybody knows because somebody knows; they google you, there's a discussion behind your back. I always say, you know, "My door's open. You can come talk to me outside of class about anything, just because there's no secrets here." And the Weather Underground lurches up from time to time. As it did with the *Weather Underground* movie [an Academy Award-nominated 2002 documentary], and so on.

But that night—as Bill's book *Public Enemy* goes on to say—we were up all night because people were emailing and texting and calling from all over the country. Clearly it was going to change our lives for the rest of the year, if not forever.

DREYER: For most people who didn't really have that background in their heads—or even if they did, you were both extremely accomplished, acclaimed scholars in your fields, and that was how you were known.

DOHRN: And as activists, but as activists in the way that was familiar in Chicago. So, everybody knew that we were peace activists and justice activists and against the death penalty and involved in prison abolition. And Bill, of course, involved in the struggles around education.

AYERS: Certainly, the mega notoriety of a presidential campaign was something we had not experienced. For fifty years we've been in and out of a kind of notoriety, but this was huge. It was also true when the movie came out about the Weather Underground, by Sam Green and Bill Siegel. Audiences looked at that movie and audiences looked at this notoriety around the presidential campaign; young people actually didn't feel that they had to ask us complicated questions like, "Why did you do this?" And, "What was your strategy?"

It's people our age who are still kind of sorting through that history. The young people look at it—and I'll tell you the response to the film, and my students that night. Their response is, "Oh, my gosh, what are the limits of protest? You guys really were committed. You were willing to risk a lot." And that's more what they take away from it than trying to figure out the nuances of strategy and tactics, which is more something *we* do because we lived it.

DREYER: And what the use of violence means?

DOHRN: I don't think they even think about it that way. Their first response is, "Holy cow, I had no idea that kind of commitment happened here." Now, of course, it didn't just happen with us, with the Weather Underground. It happened with the Vietnam vets who deserted and resisted the military. We all know what happened with the Black freedom movement and the tremendous war against them.

But I think that what they're amazed about—which we were amazed about as we looked back into the abolitionist movement and the war to end slavery—was this long thread in American life around labor struggles, around human struggles, around freedom, and around women's rights and around ending wars.

The other thing is that the *Weather Underground* movie came out in 2002. And, of course, the interviews happened before 2001. But as it screened, people are aware that there's a new war, and a new war, and a new war. And so they see that in the line with the Vietnam War and the kind of turmoil that it created.

DREYER: When we look at American society today, two areas that you're involved in could be seen as among the most significant problems we face—and that would be criminal justice and education—public education.

DOHRN: Before we talk about prisons and criminalization and militarization of domestic society, I want to talk for one minute about war and peace. Because I think that that's the other thing that we feel very devoted to. And I think that we're at a unique moment right now. When the president [Obama] made a move to bomb Syria, an amazing thing happened in the United States, in my opinion, that we all need to take notice of and not take for granted at all.

And that is that there was a wave—maybe not a wave—okay, a series of ripples across the United States, with all kinds of people, right, left, middle, political, unpolitical, women, men, young people, old people, who said, "No more war." It couldn't have been clearer if you were listening and had your eyes open and were paying attention. I think that took all of us activists by surprise, took me by surprise. People actually knew that drone strikes kill civilians and thought that was a bad idea.

". . . one of the urgent things on our agenda, that is critical to every other piece of work we do—prisons, workers' rights, rich and poor, the environment, teaching and education and health care—one of the critical things is war and peace."

So, I think that one of the urgent things on our agenda, that is critical to every other piece of work we do—prisons, workers' rights, rich and poor, the environment, teaching and education and health care—one of the critical things is war and peace. And I feel that it's urgent that we link that with everything else we're doing. Here is the Pentagon and the domestic national-security state spying, you know, militarizing the border and so on, in the name of peace.

DREYER: And I think, too, that in the late '60s a lot of what the movement really was addressing was the fact that no matter what was happening in this country, we had to deal with, we had to take responsibility for, what we were doing to the rest of the world.

DOHRN: That's right, what's being done in our name. And of course, one of the leading forces in that, then and now, is vets coming back from war and telling the truth. And so, the big NATO demonstrations in Chicago that shut down the city [in May 2012] were an extraordinary display of military power at home, by the state. And also, the determination of people to speak up was led by these very young people, men and women, coming back from war, standing up, risking their future, and throwing their medals back at the NATO generals—and the US generals were standing right behind the screen. It was like *The Wizard of Oz*.

AYERS: It was a sight; it was brilliant.

DOHRN: It was extraordinary. But let's move on to prisons and criminal justice, because I think that they're related, of course. Part of the militarization at home—that goes with having endless military bases and war abroad—is this astonishing gulag that has grown up in the United States. You can't look five miles in any direction without seeing a massive jail or prison, almost no matter where you are in the country. And yet, they're invisible to many people in the United States.

Of course, it's a totally racialized and discriminatory system. Latinos and African Americans are in prison for nonviolent offenses, robbing communities of their core people—young men, young women who belong at home and in school and inventing new ways of the arts, the humanities, technology, and work.

One of the things that I feel hopeful about—as I do around war and peace—is that you can see it falling apart. The prison-industrial complex that we have built and paid for cannot be sustained. No governor in any state can sustain it anymore, and so you find these odd things. Illinois shutting three prisons a year ago, including the supermax prison that had only been built ten years before. So you can do it, actually, you can do it. And I think one of our urgent tasks is to shut prisons. Maybe not all of them, maybe we'll leave one open in every state, but, you know, almost all.

Who likes drunk driving? Who likes domestic violence? Who likes robbery? Nobody likes any of that stuff, but the remedy has been an elaborate criminal justice system and then incarceration and solitary confinement—for what?

You need consequences, but you surely don't need that.

DREYER: And can this be separated from the drug war?

DOHRN: Well, it boomed with the drug war, but you can see that there's strategies to criminalize the next thing that will be very much like the drug war.

DREYER: Is this fear or is this economics?

DOHRN: You know, what is it? That's a complex thing.

AYERS: It's both.

DOHRN: I think it is a culture of fear, of constant fear that there is danger here and your children and your grandchildren are in danger. On the other hand, what is more failed than the war on drugs? Forty years later, nothing. Same quantities of illegal drugs coming in, same gigantic profits at the top, same incarceration and demonization of young people at the bottom, people of color at the bottom, and massive consumption by US citizens. So, now we have the big change, of course, which is the legalization of marijuana [first legalized for recreational use in Colorado in 2012]. And that's huge.

AYERS: I think that there is an economic aspect; if you let two and a half million people out of prison, what would our unemployment rate be? I mean, in some ways, when I look at schools in Chicago, the concept of the school-to-prison pipeline is very vivid, very real.

So, it's economic, but it also has a life of its own. In a capitalist system that drives us all, greed and fear are basic to it, and so it takes on a life of its own, it has a culture of its own, and every crime deserves a punishment. Every punishment has to involve incarceration and then we end up with a big business called the prison-industrial complex.

DOHRN: And of course, now the biggest boom in prison building is immigrants, who are not criminals but are being held in prisons, and that's the biggest area for private-prison growth, as well. So, we've now added a whole gigantic population of undocumented people who come here seeking a slightly better job and being able to send money home. And end up being held in these giant concrete gulags.

DREYER: Thanks to the Occupy movement, there's much more public consciousness of income inequality. But as we all said for a long time, the problems in our society and the problems with racism are all systemic. They aren't just people who have bad thoughts, you know; it's about economics, and that affects who we put in prison and what that does to their lives, and it affects how we organize our educational system.

DOHRN: Now let's say a word about Occupy. So exciting. Here's a metaphor that comes kind of out of nowhere. Who could have imagined pointing at the 1 percent and putting all of the rest of us in a pie? And I think the replication of it across the country has created a whole new generation of experienced activists and people committed to organizing.

You can see the spillovers in the responses to hurricanes and natural disasters, on the South Side of Chicago around housing, and so on. But also, these incredible new workers' rights campaigns that are going on. Look at what's going on with domestic workers across the United States. Look at what's going on with the Workers Defense Project here in Austin.

Look what happened at Sea-Tac Airport in Seattle, with a fifteen dollar minimum wage for every—primarily immigrant—worker who works in that airport. Or the strike of Chicago teachers a year and a half ago, which inflamed the city and had all kinds of community and parent support. I think it's tied to Occupy, this growing strength.

DREYER: I understand the thinking that Occupy was just this sort of spurt of activity and consciousness but that it failed because it built no continuing organizational presence. It didn't, you know, but danged if it didn't take our consciousness in this country and grab it by the throat—to mix a few metaphors here—and shake it and make us very aware of the problem that may be central to all of our lives.

AYERS: It changed the frame, it changed the conversation, and I don't know what we expect from a tent city, but that's a hell of a lot to accomplish. I wouldn't call it a failure.

DOHRN: You could say that about sit-ins, if you just wanted to take a tactic and turn it into a whole policy. So, it's grumpy and depressed people saying that.

DREYER: I did want to talk a little bit about the work that you've done about our educational system and how it's at the absolute core of so many of the problems that we face. And that includes the fact that we're so open to misinformation. We're open to all this antiscience, antifact stuff. And schools are losing art teachers, we're losing humanities, we're tied to this unholy addiction to test scores—or to this new, you know, what they call "educational reform."

AYERS: You raised this question of reform, and of course there is a corporate reform agenda and that corporate reform agenda is pushed by Republicans and Democrats alike. Arne Duncan [US secretary of education under Obama] is the current pusher, and he's basically Margaret Spellings in drag. I mean, he's the same as George W. Bush's secretary of education.

And that agenda is a profoundly backward agenda. It's an agenda based on reducing education to a score on a standardized test. It's based on stripping teachers of any professional responsibility and any collective knowledge they might bring to the enterprise. And it's based on privatizing the public space.

But I think the place to begin—as this debate rages in Texas and throughout the country—is to say, in a democracy, what is the requirement of education? What is different about education in a democracy from education in any autocratic or authoritarian regime anywhere in the world?

I mean, look, fascist Germany or Soviet Romania or medieval Saudi Arabia, they also wanted their kids to do their homework, show up on time, learn their subject matter, not get pregnant, stay away from drugs, all those things we want, too.

But is there no difference with education in a democracy? I would argue that the difference is profound and fundamental and that the difference is this: in a democracy, education is based on a precious but fragile ideal. And that ideal is that every human being is of incalculable value. And in a country founded on the notion of equality, we spend a hell of a lot of energy in our schools trying to find a basis for inequality.

> **". . . in a democracy, education is based on a precious but fragile ideal. And that ideal is that every human being is of incalculable value."**

What we should be doing is saying, for example, just as a metaphor, whatever the wisest and most privileged parents have for their children, that's what we as a community want for all of our children. That sets us on a direction that's away from standardized test scores into the music and the arts, into clubs and sports and games, and all the things that people need for a healthy, holistic development of their personality.

In fact, that makes me think of Article 26 of the UN Declaration on Human Rights, and what it says is that every human being is entitled to a free education that's geared towards the development of the full human personality. That was written in 1948, and that's a good place to start.

DREYER: How about teachers? How about the idea that teachers are important, significant members of our society who are worthy of being paid well? Are not people to hire on a temporary basis and then discard.

DOHRN: Our middle son Malik is a middle school teacher, math and science and Spanish. And you go to see his class and he has forty children in his class. But, of course, the president and the secretary of education and the mayor of the city of Chicago have twenty—at the most—kids in their children's classrooms. It's so shocking.

The mayor of Chicago has not only stripped the school budget, closed fifty schools, public schools, recertifying and spending tax dollars on private charters, but he just shrunk the budget of every public school in the city. Our granddaughter's public school, for example, lost an art teacher, a music teacher, one social worker, and one whole special ed class.

And they have to bring their own toilet paper in September and January.

AYERS: Two rolls.

DOHRN: Two rolls of toilet paper. Who thought of that? The mayor thought of that? And his kid's going to this highly privileged school, where actually the teachers at the University of Chicago Laboratory School are unionized and work with the idea that after five or six years of teaching you might become a really good teacher. That certainly you're not a really good teacher the first two years—because it's one of the great art forms ever invented; it's a very difficult and challenging field.

So, you know, it's so outrageous what's happening here. And it's not about competing with China in the next century. It's about, as Bill said, treating everyone as if they have tremendous possibility. And opening up a life and living a rich life.

DREYER: Are we creating a generation of young people who will have some skills in math and sciences but won't know how to make decisions about their lives?

AYERS: Well, that's part of it. I think that's part of it, but I also think we've got a really profound class and race division system going on in our schools. And so in Chicago you have Winnetka, the North Shore, you know, tony schools; they educate their kids to the tune of $50,000 per kid per year. And in the south suburbs, where the population is poor and African American, they have less than $5,000 per year per kid.

What that tells kids very clearly—that savage inequality communicates to children—is that we have a single policy for youth in this country and the policy is to choose the right parents. If you choose the right parents, you're going to do fine. If you choose the wrong parents, you're on your own.

And that is cruel, unusual, and backward, and it doesn't bode well for where we're headed. What we ought to be doing is investing money in teachers. We ought to get class sizes down, we ought to pay teachers for sabbaticals, for rejuvenation, for mentoring, all those things.

And teachers, Thorne, are going into teaching for the right reasons. They love kids or they love the world or they love an aspect of the world—art or poetry or history or the English language—and they want to share it with kids. We ought to support those young people to have a career in teaching, not two years and out but a real career, where you can learn how to do the craft and stay with it and get some rewards for life.

RIGHTS FIGHTERS

Civil rights pioneer and oncologist Leon McNealy (*right*), pictured here with Thorne Dreyer, was our guest on *Rag Radio* on May 6, 2011. *Rag Radio* photo.

LEON McNEALY

There just wasn't enough penicillin for Black people.

Texas civil rights pioneer Leon McNealy shares his eclectic experiences and often humorous recollections of fighting segregation in Austin and Houston.

Dr. Leon B. McNealy is a radiation oncologist now living in Marshfield, Wisconsin. McNealy first became active in the civil rights movement when he was a seventeen-year-old high school student in Houston. In 1958, as a student at the University of Texas, he became involved in sit-ins at lunch counters in downtown Austin. In 1960, he and two companions confronted then university president Logan Wilson about segregation on the UT campus, leading to a series of large demonstrations. A few years later, McNealy was a major figure in the "stand-ins" that led to the integration of movie theaters on the university Drag and throughout the South. McNealy was the object of death threats and the victim of substantial violence stemming from his efforts.

With at times playful irony, he regaled us on the show with his adventures from his civil rights days and shared with our audience some little-known but important history.

In 2019, McNealy, who was a 1963 journalism graduate at UT and who worked with the Daily Texan (which has won more awards than any other college newspaper in the country) and the Texas Ranger *humor magazine*, was named to the Daily Texan Hall of Fame.

MAY 6, 2011

THORNE DREYER: I went to a gathering—a "stand-in reunion" in December 2010—which was made up of folks who were either involved in the early civil rights movement in Austin or who wished they had been. I heard Leon McNealy speak and I must tell you, he's not only inspirational but he's very funny.

Welcome to *Rag Radio*, Dr. Leon McNealy.

LEON McNEALY: Thank you very much for having me.

DREYER: Tell us about the stand-ins, which started in Austin, and events that led up to them. People always know about the sit-ins, but I don't think a lot of people know about the stand-ins—even know that term. Then I want to go back to your early days, because you have some wonderful stories to tell.

McNEALY: Before the stand-ins happened, there was a principally Black movement started mainly by the Black students that lived at the YMCA in Austin. It was the late Dr. Joe McBride, it was Roby Hilliard, the late professor Donald Hill. And Mary Simpson was another student who was involved.

DREYER: What about the stuff downtown, the sit-ins at the lunch counters?

McNEALY: I'm not really sure of the year, it was either '59 or '60. We were listening to the radio one day and we heard about the demonstrations in Oklahoma City; they had sit-ins and they were successful. I think this was before Greensboro.

And I don't know how many there were—how many people or how many times we did it—because we were doing it between classes. I know Louis Woods was there and probably Robert Bell and Joe McBride, and so we went down and sat at the lunch counters. And we were very successful, very quickly.

One thing that I found inspirational about it was that while the unfriendly forces were putting cigarette butts out on us, an older man came up and intervened—and that was St. John Garwood, who was the Texas Supreme Court justice.

Then we had some meetings, and I know John Henry Faulk [the

Texas-based humorist, radio personality, and target of McCarthyism] was there, and I'm not sure if Cactus Pryor was present, but there were some of the more liberal figures. Austin had this tradition of having a strong, liberal voice from white people. There were the Mavericks, the Clintons, and so forth. Walter Prescott Webb, Fred Gipson, who wrote *Old Yeller* and who lived out in the hills. After the sit-ins, we started a citywide group of Black students, but a lot of political pressure came down on those from Huston-Tillotson, where my uncle was the registrar.

DREYER: Huston-Tillotson is what they now call an "historically Black college" [HBCU], in Austin.

McNEALY: They were the bulk of our demonstrators, but pressure was brought on them and they broke up because they were ordered by their professors and administrators not to attend.

And then came the stand-ins in 1960 and '61. The inspiration for the idea came from a couple of men, Chandler Davidson and Houston Wade. They were the ones that really put it together. Frank Wright allowed them to have their meetings at the YMCA, where he was director. Frank Wright was a Quaker and took a lot of heat and it took a lot of courage. He had also allowed Black students to live in the Y, which was also quite controversial.

So we formed these lines in front of the Texas Theater and the Varsity on the university Drag [a stretch of Guadalupe Street that borders the western edge of the UT campus], and the white students would go up and ask for a ticket. But they would say, "Only if my Black friend can come along." When they were told "no," they would go to the back of the line and start over. At first there was really strong resistance; they had some goons that kind of pushed and shoved on people.

I think the most memorable day was when the movie *Exodus* came to town. Some of our Jewish friends wanted to see the movie, so they joined for a while and then they went into the movie. Some of the Arab students were there demonstrating against the movie *Exodus*, but they were also on our side. And you had some of the rednecks demonstrating against the Jewish students and the stand-ins and the Arabs—so it was a really confusing day.

DREYER: Beverly Burr wrote that "initial participants in the student movement for racial equality at UT were few in number. They were mostly Black, poor, and very dedicated. They were not only UT students but also Huston-Tillotson students who participated in the early sit-ins. The actions during 1960 by this relatively small group of committed activists had earned them a following of many whites in the university community by spring of 1961."

That was a critical period there, right, those couple of years? And Texas actually was fairly early to integrate—such as it was—the undergraduate school?

McNEALY: The undergraduate school was 1956. One student was Marion George Ford; we were classmates at Wheatley High in Houston. But he had the right personality for being a pioneer.

I recall the day when we were on the city bus and I was in ROTC—we had the only Black ROTC in the South—and we were the first African Americans to be allowed to march in a military parade in the South.

DREYER: Now this is back in Houston, when you were in high school.

McNEALY: Yeah. So, Marion was on the track team and he was on the front of the bus. There were hardly ever any white people on the Nance Street bus coming home from Wheatley High School, but a white man got on the bus and ordered a little Black lady out of her seat. And Marion gave him and the bus driver a good beating, and I fled to Sawdust Alley with the police onto my trail. And I hid under a house and a Black lady comes out and says, "No, sir, I ain't seen no kids. Maybe over yonder."

So, that was Marion Ford. He was probably the smartest guy I've ever met, but he also had a really tough, tough streak about him. He was obsessed with getting into the University of Texas. I have some old articles, which I've turned over to Laura Burns and she's going to publish them on Dirty Nothings.

DREYER: I should tell people that there's a Stand-Ins and Dirty Nothings website. "Dirty nothings" was how UT Board of Regents Chairman Frank Erwin characterized student demonstrators.

And there's a lot of very interesting historical material that Laura Burns has posted there, including old stories from the *Texas Ranger*—which was the UT humor magazine that Gilbert Shelton and Lieuen Adkins and Jack Jackson, a number of famous countercultural personalities from Austin, were involved with. And I believe that Leon McNealy was involved with that publication, as well as the *Daily Texan*.

McNEALY: Yes, I was. It gave me an outlet. I was really angry, but the *Ranger* gave me an outlet to release it and also to be a bit of a social critic and make people laugh at segregation.

DREYER: Dr. McNealy is known as a satirist and tends to produce these wonderful, often funny stories that at first you're not certain whether they're true or not. And I said, "Be careful about that on the air because people can't see that twinkle in your eye."

McNEALY: Well, you know that's why I did bring my documentation with me.

DREYER: He brought his birth certificate, ladies and gentlemen, and his passport—and what else do you have there with you?

McNEALY: I have my Sigma Delta Chi journalist society from Texas. I brought my name change, my high school diploma. I have my official birth certificate from Texas, and I'm proud to say that under the box where it has "legitimate," mine is checked "yes." And I also have a picture of Houston Negro Hospital and my hospital birth certificate that has my footprint on it.

DREYER: How do we know that these aren't forgeries? We have no way of knowing.

McNEALY: No.

DREYER: So, okay, you had a pretty amazing history in Houston, and you have some wonderful stories, and I think your activism—or your rebellion—started pretty young, like in elementary school? You had an incident with the Pledge of Allegiance, I believe? Tell us about that.

McNEALY: We had this old broken-down school, and you'd come up the steps on the outside—the steps to the second floor. It's a big open area with classrooms around and the principal's office over on the left. And Ms. Flood, she would pound out songs and we'd have hymns in the morning and prayer—"Tell me the stories of Jesus!"—and then we'd say the Pledge of Allegiance to the flag. So they got to the part that says,

"With liberty and justice for all," and I had my fingers crossed and the old bat saw me. So I got my buttocks whipped.

My mother told me that night that when you're around adults, don't cross your fingers, cross your toes. But the reason why I crossed my fingers was because I didn't want God to think I was lying.

We had a couple of incidents. Florence Myers, she threw up on me during devotion—not a lot but just a little bit, and it was kind of green—and she grabbed her side and walked towards one of the empty classrooms, where she collapsed.

Well, nobody in those days had cars, so the principal and Ms. Flood, they went around the corner to Ross Rest Home, which was the big funeral home, and they brought this funeral hearse back to transport her to St. Elizabeth's Hospital. And our doctor—this was '47, just two years after the war—he knew a white doctor at the Texas Medical Center, and he went and got penicillin.

Now, penicillin was in very short supply, and, you know, you have to set your priorities in medicine. There was rationing and there just wasn't enough penicillin for Black people. So, this saved her life. That's why I like Orson Welles's *Third Man*, because there's a penicillin racket going on.

Anyway, another incident: Joann Ross, whose family owned the Ross Rest Home, had a nosebleed and she had—my mother called it cancer, but we now know it was acute lymphocytic leukemia—and so she wasn't good enough for the University of Texas MD Anderson Medical Center. But they had money, which again is very important in medicine. If you have money, you're good. If you don't, well, I can't say the word. But anyway, they went up to the Mayo Clinic and I remember my mother and father saying, "It's mighty fine they have money."

DREYER: So money could actually trump skin color?

McNEALY: Yes.

DREYER: Okay. I wanted to make sure I had that straight.

McNEALY: So, my brother said, "Yeah, they're rich, they're 'blank' rich, N-word rich." And my father kicked him in the butt.

So that made a really huge impression on me. It was one of many,

many deep hurts in life. That hurt, I think, was a motivating factor to want to take care of the defenseless, the weak, the poor.

[*A Buddy Holly recording is played.*]

DREYER: We often ask our guests to suggest music that they relate to or that played some role in their lives. How come Buddy Holly?

McNEALY: Well, I loved Buddy Holly. One night, we were sitting-in at this hamburger place and we were about to get thrown out. They started on one end of the room—and I was trying to inch back further away because Buddy Holly's "Heartbeat" came on. It was the first time I'd ever heard that song, and I just loved it. So I was trying to delay getting thrown out.

DREYER: Okay. How many places did you get thrown out of?

McNEALY: Many. And the Y.

DREYER: Did you get busted? Were you arrested at all?

McNEALY: You know, I was detained a couple of times. The most memorable time was when I was in the Chuck Wagon at UT [the café in the Student Union], and this white kid struck up a conversation with me. I had gone there one lonely Saturday night because the chairman of the Campus Interracial Committee, Billy Spearman, had taken my girlfriend, and I didn't want to go over to Almetris Co-op—that's where the Black girls lived—and watch them play tonsil hockey or anything like that.

So, a white kid struck up a conversation with me and we started talking about music. He invited me to sit with them—and that was the late and the great Chet Helms. So, I guess someone called the police, and we came out with his entourage—he was in front of me and I was like a couple of steps back, and the rest of his entourage was maybe ten yards ahead.

The police were behind this retaining wall and they grabbed me. And Chet, he's still talking to me and proceeding—and he looked around like, "Where is he?" And by that time, I'm in the police car, and Chet goes up to them—and he was extremely soft-spoken and extremely reasonable. And they would have nothing of that.

So, he walks and sits down in front of the police car. And his friends, they sat down, too. And I didn't even know any of them. And the police were so startled that young white kids would defend a Black kid, they let me go.

I ran into Chet in front of the Student Union—I don't know if it was days or months later—and we were talking about segregation and he was more radical than I was. I thought maybe things that were government owned or state owned, or city facilities, could be integrated. And he said, "No, we can integrate everything here."

So I said, "Where do we start?" And there on the poster, on a tree, was a sign about the Texas Cowboys' blackface minstrel show—and it was Jessica Darling, and she was going to play this "N-word whore" in the minstrel show. Jessica Darling was, I guess, kind of the darling of sorority row. She was, I believe, a cheerleader.

DREYER: Incidentally, Chet Helms became a music impresario and went on to start the Avalon Ballroom in San Francisco and the Family Dog. Something of a counterculture icon. He helped recruit Janis Joplin and managed Big Brother and the Holding Company.

So, tell me about the minstrel show. What did they do? What *was* the minstrel show? I mean, obviously you didn't see it.

McNEALY: I never saw one, but Chet and I started a petition to abolish the minstrel show. And I remember they had a "Roundup Jail" right next to it. And Mike Gipson, the boy in *Old Yeller*, came up and tore down the Roundup Jail. And an English instructor, Claude Allen, showed up with a sign that said, "Segregation is an anachronism." I had no idea what that word meant. We lost that struggle.

DREYER: Of course there were a lot of fronts on which that battle was fought, and there were the UT dormitories, Kinsolving dormitory.

McNEALY: That was a great one. The university had published some adverse rules, rules to make you mad. And then, if they could make you mad, they could put you on disciplinary probation and throw you out of school.

DREYER: What kind of rules were these?

McNEALY: The rules were that if you were a Black man, you could not

> **"The university had published some adverse rules, rules to make you mad. And then, if they could make you mad, they could put you on disciplinary probation and throw you out of school."**

go to a dormitory where white women were. If you were a Black woman, you could go to a white woman's room, but you couldn't use any of the public areas or their water fountains or their restrooms.

So, I came into the Chuck Wagon one morning and James Strickland and Mike Gipson were there, and they had the newspaper with the new dormitory rules and they had cans of black paint. So, they went around the campus painting, "Regents is pigs."

Yours truly—and I mean *yours truly*—went to Kinsolving, and I drank out of the water fountain, I used the toilet. People were screaming, and shortly thereafter I went along with Mary Simpson and Sherryl Griffin—we wanted to go talk to UT president Logan Wilson. We thought we could convince him that segregation was wrong—and they told us to have a Coke and a smile, and we'd never get to see him.

So we went outside the Tower [the main administration building], and I know Sherryl started to pray—she's become a minister. And we vowed to come back every day. And after a few days, there were a lot of police, campus police. So, people started asking us what we were doing, and we told them that we pay the same tuition they pay and we should have the same rights that all students did: the band, the drama department, Plan II, the dormitory, athletics.

A number of kids from the Hillel Foundation joined us. The Jewish students were often quite important to the demonstrations. And then one day we had to work out a compromise over what to say. Some students, particularly some of the Jewish students, were uncomfortable with the prayer. We worked out a compromise where we would recite the university motto which was over the door: "Ye shall know the truth and the truth shall set you free." So, we would speak that for about five minutes every noon. And one day there were five thousand mostly white students there.

DREYER: Chandler Davidson, who is a professor emeritus at Rice University and whom you know, you worked with, was one of the organizers of civil rights activity in Austin—I guess the stand-ins especially. [Davidson, who became a leading voting rights scholar, passed away on April 10, 2021.]

Chandler emailed us, since you were going to be on the show. He said, and this is a quote, "The civil rights movement in Houston and Austin, seen from half a century's distance, might seem to a younger generation to have been led by serious, solemn upright soldiers in the battle for racial justice. My own memories of the times, however, suggest that while the civil rights soldiers were serious, and often brave as well, there was, as with any youth movement, a lot of wild and crazy stuff going on. Things that would bring a chuckle, or even a guffaw, when told today. Would you agree?"

He was giving this to me as a question for you, Leon. What comes to mind that you can tell us on the radio?

MCNEALY: Well, let me say that Chandler Davidson and Houston Wade and Casey Hayden, I'm in awe of their brilliance. At the sit-in reunion, just to hear Chandler's recounts—and I said, "No wonder we won, those were some smart people."

DREYER: So, were you a bunch of wild and crazy guys?

"I was often in the wrong place at the wrong time, and I was usually more innocent than guilty."

MCNEALY: Yeah. I was often in the wrong place at the wrong time, and I was usually more innocent than guilty.

DREYER: And you're sticking to your story.

MCNEALY: Yeah, but we used to have some really fun times, with some of the white kids at the Y. We had this game, "cowboys and the N-word," and what I know now is I should have been one of the cowboys. I didn't know there were Black cowboys then. And so they would chase me down Guadalupe Street, and I was really fast, and they would say, "Stop that N-word." That was kind of fun.

DREYER: It beat the minstrel shows.

McNEALY: Another time I went to Renfro's Drugstore and one of them drove up on the curb. They grabbed me and threw me in the back of their car and one of them said, "Get the witnesses!" And people were hitting the ground. That was kind of fun.

DREYER: Tell me about Houston Wade. I believe he has since left us; tell me about him.

McNEALY: Well, Houston, again, was a brainchild of the movement and he had this very soft-spoken, very gentle style. And they used to drink beer—which I didn't—but they would have a few beers afterwards and they would sing songs, you know, "Workers' flag is deepest red, it often shrouds our hallowed dead." I remember that.

DREYER: So it *was* a bunch of commies. I knew it.

McNEALY: Well, you know, the *Dallas Morning News* ran its article on leftist influence at the Y, which resulted in us getting bombed.

DREYER: Yeah. Casey Hayden, of course, went on to become a very important figure in the movement. In the Deep South she worked with SNCC [the Student Nonviolent Coordinating Committee].

McNEALY: Uh-huh.

DREYER: And she wrote critically about the role that women played in the civil rights movement in the South, which got a lot of attention and really was an inspiration for a lot of women who then helped initiate the women's liberation movement.

McNEALY: Yeah, she was brilliant and a great leader. And of course, you know, my mind was always on a very high plane, and so I wasn't one of them—"Like say, man, she sure is fine." I wasn't one of those.

DREYER: No, certainly not. We're glad to know it, too. When you look back at all of that, you know, there was a lot of excitement and it was kind of scary at times.

McNEALY: I think the thing that struck me the most when I was there, I didn't know if we were going to win. That was the major anxiety. Were we going to lose the sit-ins and the stand-ins, were we ever going to have integration in the community as a whole?

But it was, I guess, the beginning of me thinking in a greater context—not just racial discrimination but discrimination against other people, discrimination against women, discrimination against gay people, and so I evolved. I was part of some of the shameful legacy that we have about discrimination against women or discrimination against gay people.

DREYER: That was a long process, that realization, wasn't it?

McNEALY: Yes, it was. In fact, I think I mentioned at the stand-in reunion that I called Anthony Henry up and apologized for the way we had behaved towards him for being gay.

DREYER: Yeah. And it was a difficult time then to be openly gay.

McNEALY: And—the other stress—I also had to pass my classes. And I thought the University of Texas was hard.

DREYER: But you passed.

McNEALY: Yes, I did.

DREYER: And you went on to become a hotshot doctor. Dr. Leon McNealy, who is a radiation oncologist.

McNEALY: Yes.

DREYER: And was a major player in the civil rights movement in the early '60s.

McNEALY: When you mention names like Chandler Davidson, Houston Wade, those were the heavy hitters.

DREYER: But we did have a biracial movement, and it laid the groundwork for what happened in the future. I didn't get to Austin until 1963, and I got involved in the New Left and SDS. And certainly, there were still the issues that were not resolved, there were demonstrations. I remember Roy's Lounge, which not only, I believe, wouldn't serve Black people but also wouldn't serve longhairs. We had demonstrations there and people got busted.

McNEALY: I recall that somebody actually got shot on the Drag, by a police officer, who was a longhair. It was an accident of course: the officer dropped his gun and it happened to discharge.

[*A recording of Johnny Horton's "Honky-Tonk Man" is played.*]

DREYER: Dr. Leon McNealy. Johnny Horton. Where did he come in?

McNEALY: Well, one night I went to the Chuck Wagon.

DREYER: The Chuck Wagon, by the way, was the restaurant in the Student Union at the University of Texas which served as kind of central headquarters for all of those who were a little bit off the beaten path.

McNEALY: I think it had some famous raid in there after I left.

DREYER: There was a police riot. Yes, a major event.

McNEALY: So, I go in the—I called it the "Upchuck Wagon"—and there was this white guy in my class and probably one of the biggest white guys I'd ever seen, all cowboy boots and big Texas buckle. And he had this beautiful blond wife who was very petite, and she had on these really short shorts and a little halter top and she's finger-popping and going on. And so, he invites me to sit down, and I knew this was not a good thing. But, you know, what can I say? I was like twenty years old. And so he sits down and he's introducing—and, "He's in my class," and like that—and he says, "My little Joan just loves to dance."

DREYER: Oh, boy.

McNEALY: He says, "I can't chew gum and walk." And so he invites me to dance with her. Now, I don't know what was wrong with me, but she grabs me, and she pulls me up and started dancing. And she's doing this—it is kind of ironic because the white kids called this dance the "N-word twist." So, you've got this Black boy and this white girl doing the N-word twist. And you know, records lasted like three minutes in those days and my life was flashing in front of me—and it seemed like an hour.

But the police come bursting in and the man gets up—we're no more than three feet away from him and his wife—and he says, "What's wrong, officer?" And he says, "This boy is breaking the rules," and he said, "What rule?" He says, "I ain't got no rule, that's what rule." You know, Jim McCulloch is sitting over there with his pipe. Like, I can't make this up if I was on peyote.

So Jimmy Horton's "Honky-Tonk Man" has special memories.

DREYER: You were talking of people like John Henry Faulk, who's a legendary name. And Maury Maverick.

McNEALY: Yes, Maury Maverick, Sam Houston Clinton, all general supporters of the movement. One of my precious memories was having seen Maverick getting his face slapped for asking a person about her affair or alleged affair with Lyndon Johnson.

You know, he was also friends with Bill Brammer.

DREYER: Billy Lee, yeah. Author of *The Gay Place*.

McNEALY: Another thing—I was at this party and we got raided because we were integrated. And so we were fleeing from the police and I helped Billy Lee lift his girlfriend—he was small, like I am—over the fence at the party.

DREYER: I was in Houston in the early '70s and we were involved in radical activities, and we published a newspaper then called *Space City!*, and we faced the wrath of the Ku Klux Klan.

But I don't think Austin had that much of an active right wing. It had always been, even back then, a fairly progressive city, and I don't think you faced here, or even in Houston, the kind of things that civil rights demonstrators faced in the Deep South.

McNEALY: I got rescued by an Austin detective in front of the Y when I got confronted by some hostile people; he drove up on the curb and pulled his gun and backed them off.

Actually, I did go through a game-changing event in my life. I used to sleep with a revolver under my pillow and, regrettably, it was used in a suicide.

DREYER: Oh, boy.

MCNEALY: So, after that I became an antigun person.

I was in the military, briefly. I was going to the next military assignment and I was supposed to turn left, but I got confused with my poor sense of direction and I turned right. And I must have been daydreaming and it turned out I was in Vancouver, Canada. So I decided to—since there were a lot of people that were draft dodgers up there—to try to persuade them to come home. And so I stayed up in Canada for a while.

DREYER: Okay. It's now 2011, fifty years since the stand-in demonstrations. We have a Black man who was elected president of the United States, and I'd like to know your opinion about that and about what's going on. Did the election of an African American president just scare a lot of people? Did it bring a lot of stuff out of them?

MCNEALY: I think so.

DREYER: Do you believe that it's racial, that a lot of the response to Obama is based on race?

MCNEALY: Absolutely. And, you know, I have mixed emotions. Suppose you had a really tough Black man elected? You know, what would they do then?

DREYER: There are those who say that one of the things Obama has been afraid of is being seen as the "angry Black man." But what's your feel for what's happening in this country right now? It's kind of scary. We had 25 percent of the country believing that Obama was not born in America.

MCNEALY: Well, it makes me feel alienated again, you know. I felt very alienated back in the '60s—that's why I moved to Canada. And I've begun to start fantasizing about which country do I want to move to. It's going to be a long time before people of color are accepted fully in this country. White America has a tremendous amount of denial and it seems like it's impenetrable.

I got busted not too long ago for taking mail out of my mailbox. When I told one of my white colleagues, he said, "Well, they're just looking out for you."

DREYER: What happened?

McNEALY: Well, I mean, what would you think if you saw an elderly Black man driving a late-model German car, obeying all the traffic laws, and he drives up to this house in a white neighborhood and takes mail out of a mailbox? I mean—it's obviously a thief.

DREYER: Do you think people were more freaked out by Barack Obama because not only was he a Black man but he was born of a mixed marriage?

McNEALY: That's the thing that, you know, nice people don't talk about, but that's what they're thinking. You know, I have to leave the room to really find out what's going on and have people tell me what people said.

DREYER: What about Obama? What do you think about what he's done? I mean, a lot of people, obviously, who worked for him and supported him have been very disappointed. So, were you disappointed?

McNEALY: Yes. And maybe I'm going to mellow out, because, you know, what is the alternative? I will probably go to the polls and vote for him.

DREYER: But you probably won't go out and work for him?

McNEALY: I probably won't be sending any money this time. I'm very conflicted.

DREYER: What about American society? Death panels, birtherism—the fact that things like that can take hold so easily. And that people are willing to believe almost anything, the rise of the whole Tea Party movement, which was essentially funded, of course, by Republican big money.

McNEALY: Well, you know, it's like, I think Goebbels said that the best lie to tell is a lie that people want to hear. And sometimes I will try to educate people when they start these crazy criticisms. Like, some people where I was working were upset about Michelle Obama's airplane that she flies on.

So, you try to reason with them and say, you know, "The First Lady can't actually go to the airport and catch a plane, and this airplane is flown by a special military unit. They fly people regardless of their political party or their color, and it's the same airplane that Laura Bush flew on. Were you upset that Laura Bush was using the plane?"

DREYER: But the question is how come these things get so much into the mainstream and are so easily accepted?

McNEALY: Part of it is the twenty-four-hour cable channels. Fox [News] is hugely influential, and at one of the places where I work, if you go in there, that's what's in the waiting room: Fox.

DREYER: So, you think that cable news and the internet, too, make it easy for misinformation to get spread all over the place?

McNEALY: And people want to believe it.

DREYER: Okay, are you involved in politics? Have you been involved in politics in recent times?

McNEALY: No, I haven't. The last time I was involved was when I lived in Iowa, because I just loved the Iowa caucus. I liked to do that—and people put on the funny hats. I was a John Kerry delegate and my ex-to-be was for Edwards.

DREYER: As a doctor, have you had problems through the years—are we beyond that?—because of your race.

McNEALY: No. You often won't get the same respect as a white doctor, from staff or patients. We have a very neat young woman doctor now who's a different generation. She says "awesome" and "totally," but she takes no prisoners if you disrespect her. I told her she's my role model.

But here's the nicest thing that ever happened to me when I was a doctor. I usually wear a suit and tie, but if I want respect, you know, I put the white coat on. So, I go up on the floor and this nurse just chews me out; there had been a spill and I think if the spill is a certain size, they have to clean it up. If it's bigger, it's environmental services. So, she thought I was from environmental services, but I hadn't brought a mop or anything.

So I got all the paper up and I cleaned up the spill. And one of the doctors said, "What's Dr. McNealy doing?" She said, "Oh, I didn't know he was a doctor." And I said, "Well, it doesn't really matter. I'm not too good to clean up a spill. But even if I wasn't a doctor, that's not the way you talk to people."

Thorne Dreyer and pioneering Houston feminist Frances "Poppy" Northcutt (*right*) after their *Rag Radio* interview. The show was broadcast remotely from the studios of KPFT radio in Houston. Photo by Marlo Blue.

FRANCES "POPPY" NORTHCUTT

Houston, we have a problem.

Poppy Northcutt talks about how she helped us fly to the moon in a time of crisis and then became a major player in the struggle for women's rights.

Northcutt, a mathematician and an engineer, gained national recognition for her pioneering role as the first woman to work in operational support at NASA's Mission Control. She was featured in the three-part 2019 PBS documentary Chasing the Moon *and was awarded the Presidential Medal of Freedom team award for work in the rescue of the Apollo 13 crew.*

Northcutt was a leader, both in Houston and nationally, of the women's rights movement. She served as the City of Houston's first women's advocate, was the founding chair of the Harris County Women's Political Caucus, and served on the national board of the National Organization for Women (NOW). She was a primary organizer of three national women's gatherings in Houston. Later she went into law and became the city's first prosecutor specializing in domestic violence.

In November 2019, during the fiftieth-anniversary year of the Apollo 11 flight to the moon, NOW honored Frances "Poppy" Northcutt "for her historic contributions to America's space mission, to gender equality and to legal advocacy for women."

I knew Poppy from Houston politics back in the '70s, and we reunited at the Texas State Capitol in June 2013, when Wendy Davis was filibustering anti-abortion legislation.

OCTOBER 25, 2013

THORNE DREYER: Frances "Poppy" Northcutt has played a very significant role in Houston history and in the history of the women's movement in this country.

Northcutt was the City of Houston's first women's advocate in 1974 and '75, under Mayor Fred Hofheinz. She was also the founding chair, in 1974, of the Harris County Women's Political Caucus, which was probably the most active of any women's political caucus in the country.

But Northcutt first gained national attention during the Apollo missions in the mid-'60s when, as an engineer, she was the first woman to work in flight support at NASA's Mission Control.

FRANCES "POPPY" NORTHCUTT: I was the first woman in what they called operational support.

DREYER: Poppy was profiled in a September 1970 *Life* magazine cover story titled "Women Arise," where she was featured as one of eight women "succeeding in a man's world." She was singled out in a 1969 AP story about women playing key roles in the space program. She was also featured in *Mademoiselle* and *Ms.* magazine and won a number of awards for her work.

But, first things first. You were "Miss Watermelon"? From Luling, Texas?

NORTHCUTT: [*Laughs*] I was the Watermelon Thump Parade Marshal.

DREYER: The what?

NORTHCUTT: Parade Marshal. I was not "Miss Watermelon."

DREYER: Well, that's a shame.

NORTHCUTT: There's a big difference.

DREYER: Alright. Most of the time you were at NASA, you were the only woman in Mission Control, right?

NORTHCUTT: That's true.

DREYER: And you were a mathematician. What did you do in relation to the Apollo missions?

NORTHCUTT: I worked on what was called the "Return to Earth" program. It was initially called the "Abort" program, but then they changed the name because they didn't want people to realize that we might have a disaster and have to abort. It was changed for PR purposes.

We wrote and designed the computer programs that were used to bring the spacecraft back to the earth from the moon, whether things went wrong or not. We were initially supposed to just do them if things went wrong, but our program was so good that they used us when things were going right, as well. Our program was used during all of the Apollo missions.

DREYER: Okay. You were not at Mission Control when "Houston, we have a problem" happened [during the Apollo 13 mission].

NORTHCUTT: Literally, no—I was not physically there.

DREYER: But you were there soon.

NORTHCUTT: I was there soon.

DREYER: And how did you deal with that? That was Apollo 13.

NORTHCUTT: My task didn't really start until they got relatively close to the moon, and that emergency occurred earlier.

I had some leisure time right at the beginning of the mission, so I had flown to the Cape [Canaveral] to go watch the liftoff. What I remember in particular about the flight going off, the liftoff, the launch, was that it took off at 13:13 hours, the number thirteen was heavily involved. And one of the flight crew was pulled off at the last minute and someone else substituted in.

I had gotten back to Houston from Florida and the news came on—and about five minutes later Jules Bergman, who was the science reporter from ABC, called me. And I thought that was interesting that he called me before I was called in by anybody else. As soon as he called me, I put on my shoes and I went to the control center. And the people there said, "We were trying to reach you, we couldn't find your phone number." I said, "Well, Jules Bergman found my phone number, what's wrong with you people?"

DREYER: As a mathematician, what was your role? What kind of work did you all do in terms of figuring out, I guess, the trajectory issues?

NORTHCUTT: It's just trajectory design. It was mainly figuring out how to optimize the trajectories. Because there's many ways you can come home, but you want to come home the cheapest in terms of fuel, and the fastest in terms of time. And sometimes you need to make trade-offs between those two things.

And certainly in Apollo 13 those trade-offs were really critical because we had lost the main spacecraft engine.

DREYER: Did you have to redesign the return route?

NORTHCUTT: Truly, I did not. The computer program that we designed was designed to bring you home. And it was designed not for a specific mission but to figure out how to do it, whatever your situation was. It was really a program that was supposed to be there to take care of whatever contingency you had.

DREYER: In *Life* magazine, September 4, 1970, you said that "the nature of this business"—and this was NASA, this was the space business—"doesn't lend itself to discrimination. If you write a computer program it either works or it doesn't. If you were a man, it is assumed you are competent until you prove you're incompetent. For a woman it's just the other way around."

They called you a "computress," right?

NORTHCUTT: Uh-huh.

DREYER: There's a wonderful interview that our old friend Jane Ely did. Jane, who used to work for the *Houston Post*, interviewed Poppy for the Houston Public Library digital archives—oral history archives.

About the term "computress," I think you told Jane Ely, "That sounds like a female computer."

NORTHCUTT: It does.

DREYER: All right. What happened when you were doing all of this and you started being singled out. The media referred to you as a "tall blond mathematician." And so you got a lot of attention and you got attention as a woman who was becoming extremely successful—as *Life* magazine said—"in a man's world." You got plugged into the women's movement at the same time this was all going on, is that right?

NORTHCUTT: Pretty much so. I became very conscious about the women's rights movement. I had been so submerged in my work—because in the early days of preparation for the Apollo program, we worked enormous hours getting ready to fly those missions. And the schedule was accelerated because there was some concern that the Russians might beat us to the moon. We were really under intense work pressure, so I barely read the newspaper.

But in a sense the media is part of what got me involved in the women's rights movement—because the media was coming to me, talking to me, and they're asking me about women's rights, and the more they talked to me, the more I thought, "I need to be involved in this."

DREYER: An awful lot of history.

NORTHCUTT: I've forgotten a whole lot of it.

I was on the national board of directors for the National Organization for Women in the early '70s. We had one of the early national conferences for NOW in Houston, and Houston was also the host for the first National Women's Political Caucus national convention.

But as we were putting these conferences together, the people from the Northeast, you would have thought that they were going to have to ride a stagecoach into town. They were so concerned about, "Well, is there a hotel?" Or, "How are we going to get there?" As if we were, you know, back in two hundred years ago.

DREYER: [*Laughs*] There was a point when there were three national conferences in a short period of time, and Houston was kind of the epicenter of the women's movement in the country.

NORTHCUTT: We were. We had a very, very strong women's rights movement in Houston in particular, and in Texas in general. We may have been the earliest big city to have a woman mayor, Kathy Whitmire, and she came out of the Harris County Women's Political Caucus. And,

"We had a very, very strong women's rights movement in Houston in particular, and in Texas in general."

you know, we had Sissy Farenthold, who was prominent on the national stage at that time. We had Ann Richards in Austin as governor in the early '90s.

So Houston was very progressive. We were the fifth state to ratify the Equal Rights Amendment nationally. And we would have probably been the *first* state if the legislature had been in session at the time. They ratified it as soon as they came back in.

We had our own state Equal Rights Amendment to the constitution that was passed overwhelmingly. We had full-time legislative lobbyists up there with the Women's Political Caucus in the early '70s and we passed equal credit laws, we passed all kinds of stuff.

DREYER: Were you the first women's advocate in the country? Were there other women's advocates in other municipalities?

NORTHCUTT: I don't know. I think I was certainly the first one in a major city.

DREYER: There was a women's strike that, I think, was one of the first things you got involved in. You came to Houston for this demonstration and you started to meet the organizers.

NORTHCUTT: August 26, 1970.

DREYER: August 26, 1970. And then you very quickly got involved organizationally.

NORTHCUTT: Up to my eyeballs, immediately. It was an incredible time.

DREYER: So it was out of that that you got involved as Houston's women's advocate? For the people who don't know, Fred Hofheinz was a young progressive mayor—certainly by Houston political standards, certainly by the standards of Louie Welch, who was the mayor immediately preceding him. He was very open to doing things differently.

For instance, the Houston police had become famous during that time, not only for not letting women in but for its infiltration by the Ku Klux Klan. And Fred Hofheinz was the first mayor who got his police chief to start trying to deal with that issue.

NORTHCUTT: I think the term "throw-down weapon" originated in Houston. "Throw-down gun" [a weapon planted by police to suggest it belonged to the victim].

DREYER: We talked about Houston in many ways being a progressive city; the Houston Police was not a progressive police force. Maybe "police" and "progressive" is an oxymoron, but we had people being thrown into the bayous; there was a lot of racism. [In one incident in 1977, officers beat to death a Mexican American Vietnam vet, Joe Campos Torres, and threw his body into Buffalo Bayou.]

And there was certainly sex discrimination everywhere. How was it that you—and the movement—came about confronting Fred Hofheinz when he was running for mayor? Confronting him about dealing with women's issues and about having a women's advocate. I know you said, "We dogged the poor man." You said, "We stalked him."

NORTHCUTT: We did. We absolutely stalked him.

We were concerned about no women on patrol. If you were a woman and you were in the police department—first of all, you were rare if you were there to start with, but you were also invisible. You were either in the women's jail or you worked juvenile.

There were very few women in the police department, and we were very committed to getting women out on patrol where they were visible, because it changes your perception of women. They had to be seen. And there were no women in the fire department, either.

So, we had a handful of us—it's amazing how few people can seem like many—that were just committed to try to be anywhere Fred was going to show up campaigning. And ask our questions—our pushy, obnoxious little question about, "What are you going to do about women in the police department?"

DREYER: So, he was confronted and he was asked to sign an agreement—

in exchange for the women's movement support—that he would name a women's advocate when he was elected. Is that right?

NORTHCUTT: He ran twice. He lost in his first bid [in 1971]. And during his first campaign someone put a microphone in front of his wife, and he took the microphone away from her—and said, "I speak for my wife." And he got a zillion "barefoot and pregnant" awards. Then when he lost, he lost in a squeaker; apparently his people thought that he lost because he didn't have the active support of the women's rights movement.

So, next time when he ran [in 1973], he called Helen Cassidy on the phone—at that time she was the head of the Women's Political Caucus statewide—and basically said, "What do I have to do to get your support?" And she gave him a list and had him sign a sworn notarized statement of his promises about what he was going to do for women. And I'd never heard of any politician doing that before.

Obviously, we don't trust people just saying stuff—we wanted a real commitment. And one of the things that he said he would do was appoint a women's advocate.

DREYER: And how did you become that women's advocate?

NORTHCUTT: Well, I went down and interviewed for the job. And I think they decided to put me in it because I may have been the only person who walked in with a laundry list saying exactly "this is what I'm here to do." Because I knew exactly what I thought needed to be done.

DREYER: And what was that?

NORTHCUTT: Well, an important thing was an equal pay study for the City of Houston, because you needed a starting place in order to figure out what your pay situation was. And another thing was the police and the fire; we needed to get women in the police and the fire and needed to do it tout suite.

And I also wanted to improve the treatment of rape victims. At that time women had to pay for their own rape [kit] collection. There was a statute saying they didn't have to pay for it, but it was not being enforced and women were having to pay for their own rape kits to be collected.

DREYER: I saw where the police chief was convinced that women were going to falsely report rape so that they could get a free rape kit.

NORTHCUTT: That was the assistant police chief at the time, who later became the police chief. And I was amazed when he said that.

DREYER: What did that mean? How bizarre.

NORTHCUTT: Well, I can't imagine. No woman that I have ever met has wanted to go in and have a vaginal examination—in her life. That's why we have cervical cancer problems to a large extent—because women are reluctant to go in and have that vaginal exam done.

DREYER: How much success did you have?

NORTHCUTT: I had a pretty good success rate. We got women visible in the police department for the first time and got them in in significant numbers. At one point—within a fairly short period of time—half the police class was women. It was harder to get women into the fire department, but that happened. And, you know, that policy about rape kits was changed. And I did the equal pay study. So, we made a lot of progress.

DREYER: And just the fact of having you and having that voice—the empowerment aspect of that—may have been even more important than the actual changes.

NORTHCUTT: It could have been. And we had for the first time an Affirmative Action Commission, and I served on that commission—I was the chair of it at one point—so we made a lot of steps forward.

DREYER: One of the things you said was that Fred Hofheinz was very cooperative and you worked very well with him, despite what he had said about speaking for his wife. Any of us who knew his wife, Mac Hofheinz, knew that no one spoke for Mac Hofheinz.

NORTHCUTT: Sometimes you get on the media and you say things that you shouldn't say, or say it in a way you shouldn't say it.

DREYER: Right.

NORTHCUTT: No. He was very cooperative and he was a very good mayor.

DREYER: And then, of course, Kathy Whitmire was mayor [1982-1992].

Before she was mayor, she was the first city controller—the first city-wide elected woman officeholder in the city of Houston—and later Houston had a female police chief, and women had a lot of presence in city government and in state and national government.

NORTHCUTT: Yes, we did.

DREYER: How has Houston changed, and how does that reflect what's happening in the women's movement in general?

NORTHCUTT: Well, if you're talking about Houston, I think it is still a pretty progressive city. I mean, we have an openly gay mayor.

DREYER: Annise Parker. Openly gay female mayor [2010-2016].

NORTHCUTT: Openly gay female mayor. I think she's the only one from a major city. So, you know, Houston is still a pretty open, progressive city. It's when you get out past the Beltway that things get weird.

DREYER: Houston has become, according to a Rice University study, the most diverse city in the country. Houston's reputation outside of the city, however, is not so good. People don't know what the city is, what it has become, what all happens here.

NORTHCUTT: That's because they're probably seeing people from our congressional delegation—and seeing the picture based on that group is a pretty scary prospect.

DREYER: And Texas is such a bad example of gerrymandering and of the Far Right taking power in districts in which they have absolutely no opposition. And in order to keep their base they just get crazier and crazier.

What are you doing now—what is NOW doing?

NORTHCUTT: I got back involved with the National Organization for Women because I was increasingly concerned about what I could see coming down the pike on abortion rights. I have remained active over the years—I've always been involved but I hadn't been really active in a particular activist organization. And about four years ago I got really worried—because I can count, I'm real good at counting.

DREYER: You're officially certified as being good at counting.

NORTHCUTT: Yeah, I'm a really good counter, and I could count what was going on in the Texas Legislature. I could see the result of that gerrymandering that was going on. I could tell that our Democratic numbers had dropped so much that we weren't going to be able to hold the line. And the Tea Party people were coming in, the right wing, you know—extremists—were coming in and they were going to try to get their stuff through.

So, I got back involved and I'm actually the president of Texas NOW as well as the Houston-area chapter. So, one of the things that I expect we're going to start doing is some actions about the veto of the equal pay act that [Governor] Rick Perry did. And obviously, we're concerned and continue to be involved in this fight about reproductive justice.

DREYER: You and I met up in the gallery at the capitol earlier this year, during the week that Wendy Davis's filibuster occurred and the whole issue about women's health came to the floor. And that was certainly a remarkable week.

What do you think about what happened there, and what do you think about how that energy will go forward? And tied into that, obviously, is Wendy Davis's campaign for governor.

NORTHCUTT: I think that women had sort of been lulled to sleep; they saw the gains that had been made and thought, "Okay, we don't have to worry about this stuff anymore." And then, during that special session, women really began to realize, "They actually are going to take away a big chunk of our rights." It really lit a fuse under a bunch of people. And suddenly they came out of the woodwork and went to Austin. I saw people I hadn't seen in decades; not just you—a lot of people.

And they're still very motivated and very energized about that.

"I think that women had sort of been lulled to sleep; they saw the gains that had been made and thought, 'Okay, we don't have to worry about this stuff anymore.'"

I was in favor of Wendy running for governor before that. [Davis ran unsuccessfully for governor of Texas in 2014.] I thought—well before the filibuster—that she was our best hope. And this was not her first filibuster; she filibustered about education—what was it—two years ago? And she's really very talented.

One of the things that these right-wingers haven't figured out yet is that when you really go in and try to suppress the vote—it's like raising that sleeping giant that they did over the summertime during the filibuster. You go in and you start trying to take away people's right to vote and you really make some people mad. And people will start standing up and coming out just because of that.

> **"You go in and you start trying to take away people's right to vote and you really make some people mad. And people will start standing up and coming out just because of that."**

DREYER: So, Poppy Northcutt, you were a mathematician, engineer, worked in the space program, you worked in the women's movement, you worked in municipal government, you worked for a short period of time as a stockbroker? And you worked as an assistant DA.

NORTHCUTT: Right.

DREYER: You were the first prosecutor in Houston working in domestic violence. There wasn't a domestic violence division before that, right?

NORTHCUTT: The DA's office decided to put one up and they needed a felony prosecutor, so I went in as the first felony prosecutor over there.

As I said, I wasn't that active in organizational stuff during the '80s and '90s, but I was always active doing something about women's rights—always. Whatever I was doing, I was doing something about women's rights. I've always tried to live my feminist beliefs.

DREYER: How did having all these different life experiences help you to better understand what's going on in our society?

NORTHCUTT: One of the things you do when you get involved in a political action movement is you become a lot more aware of your state legislature and your city council and your congress and all of those people and how those bodies actually work—not what you were taught in school, which is just a pack of lies. I mean, it may be theoretically true, but it's not practically true.

DREYER: I want to come back to something that we just touched on. In 1977, I believe it was, when they held the National Women's Conference in Houston. It was one of three major conferences held in Houston during that short period, about a year and a half period. It came out of International Women's Day. It was organized by the state department, and you were the on-site coordinator for that and you also were involved in coordinating the other events that happened.

NORTHCUTT: Yes.

DREYER: You were the go-to person for this kind of thing.

NORTHCUTT: Yeah, I'm a nuts and bolts person.

DREYER: You handled the bolts as opposed to the nuts, I understand.

NORTHCUTT: Exactly. Helen Cassidy and I were co-coordinators on the ground in terms of site management. We always said, "I handle the bolts and you handle the nuts."

DREYER: And there were a lot of nuts to handle, too.

NORTHCUTT: There were a lot of nuts to handle. We had bomb scares being called in. We had all sorts of stuff going on.

DREYER: Did you have much direct conflict or contact with the Klan—because the Klan was very active in Houston during this time.

NORTHCUTT: Well, yeah, they were very active. I remember one time I was threatened by the Klan. I was up talking about their trying to rescind our ratification of the Equal Rights Amendment and there was some Klan guy that accosted me. And my friend Helen grabs me and she says, "Do you know who the hell that is that you're getting in the face of?"

DREYER: Louis Beam?

NORTHCUTT: Yeah.

DREYER: And Louis Beam was one of the Klansmen implicated in the Pacifica radio bombing and other vigilante activities.

NORTHCUTT: The Women's Political Caucus was up and running when McGovern was campaigning for the Democratic nomination in '72. We took a challenge to the National Democratic Convention, challenging the underrepresentation of women. The McGovern-Fraser rules had been passed, which said that we had to have at least a third of the delegation be women, and that was the first time that had happened.

But in fact, up and down the line, lots of delegations were not representing women like they were supposed to.

DREYER: Including the Wallace delegation, I understand. You ended up working for the women supporting George Wallace?

NORTHCUTT: We did. We worked for all of the women because we were not there trying to change the political makeup of any delegation; what we were there to do was to try to increase the representation of women. We were one of the few states that had organized from the precinct level all the way up, because we were very, very well organized in Texas.

So, we were heard; we actually had a hearing before the hearings officer at the Democratic National Credentials Committee. And the guy who was defending the party said something about there not being enough women to fill these delegate spots. And in the audience, we suddenly had women shouting out.

They were standing up, saying, well, "My name is so-and-so and I was a Wallace delegate and I'm a woman and I was ready, willing, and able, and they wouldn't let me." And we had them from Humphrey and Wallace and everything. It was very funny. The whole room cracked up when that happened.

DREYER: But I understand the Wallace women were very appreciative and worked with you.

NORTHCUTT: Yeah. We were trying to get everybody a seat at the table. They didn't grant the challenge on women, but we have never had a convention since in the Democratic Party where women were not fully and fairly represented. So, even though we lost at the time, we actually won. We won the war.

DREYER: You have said that when you were in the women's movement and the Women's Political Caucus, there were Republicans involved as well. That's because there were Republicans back then that were moderates, that were pro-choice.

NORTHCUTT: Exactly. Lots of them. And there still are. They're just afraid to open their mouth.

DREYER: And we saw some of them at the state capitol during Wendy's filibuster.

NORTHCUTT: I think for a lot of Republicans, when Karl Rove and so forth started bringing in this extreme religious right, a lot of people saw this and thought, "We just have to put up with them and sort of nod to them and we won't really have to do anything."

So, I think a lot of Republican women thought, "Oh, well, you know, they're not really going to get rid of our reproductive rights. They're not really going to come after birth control. They're not really going to come after abortion. They may say it, but it's not going to happen."

DREYER: A lot of the wars have been won. Certainly, the times have changed substantially, especially for women; the opportunities are much greater than they were before you got involved in this whole process, but there's still lots to do, right?

NORTHCUTT: There's a tremendous amount to do, and I think there's one thing that people have to be cautious about. We have so much internet involvement—and I love the internet, it's wonderful—but it's boots on the ground that really makes the difference in politics.

Make no mistake about it. Pushing a button and signing a petition over the internet doesn't do it. You've got to get in people's faces.

Historian Roxanne Dunbar-Ortiz (*right*) with Thorne Dreyer at the KOOP radio studios in Austin, May 30, 2014. Photo by Roger Baker.

ROXANNE DUNBAR-ORTIZ

An Indigenous people's history.

Historian Roxanne Dunbar-Ortiz talks about her grandfather and the Wobblies, why she's an "outlaw woman," and her work with the Indigenous movement.

Dunbar-Ortiz is a scholar, an author, a historian, a social activist, and a pioneering feminist who has been an organizer in antiwar and antiracism movements and the American Indian Movement. Dunbar-Ortiz helped lead the women's liberation movement, also known as second-wave feminism. Along with a small group of dedicated women in Boston, she produced the first women's liberation journal, No More Fun and Games.

Roxanne's book Outlaw Woman: A Memoir of the War Years, 1960–1975 *is the story of her odyssey from Oklahoma poverty to the urban New Left. Her other books include* An Indigenous Peoples' History of the United States, *which won a 2015 American Book Award, and* Red Dirt: Growing Up Okie. *A native of San Antonio and longtime resident of San Francisco, Dunbar-Ortiz is part Native American. Her grandfather had roots in the Socialist Party and the Industrial Workers of the World (IWW).*

MAY 30, 2014

THORNE DREYER: Roxanne Dunbar-Ortiz, how wonderful to have you here.

I'm quoting: "Roxanne Dunbar-Ortiz has defined the term 'engaged intellectual' through a life spent on the front lines of the past four decades of social struggles. . . . She has never abandoned her roots through the process of becoming one of the most respected left academics in the United States." That's from James Tracey in *Left Turn*.

Your book *Outlaw Woman: A Memoir of the War Years, 1960–1975* is now in a reprint edition from the University of Oklahoma Press. Let me start by asking, why "outlaw woman"? Did you identify yourself as an outlaw?

ROXANNE DUNBAR-ORTIZ: At one level I consider myself a Marxist, feminist, intellectual, academic historian, specializing especially in Indigenous studies. But at another level are my roots; sometimes I feel like I'm almost two different people, and I don't even like to think where I would have gone with other trajectories.

I had as my heroes the Wobblies [Industrial Workers of the World] and the Socialist Party. My grandfather had been a member of the Socialist Party and the IWW, which were portrayed to me by my father as probably more outlawish than they were.

My grandfather was a pretty staid person; he was a farmer and a veterinarian. But my father told the stories as if they were outlaws, and it blended in for me with Billy the Kid and Jesse James and Belle Starr. And these were very beloved people. Of course, Belle Starr was heroic to me because she was a woman. And Bonnie and Clyde later—in the Depression era. But mostly from the 1880s, these bandits, the train robbers, and those who were fighting the federal government were heroes.

It was not until I was at San Francisco State that I learned that they all—these heroes of mine in Missouri—had been Confederate guerrillas with Quantrill's Raiders. I was having this lecture in US history where they were talking about Quantrill's Raiders as something horrible. And I said, "These are my heroes, what are you talking about?"

I was so antiracist—that was my very first consciousness as a teenager in high school—and so I couldn't believe it. I had to rethink an awful lot of things. I'm writing a book on Belle Starr where I'm trying to figure out why these people—whose families were not slave owners, were not rich—what was their investment? And then I get into the Cherokee nation: what was its investment in siding with the Confederacy instead of the Union?

I would hear Kris Kristofferson and Bob Dylan and all singing Woody Guthrie songs, and singing about the day old Dixie went down—and the Band, you know—and it just grated on me because it's like they weren't conscious of what they were doing.

But I am trying to figure that out, and I think it's kind of key to understanding this really strange, screwed-up country we live in. What's at the heart of it and what's at the heart of the Tea Party, what's at the heart of the hatred for the federal government. And we contributed a lot to that in the '60s, you know—kind of a poisonous hatred for the federal government.

So "outlaw woman" is what I kind of became on the left. In the old English sense of the word—because an outlaw in England was someone who literally was outside the law. They had no rights whatsoever, and anyone who ran into any of them could kill them, legally. They were considered wolves, wild wolves.

That's kind of how I saw myself: it was a combination of those childhood heroes and how I came to reconsider them as heroes. But also how I, myself, behaved as not quite within the parameters of anything that I could find. And yet, not wanting to be an individualist, you know. Although I did read Ayn Rand in the 1950s. This Irish writer in San Francisco asked me, "What's your favorite writer?" And I said, "Ayn Rand." And he started laughing—he could hardly get up off the floor laughing—and that kind of cured me of it.

DREYER: She created this sort of rugged artist, individualist kind of concept.

DUNBAR-ORTIZ: Yeah, living for ideas and principles. She just happened to be a fascist.

DREYER: Yeah, there was that.

Okay, unlike Bernardine Dohrn, who was on the show recently, you weren't actually "wanted" for anything, were you?

DUNBAR-ORTIZ: No. I wasn't a fugitive.

After three of us went to Cuba on the third Venceremos Brigade [a coalition of young people showing solidarity with the Cuban Revolution by working side by side with Cuban workers], we were followed by the local red squad, the FBI, and god knows who else. David Duke, who was the head of the Klan and based in New Orleans, was calling on the phone, threatening us; we had a firebomb thrown in and we were sleeping in different places every night.

So we decided—just to be able to continue our work trying to organize oil workers—that we would just go underground. So we had about five months of preparation and then we were underground about five months.

DREYER: One of the things you talk about is how you moved on from one kind of experience to another in the Left.

DUNBAR-ORTIZ: I moved from my antiwar and antiracist days and farmworkers—all that at UCLA—and anti-apartheid campus stuff and working in the community, too. I went from that to gradually getting angry about the status of women within the Left. And I said, "Until women are liberated, this is going to be a really stunted movement, because we can't get anywhere angry all the time, resentful of these guys behaving this way."

So, that was just in the air, you know, and different places all over the country, this consciousness was happening on the left. And of course, it was happening in general society: Betty Friedan's book [*The Feminine Mystique*] had come out and Kennedy had introduced that Commission on the Status of Women. The UN had declared interest in women's status.

It was literally in the air. But I entered it from the Left with other leftist women, SDS women, especially women from the civil rights movement. There were a lot of women doing this work, and I thought unless anti-imperialism and antiracism and class consciousness were built into the women's movement, that it would actually be a negative.

It might, you know, help the status of women in some ways, but really would not help poor women or African American women or Native women. And I was right, you know. Those of us in the anti-imperialist women's liberation movement did not win the day. Although we left some paths, I think. But feminism has a very bad name among young women activists today, because of the obliteration of that history.

"Those of us in the anti-imperialist women's liberation movement did not win the day. Although we left some paths, I think."

And so that's another reason I wanted to do the book: to say this was not the whole story of the women's liberation movement.

DREYER: Okay, here's a quote I think I stole from your website. It's from Ken Kesey: "I think of myself as an Okie. Let me tell you what that means: being an Okie means being the first of your whole family to finish high school let alone go on to college. Being an Okie means getting rooted out of an area and having to hustle for a toehold in some new area. Being an Okie means running the risk of striving out from under a layer of heartless sonsabitches only to discover you have become a redneck of bitterness worse than those you strove against."

DUNBAR-ORTIZ: I love that.

Well, I'll tell you the sad thing about the state of Oklahoma that I grew up in. Oklahoma was the most militant state. Twenty percent of Oklahomans were Socialists—voted Socialist in the 1910s-1917 and the Green Corn Rebellion, the uprising against conscription by the tenant farmers, Indian, Black, and white.

Then that was all crushed and even the Communists were unable to organize in the '30s in Oklahoma. The Cunninghams got run out [William Cunningham was an acclaimed leftist writer], and Woody Guthrie left. Pete Seeger has told these stories about how it was absolute surveillance—a police state—in Oklahoma. And so that's what I came out of.

I think my politics had to come from the stories I heard from my father, and also observing the conditions I grew up in. But that doesn't always have a political effect; it can make you angry, it can make you resentful, like Ken Kesey says, worse than the people you dislike.

But I had this grandfather, my father's father, Emmett Dunbar, Scots-Irish from the old family from back in the French and Indian War who migrated from Northern Ireland. And these were those who settled the frontier. I call them the foot soldiers of empire, but many of them became very militant and many of them were farmers, as my grandfather was.

And he joined the Socialist Party in 1905, in Missouri, just before they moved to Oklahoma in 1907, the year my dad was born. He also joined the Industrial Workers of the World. They were there organizing the wheat threshers and the oil workers, the migrant workers, the coal miners, while the Socialist Party was organizing the tenant farmers and sharecroppers. And so he was involved in both.

He named my father Moyer Haywood Scarberry Pettibone Dunbar. That long name. And he would tell me the stories—through his name—who these people were. Of course, those were the founders of the Industrial Workers of the World. And my father never went past the ninth grade and he was just a kid, you know, during this period of militancy.

He saw my grandfather, the family, suffer a lot. There were nine kids and the Ku Klux Klan and the Palmer Raids [conducted by the US Department of Justice in 1919 and 1920] against the Socialist Party, against the IWW—anyone who opposed World War I. And many were imprisoned, deported. Big Bill Haywood was not an immigrant, but he chose to leave with those who were deported and is buried in the Kremlin Wall.

My mother was a Hard Shell [Primitive] Baptist—I was a Hard Shell Baptist—but being told these stories over and over and over again. And so, it was a history, a kind of secret history I knew and that I didn't really know what to do with, from this heroic grandfather.

When I moved to San Francisco, other things happened, like civil rights. I moved to the city to work and finish school in a public trade school, and my last year of high school was the first year of integration in Oklahoma. And my school was the first high school integrated. There were race riots there all the time. That is, whites beating up on the very, very few African Americans brought in.

They had a very good community school, the Dunbar High School. They stole a few of the athletes, the good athletes from Dunbar School, and brought them to Central High—and it was the first time I had been forced to look at a situation and say I'm on one side or the other. And I could not be on the side of these snarling, angry young white men—and women. The girls were also beating up on the African American girls. I was called an "N-lover."

I changed from the secretarial trade to journalism because they actually had a daily newspaper and the boys studied printing. I was one of only two girls in journalism, and there was a hotbed of a few radicals, you know, and the teacher was gay. You had to be subversive in Oklahoma at that time.

But this didn't really hook me up with this IWW-Socialist Party radical past. That didn't happen until I went to San Francisco in 1960. The students at San Francisco State were getting ready for the Freedom Rides and everything, and they invited Norman Thomas to speak on campus. And I knew that name, you know; I knew nothing about the Left but I knew that name. My dad used to tell me about him.

So, I went up to him after his speech and I told him my grandfather's name and about my father, and he was so sweet. He was very elderly, and of course he wasn't as radical as he used to be. But that awakened in me, you know, this sense of all those stories.

DREYER: For people who don't know Norman Thomas, he was a six-time Socialist Party candidate for president.

DUNBAR-ORTIZ: I guess it's really why I became a historian—that I had so much oral history—that I did really well in history. To me it was stories of the past—but most of them were falsely told. I kind of knew they weren't true because I'd had this other perspective built into my mind.

So I became an organizer, trying to find ways to organize the working class and poor. And in much of my life—in the last forty years—Native American communities. But I didn't put anyone in a slot as being this or that, you know, because my oldest brother became a raving kind of right-winger racist—and my older sister.

My dad told me these stories that he didn't even tell the other kids. I was the youngest kid and I was an asthmatic, sick all the time, so I was a great listener because I couldn't talk. And so he would tell me stories just to kind of comfort me.

DREYER: You also had some interaction with music and Beat culture, right?

DUNBAR-ORTIZ: I got married at eighteen and my husband was just turning twenty when we got married. We met at the University of Oklahoma, my first year, his second. He thought of himself as a beatnik. He had his hair kind of shaggy and wore black turtleneck shirts. I just fell in love with him, and he was so different from all these buttoned-up guys with suit coats on.

He loved the blues. The East Side of Oklahoma City is filled with juke joints and booze clubs, and so he introduced me to the blues. I had never really heard the blues, the Mississippi blues, just country music and folk music, you know. Old folk music. And he introduced me to jazz.

At Norman, at OU, there was actually a little coffeehouse called the Green Door, a beatnik coffeehouse. And there was a very rare group of people who went down there and read—and posing, you know, wearing leotards.

We had the dream when he graduated from OU to go to San Francisco and find the beatniks. So we came in 1960 and unfortunately quite a few of them were gone by then. Allen Ginsberg had moved to New York and Gary Snyder moved up north, where he still lives. Lawrence Ferlinghetti was still there, and of course City Lights Bookstore was still there. And City Lights published my book the first time it was published.

DREYER: And boy, what a role City Lights Books has played, not just as a bookstore—as a community center but also as a publishing house. So many important writers were first published because of City Lights Books.

DUNBAR-ORTIZ: Exactly, and poetry would probably not have thrived as it has in the United States without City Lights publishing chapbooks and things that didn't sell much—but that wasn't the point. They also introduced the pocket book—you know, the pocket books were just genre books before.

But once we got to San Francisco my husband started working for Bechtel [the engineering and construction company]. He went into civil engineering instead of architecture, because it is very hard to make a living in architecture. He became more and more conservative while I went to San Francisco State.

The deal was that I'd send him to college for three years and then he would send me until I graduated. And I went to San Francisco State, which from day one when I was there was volatile. The second month I was in San Francisco was the HUAC hearings, the famous HUAC hearings in 1960.

DREYER: House Un-American Activities Committee.

DUNBAR-ORTIZ: Yeah. Where all the students were water hosed because they had disrupted the hearing. And I was at the library and came out and I saw this happening and I thought, "Oh, my god, what's going on?" You know, these fire trucks and people up in the air and crashing on the granite stone. And I was afraid to even go up closer—police all around.

DREYER: HUAC actually just packed up and left town, didn't they?

DUNBAR-ORTIZ: Yeah. They packed up. These are the same people that later started the free speech movement at Berkeley, but San Francisco State became the most radical campus. They have a School of Ethnic Studies; it's the only one in the world, I think. [In 2019, California State-Los Angeles announced the establishment of a College of Ethnic Studies, only the second in the United States since San Francisco State established its college in 1969.]

DREYER: You have a new book coming out from Beacon Press this September, *An Indigenous Peoples' History of the United States*.

DUNBAR-ORTIZ: Yes.

DREYER: And you were involved in the American Indian Movement [AIM] and are part Native American. So tell us a little about this book.

DUNBAR-ORTIZ: Howard Zinn wrote *People's History of the United States* in 1980 and it was published by Beacon Press. And so, before Howard passed away, he suggested to all the editors that they do a series of different peoples' histories: women's history of the United States, queer history of the US, African American, all of them. It's reenvisioning United States history through different perspectives. And he said "Indigenous"—well, he said "Native American"—and you should get Roxanne Dunbar-Ortiz to do that.

So, when they called me in 2007 and asked me to do this, I said, oh, absolutely. I thought this would be so easy—this is what I've been writing on for thirty years. Well, it wasn't so easy to bring into a trade book; this isn't an academic book, and it's not a history of Native nations in the US, it's a history of the United States from this perspective. Very, very tricky. It was the hardest book I've ever written.

But, yeah, I joined the American Indian Movement right after Wounded Knee in 1973 [the occupation in South Dakota by Oglala Lakota and followers of AIM]. There had been a wonderful missionary for Indigenous peoples, a man named Mad Bear Anderson who is Tuscarora Indian. He marched at the front of the Poor People's Campaign [in 1968], their first march. He was recruited by Martin Luther King.

He went all over the hemisphere trying to bring Native people together into what he called the "rainbow coalition"—this was like pre-rainbow coalitions—and he had a newspaper called *The Rainbow* that was in many different Indigenous languages.

When I was living in New Orleans he would stay over in the Seamen's Hall, which was down the street from where I lived in the Irish Channel. My name was in the paper and it described me as part Indian and so one day he knocked on the door. He wanted to talk to me. I said, "No, I don't know anything about being Indian." I grew up in a white town, white church, and my mother hated the idea of being Indian; she was ashamed of it.

But he kept coming back. He had this mission of rescuing the Indians who had been lost. That's really what the American Indian Movement was about; it was a pan-Indigenous movement.

After Wounded Knee I said, "Yeah, I think I want to make a commitment to this," and I got recruited. I was in law school—Santa Clara Law School—and one of the lawyers for the Wounded Knee defendants practiced nearby in San Jose and he was always coming over and recruiting people at the law school. So, he recruited me to work on the Wounded Knee legal defense and that's really how I came in.

DREYER: One of the things that you are known for in your writing, and especially in *Outlaw Woman*, is that you tell your history and you tell the history of the movement but you tell it without a lot of value judgment.

DUNBAR-ORTIZ: I just kind of tell my own story. And I did find that

"We can never reinvent what was then, but the younger generation is finding ways to create another world that I find very exciting."

when the book came out in 2001, that people did respond with their own stories. When I would have public events and all these people started talking about some of the trauma that they felt, bitterness.

But let's end on a positive note. We can never reinvent what was then, but the younger generation is finding ways to create another world that I find very exciting. I'm here at a conference with all these young Native Americans, and all of them are working with their own people while they're becoming university professors, getting doctorates—and that is very unusual. It's going to change the universities, their presence.